WHAT ALL CAN GO WRONG AND HOW IT DOES

The Diary of an IITian

SHRIKANT JOSHI

BLUEROSE PUBLISHERS
India | U.K.

Copyright © Shrikant Joshi 2023

All rights reserved by the author. No part of this publication may be reproduced, stored in a retrieval system or transmitted in any form or by any means, electronic, mechanical, photocopying, recording or otherwise, without the prior permission of the author. Although every precaution has been taken to verify the accuracy of the information contained herein, the publisher assumes no responsibility for any errors or omissions. No liability is assumed for damages that may result from the use of information contained within.

BlueRose Publishers takes no responsibility for any damages, losses, or liabilities that may arise from the use or misuse of the information, products, or services provided in this publication.

For permissions requests or inquiries regarding this publication, please contact:

BLUEROSE PUBLISHERS
www.BlueRoseONE.com
info@bluerosepublishers.com
+91 8882 898 898
+4407342408967

ISBN: 978-93-5989-023-4

Cover Design: Muskan Sachdeva
Typesetting: Pooja Sharma
Editor: Narayanamurthy Raghupatty

First Edition: December 2023

Background (2005)

During the last few years, the Indian Institutes of Technology (IITs) have gained significant popularity. Coaching classes for the Joint Entrance Examination (JEE) have sprung up in every town and city across the country. Millions of parents dream that their child will one day enter an IIT. They believe that once a youngster gets into an IIT, his / her future is secured. After graduation, they expect that the young IITian will get opportunities to go to the USA and mint money. Name and fame would follow. Or maybe he would get into one of the IIMs and later join some Multinational for a fat salary.

The IITs certainly have made their mark, not only in India but also in the developed countries, particularly the USA. Recently '*The Times of India*' published a news item titled "IIT Grads earn place under American sun." It was a pleasure for me to read the article. It made me feel proud of being an IITian. I am quoting the first three paragraphs from the article:

"**San Jose 18th Jan 2003**: As hundreds of Indian Institutes of Technology (IIT) alumni gather here in Silicon Valley this weekend to mark the golden jubilee of their celebrated school, a fancy new equation is bandied around in the US: IIT = Harvard + MIT + Princeton.

The economium comes from CBS's highly regarded '60 Minutes', the most widely watched news programme in the US. In a rah-rah story last Sunday CBS told its over 10 million viewers that IIT might be the most important university one could have heard of.

'The US imports oil from Saudi Arabia, cars from Japan, TVs from Korea and whisky from Scotland. So what do we import from India? We import people, really smart people,' co-host Leslie Stahl began while introducing the segment on IIT. 'The smartest, the most successful and the most influential Indians to US seem to share a common credential: They are IIT graduates. Put Harvard, MIT and Princeton together and you might begin to get an idea of the status of this school,' Ms Stahl reported".

Back home, Indian Newspapers and magazines, have been reporting success stories of IITians. I recollect reading about one young IITian who, a couple of years ago sold his dotcom company to a large Internet provider for over Rs. 500 crores.

All this makes one believe that if one is an IITian, one must be successful and must be rolling in money. By and large, this may be true, but it certainly is not true in all the cases. Sometimes things go wrong and for some people all the time things go wrong. True, I am writing about extreme cases, which are beyond the three-sigma limits' and I am one such specimen.

Besides me, my son too went through these hallowed portals, which was rare for my batch-mates. I joined IIT Kanpur in 1970 and earned my B. Tech in Mechanical Engineering in 1975. It was a five-year programme then. Subsequently, I completed my post-graduation in Industrial Engineering from one of the most coveted Schools, the National Institute of Training in Industrial Engineering (NITIE), Mumbai. NITIE is considered equivalent to IIMs in terms of starting salaries of students passing out from the Institute. My eldest son passed out from IIT Kharagpur. He was the topper of the Electrical Engineering Department, and did his MS/PHD programme from Stanford.

With this background, I would like to turn to the main theme of this book. During the last twenty-eight years something or the other seems to go wrong with whatever I plan, whatever I try to do and whatever I did. And this is an attempt to narrate, "How things go wrong."

Many close friends say that statistically it is impossible to be on the wrong side of the Lady Luck all the time. My answer is a small episode from a Russian book of statistics meant for beginners.

A young lad, having studied a bit of statistics, wagers a bet with a professional gambler. While they are sitting near a window in a coffee shop, they start discussing probabilities.

"What is the probability of the first person we see from the window walking across the street, being a male?" asks the lad.

"Half" is the obvious reply of the gambler.

"And so what is the probability of the first ten persons we see from the window walking across the street, being all males?" inquires the lad.

"Very less" replies the gambler.

"If we increase the number to hundred, and not one being a female?" asks the lad.

"Next to impossible. OK, but for the sake of it, let us have a bet. One to hundred." The gambler throws in the offer.

As soon as the lad accepts the bet, to his misfortune he sees an Army Battalion parading down the street.

Well, when things go wrong, one faces difficulties. And when many things go wrong in succession, there are extreme difficulties to be faced, those who come out of the situation and rise to the top write autobiographies, which get sold and appreciated. However, I am sure there are some capable people who do not reach any milestone, and hence do not dare to write about themselves. I am however making an attempt.

This reminds me of a book authored by Lee Iacocca who redeemed Chrysler Corporation out of an extremely difficult situation. He writes about his trying period, "Every time we saw light at the end of the tunnel, it turned out to be a train approaching us from the opposite direction."

In my case, I wish to add that the trains coming from the opposite direction had a frequency of Mumbai Locals. **Maybe I was always on the wrong track.**

In the strictest sense, this is not a diary, as I am not in the habit of writing one, but I intend to keep writing about various episodes as I keep remembering them. Maybe later I might shuffle the chapters once I complete the book. To kill the monotony, I have also inserted some interesting episodes, which are not related to the main theme. Who likes to read hundreds of pages of tragic episodes non-stop?

I do not postulate any theory nor do I expect the readers to draw any morals or conclusions. Nor do I expect the readers to sympathize with me. I only expect that at the end the readers would say to themselves **"Oh! This too can happen to an IITian."**

I started writing this 'diary' or ramblings of a mind as one would say, some time in Dec 2002. I wrote in fits and starts. Once there was a gap of over three years. Having completed over two hundred pages, I gave copies to a few of my friends and acquaintances for their comments. Surprisingly, the older generation enjoyed reading it, and was eager for the remaining chapters. My friends also appreciated my writing. There were, however, some suggestions from everyone. Some of these which were common, but which I have not followed, need to be addressed here.

My critics suggested that I should advise (based on my experience) the younger generation about dos and don'ts in life. I have so far refrained from doing it, primarily because I strongly believe 'advices' based on one's experiences need not be applicable in another situation.

The second common suggestion was that I should have written in a chronological sequence. This I have not done. Firstly, I did not want to write my autobiography. Secondly if I did write chronologically, it would appear as if I am trying to justify why I have not succeeded in life. And most importantly I was afraid it would become a Harishchandra Taramati story. In a contemporary environment, not many are interested in such tragic stories. For the convenience of readers, however, I am giving a brief sequence of my professional engagements since my IIT days, before I start the first chapter.

One very worthy question from a reader was whether I ever did any retrospection? Well, I never did it consciously. However, as I wrote I realized that on some occasions I too took wrong decisions. Who does not slip? Even Sachin Tendulkar does many times. Later, taking a clue from Chetan Bhagat, I have covered 'Three mistakes of my life.'

While writing, I also realized that one is (or becomes) what one goes through. A person's decisions and judgments are influenced by his/ her previous experiences. This probably could be one of the morals of my story. If one realises this, one will stop criticising people, their actions and decisions, at least half the time.

December 2020 :-I have now completed the book and plan to publish it by next quarter. Two things I want the readers to keep in mind: Each chapter has been written as a stand-alone chapter and hence there could be some repetitions which the readers could overlook. And secondly, most of the situations are pre smartphone / pre net banking days even pre email, pre mobile phone days.

MARCH 2023:-

Once again, for some reason or the other the publishing has been getting postponed. Now however the situation demands **'NOW OR NEVER'**. **THE LAST CHAPTER ELABORATES THE REASON.**

As Mentioned, Since Most Of The Chapters Are Independent Of Each Other (Stand- Alone), Readers Are Requested To Though My List Of My Chronological Engagements For Better Appreciation And Correlation.

My Professional Engagements

July 1970:- Joined IIT Kanpur For Five Years B. Tech. Programme In Mechanical Engineering.

April 1975:- Passed Out From IIT Kanpur.

June1975 - Aug 1975:- Down In Bed.

Sep 1975 - Jan 1976:- Worked As A Graduate Engineering Trainee At Gajra Gears Ltd, Dewas.

July 1976 - May 1978:- Did Post Graduation In Industrial Engineering At National Institute For Training In Industrial Engineering (NITIE), Mumbai. Now IIM Mumbai

July 1978 - April1979:- Worked With Kirloskar Consultants, Pune, As A Project Engineer.

May 1979 - April 1982:- Joined Steel Tubes Of India, Dewas, As Industrial Engineer And Left In April 1982 While I Was Manager, Planning Industrial Engineering.

May 1982 - Dec 1982:- Was Works Manager At Atma Tubes, Chandigarh.

Jan 1982 - July 1989:- In Jan 1982, Worked With Caldyne / Migma Group, Initially At Delhi, And From May 1985 Onwards At Indore, To Set Up A Foundry.

Aug 1989- Jan 1992:- Worked On My Own In A Consultancy Outfit At Indore.

Jan – 1992 –May 2020:- Bought And Managed Static Transformers Pvt. Ltd. We Manufacture Electrical Equipment Used For Marine Applications.

June – 2000 - Onwards :- Free-lance Consultant And Mentor Of Static Transformers Pvt. Ltd.

--xxx---

Contents

The Whistle Blowing Act (January 2004) 1

The Intellectual Property In India (1999-2000) 19

American Systems V/S Danish Human Touch (Dec 2001) 24

Labour Pains 36

What If 45

Static Proposes And Bhel Disposes (June 1995) 49

The Biggest Gamble 56

Until Things Did Not Go Wrong 82

Oldie's Day Out Or *Ye Mera India* (Nov 2004) 90

The Thugs Of Delhi And The Gullible Indians (1996) 97

Heads You Win -Tails I Lose Or The Power Of Zero (1998-99) 103

Miraculous Memory (2004) 108

German Thieves V/S Danish Honesty (1998) 114

The Cow And The Tiger 120

Talhunt 125

Fruits Of 'Progress' (2000) 130

Wild Goose Chase (2005) 140

Golden Days Again 151

My Good Days With Steel Tubes 160

The East India Company 173

Tragedy, Comedy, Or Horror Show (2005) 180

The Last Straw On The Camel's Back Or How I Started Writing 191

Drama In Real Life (2012)	198
Mixed Pickle	204
My Consultancy Days	217
Again, Again And Again	234
The Oxymoron: Tough Tender	244
Management Gurus	253
Going Chronologically Or The First Mistake Of My Life	261
My Days With Migma Equipment Or The Second Mistake Of My Life	271
The Third Mistake Of My Life	282
What All Can Go Right And How It Does Not	304
All Is Well That Ends Well (October, 2023)	309

THE WHISTLE BLOWING ACT (JANUARY 2004)

THIS CHAPTER IS DEDICATED TO

THE MEMORY OF

SATENDRA DUBE

FOR

HIS VALUES

AND

HIS GREAT COURAGE

The Whistle Blowing Act
(January 2004)

A few days back, I read the sad news about Satyendra Dubey; a young IIT Kanpur graduate who was gunned down on 27th November 2003, reportedly by the Road Mafia in Bihar. He was working with The National Highway Authority of India and had complained of corruption in Bihar stretch of the Golden Quadrilateral Project. Apparently, in spite of his request that his complaint about siphoning of money from the project be kept a secret, and his identity not disclosed, his name had been leaked out.

Since the news first appeared in The Indian Express, people from all walks of life expressed anguish over the incidence. The judiciary, politicians, bureaucrats, academicians, print media, television channels - all got involved in a kind of national debate. The Supreme Court asked the Central and the State Governments to provide protection to the whistle blowers. Commission of Enquiry was set up, and the CBI was handed over the case for investigation.

During my thirty-four years of professional career, I too have blown the whistle a number of times. As a matter of fact, I would say that I have not only blown the whistle but have also played the bugle, and in a few cases have been lucky to bring the guilty to justice.

THE BACKGROUND

I had bought majority shares of Static Transformers Pvt. Ltd., a company primarily engaged in manufacturing and supplying electrical equipment to the Indian Navy. I joined the Company as the Managing Director on 6th January 1992. Earlier the Company had supplied Helicopter Starting Rectifiers to the Indian Navy, four of which were fitted on K class frigates.

It so happened that in 1993, some of our warships went to Somalia. During this action the rectifier fitted on board INS – Kuthar developed a snag and created a panic situation as one admiral had to fly off in a helicopter.

The Indian Navy decided to check all the rectifiers fitted on K class ships and found one more rectifier out of order. They therefore asked us (being the Original Equipment Manufacturer) to quote for repair and testing of the rectifiers. We sent our offer and after negotiations, were awarded the contract of repair of the equipment and supply of spares for two Helicopter Starting Rectifiers for a few lacs.

We collected the units from the ships and subcontracted the job to one Mr. Date who had a factory at Mumbai. The fact was that these units were originally built at Indore using Date's design and electronic control cards. By subcontracting, we also were able to save freight charges.

After Date completed the work, the units were shifted to INS – Kunjali, a Naval Base in Colaba, Mumbai, for Helicopter Starting Trials. Our team of engineers and electricians went to Mumbai for trials. The trials, however, were not successful. Our engineers checked the settings, which were perfectly fine. The Helicopter Starting Rectifiers were giving the required output voltage; however, as soon as the pilot pressed the ON button, the helicopter's relay would trip, which would not permit the electrical circuit to complete. Our team returned to Indore without a clue.

In June 94 I visited Mumbai with my electrical engineer and witnessed the trials. It was the same fiasco again. We tried our best for a week to solve the problem. Every morning we used to go from our hotel at central Mumbai to Kunjali, which is at one end of the Metro; and after unsuccessful trials we used to travel to Goregaon, which is at the other end of Mumbai; discuss our observations with Date, a very brilliant and knowledgeable electrical engineer. Every evening we would conclude that there was nothing wrong with our equipment.

I am a mechanical / industrial engineer. I, therefore, had to double-check my analysis with experts in electrical / electronic field. The problem here was that due to frequent failures, cooperation from naval officials was diminishing. Secondly, we did not know anything about the helicopter's internal circuitry. Moreover, we were not allowed to take any measurement while the trials took place on the helicopter except from the meters of the helicopter and those fitted on our equipment. From Date's office we tried to call Avinash Abhyankar, another Electrical Stalwart based at Pune, who, we thought, had some knowledge of helicopter's electrical circuitry. It did not help us much. We could not doubt the helicopters as the same were started for sorties by simple battery carts every day.

After a weeklong futile exercise, I returned to Indore. I planned to search for a solution by either going to some technical expert or to Hindustan Aeronautics Limited (Manufacturer of these helicopters) to find details of the circuitry / electrical characteristics.

We had no access to any one working in this field in Hindustan Aeronautics. However, we thought my cousin Jayanta Apte might be of some help. He is an electrical engineer and at that time was working with the Indian Air Force. He was a Group Captain during that period and was stationed at Delhi, at the headquarters of Western Air Command.

And so, I went over to Delhi to meet him and to discuss the problem. He gave the circuitry of Chetak helicopter (The starting system), which was fairly simple. After detailed discussion we concluded that the cable and the connector that was connecting the power from our unit to the helicopter must have a loose contact somewhere.

To confirm this point, there was a simple procedure, which I suggested to the Navy. I wrote that first a helicopter be started using a battery cart to confirm that the hello and the connecting cables were OK, and then without disturbing the connection at the hello end, the battery cart be removed and replaced by our Helicopter Starting Rectifier. Helicopter may then be started with the rectifier. This would eliminate the doubts regarding bad connection / contact at the hello end, or bad cables. The concerned naval officer did not however understand this idea.

I therefore, personally visited Mumbai in July and met the naval officer at the Dockyard. And that is where I came across V. Kumar who was a Captain by rank and was the boss of the person in charge of our contract. During my first meeting with him I told him that in case my suggested procedure failed to start the hello, Navy was free to start the same with their battery cart, lift the Helicopter Starting Rectifiers, and using the hello dump them in the sea; we would pay for the loss. This kind of language was totally unlike a small-scale vendor.

V Kumar got impressed by my bravado and agreed to my proposal. Next day trials were planned and V Kumar deputed his officer for organising all the logistic support. He also personally visited Kunjali to speed up the trials, and made sure that pilot / helicopter was available.

THE TRIALS

As suggested, a helicopter was started using a battery cart. Cables were then disconnected from the cart end and our Helicopter Starting Rectifier replaced the cart. Helicopter was then started. The deafening noise of its engine was music to my ears. The helicopter was started a few more times until the pilot refused to continue the trials as the engine of the helicopter got hot due to frequent starts.

The second Helicopter Starting Rectifier was also tried out in similar fashion. The trials gave positive results. Due to frequent rest periods required between starts, the trials were completed only by evening.

V. Kumar again visited Kunjali towards the end of the trials. At the hello base, apparently impressed by the result, he took me aside and asked me to join him for a drink in the evening at his residence. This was very much unlike a senior naval officer of captain's rank. Not to displease him, I agreed.

I went by his car to his flat in Navy Nagar. He was staying alone in the officers' mess while his family was at Delhi. After the pleasantries, I requested him to help me to get my payment released early, as a lot of time was already lost in the trials. He immediately came up saying, "Sure, Mr. Joshi, I will help you get your payment but you too have to help me." I was already suspecting that he wanted some gratification from us. In spite of my anticipation of his demand, I was, for a moment, taken aback. I only said, "What help?" He immediately added saying, "You see, Joshi, you are a bold and outspoken person, I have taken a liking for you, I will get your payment released very soon. How much is it? Three lacs thirty-five thousand, is it not? OK, you pay me thirty-five and you get a lot more business from Navy."

I agreed to pay but added that I would do it only on receipt of payment from the Navy. I did not have the guts to refuse and displease him. Else he would put spokes in the payment process. It is common knowledge that no one individual in the Government can help you get your work done, as he is only a small part of the system. However, even a small fly can stall your work at the government departments.

I did not want to continue my meeting and so I excused myself, saying that our team wanted to celebrate the day's success. I returned to the hotel and took our team to a good restaurant for dinner and had a good night's sleep thereafter.

THE IRRITANTS

V Kumar's asking me for a bribe was not the first incidence of corruption. I was already paying to fulfil the demands of someone or the other though quite unwillingly. Just after taking over Static Transformers, our accountant Uday came to me saying that he was going to CAT (Centre for Advanced Technology) to pay Rs. 1000 to Nodwel so that our payment worth one lac would be released. It was a standard practice to pay one percent to this accounts officer, he informed me. This practice continued for some time until one day, I objected and stopped it.

This fellow, Nodwel, had the audacity to keep phoning for payment to Uday. One day, I took his call. He asked me for Uday and I shot back "Look Mr. Nodwel, we are no longer going to pay you. You get your salary from the government for your work. And if you continue making calls or stop our payment, I will make sure that you leave Indore."

"What can you do to me?" he asked, not quite politely.

I was already quite irritated and was about to lose my temper and so I reacted, "You are new to Indore Mr. Nodwel. Do you want to be physically hurt?" And I put the receiver down.

Later, I got a call from his boss, one Mr. Patel. Nodwel had complained of my threat. Patel called me and questioned me about my threat. I remember saying "Sir, if someone asks me for a bribe, I will do exactly what I said".

Then onwards we never got a call from Nodwel. Our payments from CAT continued to be received though with some delay.

The most interesting part of this story was my meeting with Dr. Bhawalkar, the then Director of CAT. One day, at my request he gave me an appointment. During the meeting I handed him a long list of payments, which were due from CAT and were getting delayed. The list consisted of ten odd entries worth about a few lacs. One by one Bhawalkar went through the list and came to an item against which we had not written the concerned indenter's / officer's name. I informed Bhawalkar that that particular payment was already under process and Nodwel was the concerned officer. I added "Since we do not pay any bribe to him, we know that the amount will get delayed for some time. But it is OK with us."

Bhawalkar's response was: "I know he takes money. You know Mr. Joshi; I have already transferred him from that section. As a result, his house construction has stopped." (Later Nodwel was transferred to BARC, Kota). What a pity! A person in-charge of thousands of crores of rupees worth of projects, employing thousands of people, is so helpless.

Later I learnt that Nodwel belonged to SC/ST category while Dr. Bhawalkar was an upper-class Brahmin and could not have taken stronger action, else it would have created a serious PR problem.

ANOTHER IRRITANT

Another irritant during that period was Commander Goyal, a naval inspector from Bhopal. Earlier when I had just taken over Static Transformers, an inspector from the Navy's Baroda Office used to visit us for inspection of the material. However, this Goyal, using his contacts with higher-ups in Navy, had gotten the inspection job assigned to Navy's Bhopal Office. He was keen to increase his domain. Navy's Bhopal office is equipped mainly for inspection of turbines manufactured by BHEL for the Warships, and therefore, is headed by a mechanical engineer. At Static we manufactured electrical equipment. For us inspection by Bhopal was a mismatch. But then we had no say in the matter.

This gentleman, Goyal, was a very cunning and greedy fellow. During my first meeting with him I openly asked, "Sir, I am new to Static and I do not want to play hide & seek, in case you desire anything, please let us know, we should not have any communication gap". He pleased me by saying "No, No Mr. Joshi, I do not take any money. Some gifts here and there would be OK".

'Some gifts' however turned out to be a relative term. It started with a drum of twenty litres of oil paint for his in-laws who stayed at Indore, then the workmen's services for painting, then a fancy telephone instrument unplugged from my cabin, and thousands of rupees worth STD calls (The rates were very high then) from our office.

During one of his visits, he picked up a small compressor from our paint shop (on returnable basis, which never came back), then a pump (we had to buy a new one). The list was growing and causing immense irritation. It would have been better if he had asked us for cash instead. Once he got his car repainted at our factory (we employed a very skilled painter then).

One day, I reached the factory at noon to find a team of my workmen fabricating a dish antenna. (Dish antennas of the first generation were around two meters in diameter.) Goyal was instructing them on the construction aspects. It was a bit too much for me to tolerate, but then he was inspecting ten lacs worth of transformers, which were to be shipped to Mazagaon Docks. I took him aside and said "Sir, I will buy you a dish antenna. But please do not insist on this fabrication work". And so, we were poorer by Rs. 15000/-.

The worst case with Goyal happened during December, 1993 when his assistant visited us to inspect ten lacs worth of transformers. He stamped the transformers (which is as good as clearing the material for dispatch). We packed and shipped the transformers to the transporter and submitted our bills to the bank. During that period, we were under tremendous financial pressure and needed funds urgently. We sent Praveen, our troubleshooter, with the bills (sealed by the bank) to Mazagon Dock's Bank at Mumbai. He collected the payment and returned to Indore.

Goyal was to issue the "I" note (Certificate of inspection without which we were not authorised to claim payment) from Bhopal.

However, Goyal visited us a couple of days later and refused to issue the "I" note stating that his assistant had slipped up in the inspection and he would inspect the transformers again. We had to bring back all the transformers from the transporter (Luckily the transporter had not shipped them to Mumbai); unpack them and carry out the inspection once again. It was a criminal offence, inadvertently committed by us i.e., collecting payment on false transporter document.

After the re-inspection, Goyal came out with some stupid reasons to reject the transformers. The fact was that he wanted his Jeep's body built at our factory and was kind of blackmailing us. I assigned the task to make Goyal change his mind in our favour to Hemant Atre, a senior supervisor employed by us. He somehow made Goyal agree to issue I note and, in the process, paid him ten thousand rupees, the cost of building his Jeep's body.

There were many such irritants I was facing at Static. However, this last event had crossed the threshold of my tolerance. To be very honest, had we been making money at Static and had we been cash surplus, maybe, I would have paid the bribes without feeling the pinch. But the fact was that there was nothing wrong with our products. They met all the specifications and quality standards and we had bagged the orders because we were the lowest bidders and therefore, I did not want to succumb to such demands. In fact, I hated paying bribes.

THE ACTION: PLAYING OF BUGLE

Our rectifiers were shipped from Kunjali to Dockyard and were installed on board INS Kuthar and Kukri. On-board hello trials were held sometime in October. During that period, I used to get telegrams from V Kumar asking me to contact him on phone and during the calls, he pestered me for early payment. I sent Rs. 5000/- through my engineer when he went for ship trials. Finally, we received the ship report and we submitted the bill for payment in November.

In the meantime, during my visit to Delhi I met Commodore Arora, a very forthright officer who was then the Director of Quality Assurance (Naval). This Directorate is responsible for quality assurance of equipment to be fitted on-board Naval Ships. During the meeting, he asked me if we were facing any problems with his inspectors.

I narrated V Kumar's episode as well as informed him of Goyal's activities. He was shocked and asked me what I wished to do. I said, "I want to kill them." He asked me to meet him again the next day. In the meantime, he was to discuss the matter with the Admiral in-charge of Personnel.

The next day he informed me that I should give him a written complaint concerning both the cases. He assured me that the matter would be kept confidential. He would personally hand over the complaint to the top brass who would initiate action. I double-checked the matter with Captain Anil Vyas who was at that time Deputy Director of Systems (Electrical). Anil Vyas confirmed Arora's credentials. I returned to Indore after handing over written complaints to Arora.

The day after I reached Indore, I got a call from NHQ (Naval HeadQuarters), New Delhi, who checked my availability. The call was followed by another call from WNC (Western Naval Command). One Commander Gupta spoke to me from Naval Intelligence. He called me to come to Mumbai immediately.

I took an overnight bus and reached Mumbai the next day, checked into a shoddy hotel near Mazagon Docks and went over to WNC. I was taken to Commander Gupta who was in plain clothes. He praised my courage and took me to the CNC's (Commander in Chief) office. I do not readily recollect his name but I believe he was Admiral Vishnu Bhagwat who later became Chief of Naval Staff.

He appreciated my courage and said that he will ensure that my bold action did not adversely affect my business. I responded saying, "Sir, I am not dependent on Indian Navy and have two hands and enough grey matter to make my living". Come to think of it, these remarks were certainly uncalled for and indicated arrogance. However, my adrenalin level had gone up and it was that state of excitement which made me say so.

Back in Gupta's office I was told that CBI would handle the matter and V Kumar would be trapped accepting bribe from me. Once again, he asked me if I wanted to back out. On my re-assurance / reconfirmation, he took me from WNC to Tanna House near Regal Cinema where CBI had an office.

Before leaving Indore, I had planned on two items. I had gone to our Bank Manager and collected a pack of fresh Rs. 5000/-worth pack of notes; noted down the serial numbers. Secondly, I had written a complaint addressed to CBI and carried the same in duplicate with me.

The decor of CBI's office was a disappointment. One might imagine it to be like MI-5 headquarters. However, it was just like an ordinary government office, with age-old wooden furniture. With files and papers cramped up everywhere, the office gave a depressing look. Inspector Shingwekar took us to SP's (Superintendent of Police) Office, one Mr. Y P Singh. I took a receipt of my complaint from him, which was necessary as proof. This would protect me against any possibility of getting framed as a person intending to bribe a naval officer.

The trap was planned in minutes and accordingly, I phoned V Kumar from SP's office. The CBI planned to tape the conversation. I thought they would have some sophisticated equipment for tapping the tele-conversation. However, it was a small palm held tape recorder, which Shingwekar was holding near the receiver of the phone.

It was 16th of December 1994, maybe it was around 1 PM when I spoke to V Kumar on phone. I told him that I had reached Mumbai and wanted to handover the payment to him. I added that I had brought only part payment, as we had not got the credit against the cheque received from Navy till then. He wondered as to why Navy's cheque for Rs. 335000/- was not cleared. I bluffed, stating that since it was a treasury cheque, it would get credited only when its confirmation reached the bank.

He called me to his office. I however excused myself saying that I was tired due to the sixteen-hour long bus journey and that I would meet him in the evening. As previously advised by CBI I asked him to meet me at the Golden Gate Restaurant, which was in the neighbouring street. He confirmed that he would be there at 6 PM.

The quality of recording of this conversation was awfully bad. However, the conversation could not have been repeated. CBI inspector then introduced me to one Mr. Aslam who would accompany me as a witness during our proposed meeting at The Golden Gate Restaurant.

The officer briefed us. The pack of hundred 50 Rupee notes was sprinkled with some powder and was kept in Aslam's carry bag. I was told to introduce Aslam as Static's new local representative. V. Kumar knew our local representative, C.V. Joshi. I was to tell V Kumar that Joshi had quit. Further, if the money was transferred, I was to wipe my face with a hanky as soon as we stepped out of the restaurant. Aslam was to switch on the tape recorder in his bag during the meeting.

THE REAL ACTION

All set and rehearsed, Aslam and I waited for V Kumar outside The Golden Gate restaurant. At around 6 PM, V Kumar appeared in naval uniform. He patted me on the back and asked me to wait in the restaurant. He would return in a jiffy once he changed to civilian clothes, he suggested. It would not be proper to be seen with us in the restaurant while he was in uniform, he said.

He was back in about half an hour and once seated we ordered lassi. I introduced Aslam to him. V. Kumar told Aslam to keep meeting him frequently. He could pick up subcontracts from Kumar. V Kumar boasted, "As long as I am kept happy, I will ensure that orders of your liking are placed with you"

I casually mentioned that the next day I was proceeding to Ranipet (Near Chennai) to negotiate some order for electrical equipment required for Trishul missile launcher. V Kumar volunteered to help me get the order using his contacts and gave me names of /some naval officers involved in the missile project. I scribbled down the name on the jacket of the flight ticket (for returning to Indore). After doing justice to our lassi, I asked him "What do I do with the money". He promptly replied, "Pass it on

". I took out the pack of notes from Aslam's bag. Kumar grabbed the pack hastily and shoved it in his safari suit's trouser pocket. We all got up and moved out.

Just as we were passing through the door, I wiped my face with my hanky while Aslam, as planned, asked him if he wanted to have a Pan. His response was affirmative. As we climbed down the steps and reached the Panwala on the footpath, Shingwekar and three other hefty CBI officers nabbed V Kumar. Shingwekar held V Kumar's hands, folded them on his back and held them tight and said "I am CBI inspector. Mr. Kumar, you are under arrest for asking for and collecting bribe from Mr. Joshi".

For Kumar, this probably was the most unexpected moment of his life. He protested, but only verbally, saying, "Do you know who I am? I am a Captain of the Indian Navy and you are only an inspector. You have no authority to arrest me". At that instance, Y.P. Singh appeared, displayed his batch and said, "I am Superintendent of Police, and have all the authority to arrest you. You have collected bribe from Mr. Joshi".

V Kumar panicked, "Who says? I was to go to Delhi next week and Joshi has given me this amount to be delivered to his relatives in Delhi. Tell them. Tell them Mr. Joshi". It was practically a high-pitched shout. In an equally loud voice I reacted, "Mr. Kumar, you wanted a bribe for clearing my payment. I did not wish to pay and so I have got you arrested by CBI. And what relatives? I have none in Delhi."

"You have cheated me. You have cheated me," he kept mumbling.

V Kumar was frisked and then his hands were rinsed in some chemical (I believe it was lime water), which was collected in a bottle. It had turned pink. It was sevenish in the evening, near Regal, in Mumbai. A crowd had already started gathering. Suddenly, two Ambassador cars screeched to halt by the roadside. Two inspectors got in on the front seat and two in the rear. Of course, V Kumar was between them.

We were asked to get into the next car with the remaining police personnel, all in plain clothes, and SP asked V Kumar's driver to follow his car and thus the caravan of all the vehicles sped to Tanna House. Mission accomplished. The event was just like a Bollywood movie scene.

Back at Tanna House, we had a round of cold drinks and sandwiches before we were debriefed. We signed some documents. It was 11 PM when Aslam and I were released and that was when I left for the hotel.

I was called to Tanna House the next day and asked to send the telegrams received by us from V. Kumar and any other documents which could be useful to CBI in their investigation. Shingwekar took the cover of my air ticket. It was then that I learnt that Kumar's driver was sent to his house to bring a spare trouser as CBI kept the one, he was wearing as evidence. Its pocket had the traces of powder sprinkled on the notes. V Kumar was grilled till early morning the next day. Calls were made to WNC / NHQ Delhi and after consultations with the top brass of Indian Navy; he was handed over to Naval Police at four in the morning.

Task accomplished, I returned to Indore the next day by morning flight. I was the only person who produced a jacketless air ticket at the check-in counter. On the day I reached Indore, *"Nai Dunia"*, Indore's popular Hindi daily, carried a news item stating "A senior Naval Official was nabbed by CBI red-handed while he was taking bribe from the representative of a company engaged in manufacturing helicopter spares." It was obvious that CBI had leaked the news. We later found out that similar reporting was done by most of the National dailies published from Mumbai.

During the next quarter, I met Shingwekar and Y P Singh a couple of times; provided them with the necessary papers. By the end of March 1995, I learnt from Shingwekar that CBI had completed its investigation and handed over the findings to Navy. The Navy then started its own probe. The Naval officials interviewed Date, CV Joshi and many others. I was called once to Mumbai to give my statement to Capt. Mohanan in his office on board INS Vikrant, the aircraft carrier. Capt. Mohanan was the Commanding Officer of the warship and was in-charge of the investigation.

COURT MARTIAL

In June 1995, the court martial proceedings started in Mumbai at INS – Angre. I was called as a witness. On the first day I had to wait outside the courtroom for the examination of Aslam, an officer of Indian Airlines, Navy's Cdr. Harsha and Cdr John, both working under Kumar, (in December 1994) was in progress.

It was the first (and hopefully the last) court martial proceedings, which I witnessed. There were five very senior Naval Officials, of the rank of Commodore and above, acting as members of the Jury, all dressed in full ceremonial uniform. They occupied the podium. Two other senior naval officials of Captain's rank, again in ceremonial uniform, holding bare swords, escorted V Kumar. They were called "Friends of the accused". They would escort him in and out of the courtroom. Mohanan was the prosecution officer. An officer who was an expert in legal matters was conducting the case. V Kumar's family members and a few persons from Navy were sitting as viewers.

The court proceeding would commence at 10 AM and then there was a break for lunch from 1 to 2 PM, and again from 3.30 to 4 PM for tea. We were offered lunch and tea in a nearby Mess where a high standard of decorum was maintained. None of the witnesses were allowed to be in the courtroom except when it was his/her turn.

The first day I spent doing nothing, only waiting for my turn, which did not materialize. The next day my turn came in the morning. My examination continued right through the day. It got over just before 5.30 PM when the session ended.

V Kumar was allowed to avail of the services of a civilian lawyer. I had to stand in the witness box throughout (except for lunch and tea breaks) and answer questions. I had to narrate the whole story. The lawyer tried various ways to make me contradict myself or to make a statement which would go against the proceedings but to no avail. My witness statements were based on facts rather than a cooked-up story. As long as I was alert, it was not possible that I would make any contradictory statement.

Even though the episode is around nine years old, I distinctly remember a part of my interrogation. At one point of time V Kumar's lawyer asked me, "Is it true, Mr. Joshi, that   Capt. Kumar liked you, your attitude, and hence tried to help you out of the way?" To which I remember having replied, "I am not sure whether he tried to help me because he liked me.

It is he who knows better. However, when I agreed to pay him the money he demanded, he certainly gave indications that he liked me."

There was a loud laughter; even the jury could not hide their smiles.

During lunch and tea breaks outside the courtroom, Kumar's family members were interacting with each other as if they were on a picnic. With their false brave faces, they thought they would bring down my (and other witness') morale. It was a childish attempt.

At the end of my testimony / cross-examination I requested the jury to permit me to make a small statement. I said, "I have tried my best to be honest and truthful throughout. You are five members of the Jury. All of you must have read the famous story by Munshi Premchand. I am a great believer of that story. It is the **"Panch Parmeshwar"** (Jury is God). And with that punch I walked out of the courtroom.

During the tea break on the second day, (my examination was in progress that day) I was standing alone, having my cup of tea. Cmdr. Prabhawalkar, a member of the Jury, walked up to me and asked me in Marathi "Mr. Joshi, do you attend court cases regularly?"

"No Sir, this is the first time I have ever attended any court proceedings." I replied.

"I am surprised! You are awfully consistent. You have not contradicted yourself even once"

My obvious reply was that it was because my statements were based on facts.

The court martial proceedings continued for a few more days. I used to contact Shingwekar regularly on phone from Indore, primarily to know when our money would be released. (Pack of Rs. 5000/- which was kept as evidence by CBI) and also to know the fate of the court martial.

A few months later, I learnt that the verdict had been announced: **"Found Guilty; Removed from service with one year's Rigorous Imprisonment."**

THE MEDIA

On that day I called two prominent Hindi dailies published from Indore and one national daily published from Mumbai. I informed them of the matter. I also told them that they could get authentic information from CBI's Mumbai office. But the matter was never reported by any daily.

A few things, which I learnt later, were quite amusing. When I collected Rs. 5000/- from CBI office, I met SP Y P Singh briefly. He told me that V Kumar had approached him and offered him Rs. 25 lacs to squash the case. Many of the naval officials later on told me that V Kumar was a black sheep and had minted money.

My regards for Anil Vyas went up many-folds when I learnt later that he was V Kumar's roommate during the training period. Their families had a close relationship. V Kumar's wife used to tie him Rakhi and Anil Vyas was her "Moo Bola Bhai" (accepted as a brother). In spite of all this background, he had kept the information about my complaint a secret because of his high moral values.

There was some sad information too, which I got from the grapevine. While the Presidential Pardon cut down V. Kumar's RI to six months, his family was socially ostracized by the naval community since the day he was nabbed by the CBI. His one son attempted suicide due to family disturbances. (Similarly, in Nodwel's case, his son became psychotic).

Ever since, none of the naval officials has dared to ask us for a bribe. I get good respect from honest officers and the bad ones keep their distance. In my heart of hearts, I thought I had not only blown the whistle, but had brought the guilty to justice and I would be rewarded for my deed. I however did not even get an appreciation letter from the Indian Navy. On the contrary, I ended up spending money from my own pocket for my visits and hotel stay. Mohanan had offered me a free stay in Sailor's Mess, which I thought was an insult for a person of my standing, and had opted to stay in a hotel. A few days later I did get a cheque of Rs. 1300/- towards the expenses incurred by me for travelling to Mumbai and two days stay there.

As far as Goyal is concerned, Navy held an internal enquiry. We could not give any documentary proof. And apparently, the news of my complaint had been leaked to him before the investigating team visited him. He was absolved of the accusations made by us. He, however, was transferred to Visakhapatnam. His reputation in the naval circles had tarnished. He resigned and left the Navy the very next year.

---xxx---

THE INTELLECTUAL PROPERTY IN INDIA
(1999-2000)

THIS CHAPTER IS DEDICATED TO

THE PEOPLE OF USA

WHO

VALUE

AND PROTECT

INDIVIDUAL'S INTELLECTUAL PROPERTY

Intellectual Property in India
(1999-2000)

Once, while I was at Static, we received some confidential documents comprising of three booklets from a defence organisation located in Hyderabad. In the past we had supplied some transformers to this organization, and were therefore aware of the hassles involved in dealing with it. The organisation was responsible for procurement of material for the ATV project (Advance Technical Vehicle), in other words, the Nuclear-Powered Submarine construction project.

The first booklet contained commercial terms and conditions of the tender (invitation to bid). The second one covered the general technical requirements. The last one had only four or five pages and gave a sketchy brief of the equipment required by them. The first two booklets of around 50 pages each were a sure cure for insomnia.

The first booklet gave commercial do's & don'ts; most of the conditions were about "How the bidder could get disqualified". Most of the technical specifications narrated in the second booklet were not applicable. It was like ordering a typewriter along with technical specifications that read, "Any equipment weighing 500 kgs or more should be provided with lifting hooks". As always, I delegated the task of reading the tender documents and preparing our offer while ensuring that it did not violate any of the general conditions.

The equipment they wanted to procure was a battery charger and a battery discharging system.

The battery charger was to be used for charging batteries at a constant current of 550 Amperes ±2.5 Amps so that the battery voltage built up from 140 to 240 volts. This would take about 24 hours. Similarly, the discharging system was to discharge the battery from 240 volts to 140 volts at a constant current of 550 ± 2.5 Amps. This was also expected to take around 24 hours.

The specifications of the discharging system were probably based on some Old Russian design and the system was to have resistors, which were to be manually switched in or out of the circuit to maintain the current constant. The charger was to provide a maximum power of 132 KW and similarly, the discharging unit was to be capable of handling 132 KW energy and dissipating it to the atmosphere.

It was quite a large system. Moreover, the number of times the resistor value was to be adjusted was very large (more than sixty) which we optimized the design to minimize the requirement of contactors and switches, though it would differ slightly from their description.

We found some contradiction in the technical requirements, which is quite a normal phenomenon in tender documents. However, we made a tentative design, following all the instructions and sent our offer.

After a few months and some correspondence later, we were called by TNC (Technical Negotiation Committee) for a meeting.

I went to Hyderabad and attended the discussions. It took me some time to explain to them my optimised system. I even offered them an auto control system for the discharging system. Finally, they understood my design. During this visit I found out that only two other parties had participated in the tender. One was Hind Rectifiers, and the other was a lesser-known company from Ahmednagar.

The next day I flew from Hyderabad to Delhi for some other work. On the flight I was thinking about this tender and felt that our chances for getting the order were good as our overheads and costs were much lower than the Bombay based Hind Rectifiers and I had never heard of the third bidder previously in connection with Naval Tenders. This bidder was likely to go cautiously, and keep extra margins.

The supply also involved environment testing i.e., testing of the equipment to withstand - 30 °C (I don't think Navy operates submarines from the Himalayan peaks), 95% humidity for 24 hours, shock, vibration and so on and so forth. The scope also included EMI, EMC testing which is the latest requirement in equipment for Defence use.

I do understand EMI, EMC but then unfortunately it had become a practice in Defence to put it in these specifications even for buying pencil cells. All this testing, which is possible only at Bangalore, New Bombay, Madras, Hyderabad (at DRDL), involves a lot of time and money. I thought that the third bidder would not be aware of this and therefore budget for a considerable amount in his quote.

I started thinking seriously about our offer. Somehow, I did not like the scheme of the discharging system. So much current and frequent changing of heavy contacts was going to be problematic. And suddenly at 33000 feet above MSL (mean sea level) I got an idea. I wondered if I could use the charger itself in series with the battery so that I could maintain the current constant without changing the resistance.

By the time I reached Delhi, the design was clear in my mind. This would save considerable cost and maintenance hassles and would practically be a single equipment instead of two. From Delhi, I telephoned Hyderabad and talked to the concerned officer. I explained the idea to him and said, "Sir, you will not be charging and discharging the battery at the same time. With my concept you can discharge the battery using the battery charger and a fixed load at constant current"

I went on to explain the concept until he sounded like he had grasped the idea. It was going to save the Navy a lot of money and I would compete with much lower costs (for more or less that of single equipment) with my co-bidders. The Captain (Naval officer to whom I had spoken to) asked me to give the details of my scheme in writing, which I sent him from Delhi itself.

For about a month, we heard nothing, until one day we got a large envelope by speed post containing three booklets with a letter requesting us to submit our offer. The first two booklets were identical to the once received earlier. The third had the details of the Battery charger cum discharger with a fixed load bank. Most of the write up was a copy-paste of my proposal. This was MY scheme. Damn it! Now the other bidders, who would quote, would have the same cost advantage.

Anyway, we quoted again and attended the TNC at Hyderabad. A few weeks later we were called for Price Bid Opening. I went to Hyderabad to attend the same. After a lot of formalities in a conference hall, Commodore Telang (Incidentally from Indore) opened the three envelopes. Hind Rectifiers had quoted Rs.12 lacs, Static Rs.10 lacs and the party from Ahmednagar Rs.3.5 lacs.

Obviously, we lost the order. I am however sure the Nagar party must have made a big mistake or it was a kind of clearance sale for them. The cost of transportation, and carrying out various tests at Bangalore & Hyderabad and cost of material itself would exceed Rs. 5.50 lacs. Anyway, this happens many times in such tenders – due to someone quoting wrongly, the deserving parties lose the order. I would not have included this episode in this diary just for this reason of getting priced out, as it is a part of the game.

But the more important point I am making here is regarding intellectual property. During my first visit to the US, I was with Sudhir Nath (my NITIE batch mate) in North Carolina. One day we were going around the downtown area when we came across a car park where we saw that most of the parked cars had a cardboard fixed inside the front glass to block the sunrays. Sudhir told me that the person who came out with this folding cardboard idea patented it and became a millionaire. We hear many such stories. Once I was watching a programme on Discovery about female millionaires in the US. One woman who came out with the idea of making small, soft plastic pads which could be slipped into women's dresses to enhance their figure had patented the idea and had become stinking rich.

Of course, I could not have become a millionaire by supplying equipment worth a million, but somehow, I felt quite frustrated at having suggested a good idea to the Government Agency. Anyway, life is like that and that may be why Rajeev coined the slogan **"MERA BHARAT MAHAN"**.

---xxx---

AMERICAN SYSTEMS V/S DANISH HUMAN TOUCH
(DEC 2001)

THIS CHAPTER IS DEDICATED TO

CITIZENS OF DENMARK

FOR

THEIR HOSPITALITY

American Systems Viz-A-Viz Danish Human Touch
(Dec- 2003)

Murphy's Law states: If things can go wrong, they will. I would add: However, God saves you from disaster. I went through an ordeal, which confirms this belief. It occurred during my visit to US and Denmark in December 2001. As a matter of fact, I always had unique experiences every time I went abroad. This was one such memorable experience.

I was to visit a firm in the US and another one in Denmark. I had planned a ten-day tour. I was to go to Pittsburgh in the US, then to Chicago to visit Apoorva (Apu), my nephew who was then a student pursuing PhD, and then to Denmark for a couple of days before I returned home.

Just before I left Indore, I got an e-mail from the Danish Company that the concerned person would not be available on the scheduled dates and that I should postpone my visit by a week. Postponing the visit would have called for rescheduling of appointments in the US, re- rebooking of tickets etc. and so we thought that it would be wiser that I proceeded as scheduled and cooled my heels for a week at my nephew's place rather than postponing the scheduled departure.

Unfortunately, my US visa had just expired. I therefore sent one of the officers with my passport to the US consulate at Mumbai for submitting my visa application in the drop-box. He was advised by the officer there that I would be required to visit in person. Since 9/11 had just taken place, getting the US visa was problematic. I had to fly to Delhi for my Danish visa and then to Mumbai for the US visa. All this caused me to skip getting myself health insurance. During those days there were no private companies and the Government Insurance companies operated five days a week. But then my visit was a short one. And I was young enough to take risks. I therefore decided to proceed without health cover.

THE FIRST GLIMPSE

I had the first glimpse of the American systems at Mumbai Airport itself. I was waiting in the queue for checking-in when I saw an airline's employee approaching me; a young girl of Delta Airlines in a well ironed uniform. I had been to US a few times in the past and was well aware of the rigmarole. Hence, before the girl started questioning me, I in a monologue said, "These are my bags. I packed them last night. I have not opened these since then. No one has given any material to be carried to US. I am not going to open the bags until I hand them over at the counter."

But Alas! She was bound by the American Systems. For her (though an Indian) the rules and regulations had to be followed. And so, she said, "Thank you Sir. But I still have to ask you some questions." And the following question – answer session took place.

Q1: - "Sir, whose bags are these?"

Ans: - "These are my bags."

Q2: - "When did you pack them last?"

Ans: - "I packed them last night."

Q3: - "Have you opened them since then?"

Ans: - "No. I haven't."

Q4: - "Has anyone given you any material to be carried to the US?"

Ans: - "No, no one has."

"OK! Kindly do not open these until you hand over the bags at the counter. Thank you, Mr Joshi, and have a nice flight."

She took out some coloured stickers, pasted them on to my bags and continued with the person behind me in the queue. For her the rules had to be followed; come what may.

THE JOURNEY BEGINS

After around forty hours of gruelling journey from Indore to Pittsburgh via Mumbai, Paris and New York, I reached the destination. The Company's representative picked me up from the airport. After driving for two hours, we reached a small town, where the factory was located. I checked into a hotel and ordered a green salad, as it was closing time for the hotel restaurant. In spite of my extreme hunger, I could hardly eat a portion of it, but then when one travels abroad; one has to be ready to face such an eventuality. The salad was full of broccoli. It was so pungent that even Jughead would refuse to eat it.

The next day was a day of surprises. The factory turned out to be a replica of Static Transformers in terms of size, hotchpotch layout, untidy appearance, and so on. We tend to form a mental picture based on the glossy & colourful catalogues, especially if the same are received from white men.

The factory tour took not more than fifteen minutes. Another surprise was in store for me. I was to negotiate a business deal with the CEO (Chief Executive Officer) and he was missing! I was politely told that he was reaching Pittsburgh the next day at 11.30 AM and that our meeting would take place over lunch there. The CEO was to catch another flight at 2.30 PM.

We had been corresponding with this CEO for the past few months and based on his emails, we believed that the said CEO was very keen to have a business association with us, which certainly would call for a slot of more than 3 hours. The luncheon meeting in a crowded restaurant was a mere formality, by the end of which it was clear that the Americans were not at all interested in the business. In Hindi there is a saying which summarises this episode. It is "Khoda Pahad Aur Nikli Chuhiya". (One digs up the whole mountain only to find a small mouse).

The CEO dropped me at Pittsburgh railway station at 2.00 PM from where I was to catch a train at 10 PM. It was mid-December and hence quite cold in the open. In addition, the CEO's cold response had frozen my spirits. I therefore spent most of this waiting period sitting at the station. For dinner I ventured out trying to find some Pizza Hut or

McDonald's or if I were lucky, some Indian restaurant. My hour-long search did not yield any result, rather inadvertently it whetted up my appetite.

After another hour's search in the nearby market, I located a Chinese restaurant, which I thought was a good bet. Most of the tables of the restaurant were unoccupied. The aroma of Chinese food was missing. The menu was quite unfamiliar. I could locate only one entry, which I believed was fit for human consumption. It was veg- chow mein costing seven dollars. The dish arrived soon. Visual examination revealed that there were exactly seven green pieces of some vegetable leaf in the heap of noodles. My first bite revealed that the cook had used Mobile Oil as the frying medium. In disgust, I walked out after keeping seven dollars on the table.

I remembered a joke I had read while I was in high school. A diner orders a meal in the restaurant. A display board says "Today's Special: - 50% Chicken with 50% Horse for just Rs.20". The diner gets annoyed when he finds only one very small piece of chicken in the serving. He calls the waiter for an explanation who politely says, "Sir, the cook prepares food using one horse and one chicken."

Before I boarded the train, I managed my dinner with a piece of pizza I could buy at the station. Apu cherished the rest of 330 degrees the next day. Early following morning, I woke up and went straight over to the Pantry for a coffee. I had removed my shoes and had dozed off in the cosy seat of the chair car. I had walked to the pantry car without putting on my shoes (and unlike many, my feet or socks do not stink). As soon as I entered the Pantry Car, the pantry man (not so politely) told me to return to my seat and put on my shoes. I had just got up from sleep and it took some time to comprehend. In the meantime, he added, "That is the Rule. Man!" Feeling a little hurt at being snubbed by a white man I went back.

I returned with my shoes on and ordered a coffee. While I was sipping the watery coffee sitting at a window seat, a young white lady entered. Just like me she was not wearing shoes. The white man snubbed her too, this time his arrogance was more distinct in his tone. The lady had probably come from a far-off bogie and did not want to go back. She started arguing with the pantry man who however remained quite stubborn. The lady suggested a via media. Having walked so far, and being already there, she suggested that she would carry her coffee to her seat and not stay in the pantry car without shoes. The pantry man stuck to his guns and said, "These are safety requirements and I am not allowed to serve you unless you are here wearing shoes. My hurt was gone. It was not a white-brown behaviour. It was the result of "The Great American Systems". My appreciation for American Systems went up.

BACK TO THE MAIN EPISODE

I reached Chicago the next day in the morning and boarded a local bus from the station. At one of the bus-stops an old lame lady was waiting in her wheelchair. The driver stopped the bus; opened the doors of the bus, pressed another button and as a result the stairs of the bus automatically got converted into a slope. The lady rolled her chair on the slope onto the bus. No passenger helped her. Once she (in her wheelchair) was inside the bus, she manoeuvred her chair to a specified place clearly marked for handicapped persons and snapped the hanging chain to her chair to secure the same. In the meantime, the driver converted the slope into stairs and closed the door. The bus started moving. No one uttered a word except the lady who told the driver her destination. My appreciation for the American Systems went sky high.

I spent a week with Apu during which I hurt my shoulder very badly. I had gone shopping and had slipped on the pavement. In the process my shoulder was badly hurt. The swelling at the shoulder waxed from the size of a TT ball by noon to a football by the evening. My tension increased in proportion until the next day when the swelling as well as pain subsided.

In spite of being a non-believer I thanked God and cursed myself for not getting proper insurance.

THE ONWARD JOURNEY

I was to leave Chicago at 9 AM, on 16 Dec. and reach Newark airport at 3 PM. I was to catch a shuttle at 4 PM to reach JFK Airport at 5 PM. All checked and confirmed on the net.

Accordingly, I boarded the flight at 9 AM on 16th December. The flight reached Newark – at 3.30 instead of 3 PM., which was within tolerable limits i.e., I had enough time margin. My wait for the baggage started. The delivery conveyor was at a standstill. The minute hand crossed 12 and the conveyor still was still. Panic started setting in. I was comforting myself by assuming that even if I miss the 4 O'clock shuttle I would catch the next one at 5 PM and would be at JFK by 6 PM, one and a half hours before the next scheduled departure. The baggage arrived 15 minutes after four by which time the 4 O'clock limo had left.

As luck would have it, there was heavy traffic and the 5 O'clock shuttle reached JFK at 6.30 PM. I took my bags and handed over 10 dollars in change to the limo driver who just about cursed me and refused to accept the change (I had earlier watched my nephew putting 50 pennies in the slot for a bus ticket, while the bus driver watched and waited patiently). But then all human beings are not the same.

I got the shock of my life when I saw a long queue for entering the airport. This was a result of 9/11. There was no point in requesting the security personnel to let me in on priority; else they would suspect that I belonged to Al Qaeda. And so, I waited helplessly in the queue. Had I been a believer, I would have started muttering Hanuman Chalisa or Ramraksha. (Religious chants invoking God)

I cleared the security and after waiting for some more time in another queue, I reached the Delta counter at 7 PM. The counterman punched in my ticket details and said, "Sorry Sir, the flight is closed" I pleaded and requested him to accommodate me in the flight. The officer did try to help. He phoned the pilot of the aircraft, but did not succeed.

I had just about 400 dollars with me, which was sufficient for a two-day break of journey at Frankfurt. I therefore had to work out a contingency plan. First of all, I went to the reservation counter to book a seat on the next day's flight (similarly to change Frankfurt Mumbai booking from 18th to 19th December. Incidentally my visa (Danish) was valid only till 19th December.

The booking clerk confirmed the ticket for New York to Frankfurt sector and asked me to pay 400 dollars towards rescheduling charges. I explained to him that never before had I paid such charges on international flights and secondly, I did not have 400 dollars left with me. He thought for a while, fiddled with the keys of the keyboard and returned my ticket after a considerable time saying, "Here you are." I heaved a huge sigh of relief.

Many nights during my college days and even afterwards I would dream that I was to appear for an exam the next day and that I had not studied or prepared at all. Scared, I would wake up only to realise that it was a dream and not reality. One could call it a mild nightmare. The few minutes the booking clerk was fiddling with his keyboard was just like déjà vu of my dreams.

I had two options for the night. I could sleep at the airport or go to a hotel. I felt quite unsafe to spend the night at the airport. Had I been younger I would have gone for that option. I worked out a contingency plan. I had sufficient money to reach Odense in Denmark where I would borrow a few hundred dollars from Elvstrom of AXA Power, with whom I had good business relations.

A nearby hotel costing about 150 dollars a night offered free Airport pick-up service. I went over to that hotel, stood in the queue for check-in for about an hour. Once in the room, I called Apu and informed him of the day's happenings and also asked him to mail Indore and Denmark to inform them of the change of my flight schedule.

The next day I checked out at 12 noon utilising the hotel's comforts to the last dollar and straight went to the Airport on vacating the room. Taking no risks, at 1 PM, six and a half hours prior to the departure time, I checked in my baggage, took the boarding card and had a sandwich for lunch. I then went over to the booking counter for confirmation of my onward journey. By then I had about 200 dollars left with me. As per my plan this was enough to cover the train ticket from Frankfurt to Odense and other expenses.

I handed over my ticket to the counter clerk, she keyed in the ticket details. She took a considerable time before she asked me for my boarding card. Unsuspectingly, I gave her my New York - Frankfurt Boarding card. She again punched some keys at her terminal and asked me for 400 dollars. It was a shock to me. Ten minutes of argument later I asked her to call her supervisor. A smart young girl in uniform appeared. Another round of arguments followed. She refused to return my boarding card and threatened to call back my baggage. I pleaded and told her about my financial status. However, she did not budge. She gave me her card and said, "Call your nephew or any one for money, but we cannot bend the rules".

I moved out from the counter and walked the entire departure lounge searching for some Indian Businessman returning to India with a hope to get some help. It was, however, like searching for a needle in a haystack.

I then called Apu and narrated the whole story. I asked him to pay Delta using the net. After 30 dollars' worth calls later, I learnt from him that 400 dollars were paid to Delta against my ticket. By 4 PM I got my boarding card. I returned the supervisor's card and casually said that I had spent 30 dollars in calls. I felt most stupid when she replied, "Why didn't you use my card?" I had not seen a calling card before.

I thought the ordeal was over but there was one more surprise waiting for me on my way home. I reached Frankfurt the next morning and took a train to Frankfurt Main and from there to Odense arriving at 9 PM. It was drizzling outside and the temperature was just above zero. I lugged my bags to the hotel around 500 meters from the station and checked in there.

The next morning, I had a heavy breakfast, which is the only familiar meal one gets there. Elvstrom picked me up and we spent time working out our business deal. Except for a small lunch break we were busy in working out the details. Mrs. Ackerman, wife of the Ex-owner of AXA Power, had informed the canteen keeper of my eating habits. And so, I could eat some raw vegetables, two boiled eggs and some bread for lunch.

We closed our deal by 3 PM. Elvstrom took me to the hotel; I picked up my bags from there. He then dropped me at the station and helped me buy my ticket to Frankfurt. Until then I was still waitlisted on the 19th Frankfurt Mumbai flight.

As per the railway timetable, I was to board a train from Odense at 5 PM, reach a small station called Ringsted at 6.20, catch another train at 6.40 for Hamburg in Germany. I was to reach Hamburg at 10.10 PM and board the train for Frankfurt at 10.40 PM. I was to reach Frankfurt at 6 AM on the 19th. From there I would take a local to Frankfurt airport which is just a few minutes journey, to board the Frankfurt – Mumbai flight scheduled to depart at 10.30 AM.

The journey from Odense to Ringsted was uneventful. At Ringsted, I checked the display on the platform "Bohr -4 (Platform 4) to Hamburg" was clearly displayed. I trust the European rails for their punctuality.

It was very chilly and the platform was totally open except for a small heated waiting room. During my 20 minutes of waiting, I checked the display four times. At sharp 6.40 PM, a train arrived on Platform 4. Including me, all the passengers (not more than 20) boarded the train. Within a minute the doors closed and the train picked up speed. Even before I settled into a seat, I sensed that there was something wrong. The train decor was not like a long-distance train and so I asked a lady passenger if the train was going to Hamburg. "I don't know" was her reply. The same was the answer I got from two more passengers. I then spotted a dark-skinned man. From his looks I could make out that he was a Srilankan (you find quite a few Srilankan refugees in Denmark) I checked with him.

He gave me the shock of my life. He said, "No! This is a local train. The train for Hamburg was late by a minute. This train will divert from the main track to another destination after a few stations"

I panicked. I was in a real fix. My visa was expiring on the 19th. My travel plan was kind of "JUST IN TIME". How would I reach Frankfurt to catch my flight? I explained my predicament to the Srilankan. I was at my wits end and it must have showed on my face.

The Srilankan also informed me that the train to Hamburg was an express train which would stop at very few stations and that the option to go back to Ringsted to catch the next train to Hamburg would mean a considerable delay. I would not be able to catch the next day's flight.

But just then the ticket checker wearing a navy-blue uniform arrived. The Srilankan immediately explained my situation to him in Danish. After a few minutes of conversation, the Ticket Checker took out a mobile phone; punched a few digits. He spoke for a minute or two on the phone and then spoke to the Srilankan. This short period of a few minutes was AGES to me. Finally, the Srilankan turned to me and with a smile on his face said, "Look, he has talked to the driver of the Hamburg train. On the next station it will overtake this local. What you have to do is to get down at the next station, cross over to the neighbouring platform. The Hamburg train will stop for you for a minute"

I profusely thanked the Danish Ticket Checker. He might not have understood my English, but certainly my facial expressions conveyed my gratitude.

The Sri Lankan volunteered to add "Look! I am also getting down at the next station. I will help you to cross over to the next platform"

At the next station, I literally ran (not-withstanding the pain in my injured shoulder enhanced by lugging my heavy bag). The Srilankan helped me and carried my briefcase. I was panting heavily as I reached the platform and just in seconds the train arrived. I pressed the button; the doors opened; I climbed in with my bags. The Srilankan threw in my briefcase he was carrying. The doors closed and the train was in motion even before I could thank the Srilankan.

Rest of the Journey is history. At Frankfurt Airport, my booking was confirmed and I reached home safely (not that I lived happily ever after). At Frankfurt airport, I overheard an American teenage girl who was using the next phone booth. She was speaking to her mother and from what I heard I could make out that she was short of money and was talking to her mother complaining that it was the airline's fault and not hers. She was sobbing loudly. Probably she was in a similar situation like what I had gone through. I thought I would comfort her and provide some help. However, as I offered help, she said, "No. Thank you" and walked away.

This small episode apart I am sure readers would appreciate why I titled this chapter **"AMERICAN SYSTEMS VIZ-A-VIZ DANISH HUMAN TOUCH"**

--xxx--

LABOUR PAINS

THIS CHAPTER IS DEDICATED TO

GIRISH PATWARDHAN

WHO

LABOURED FOR US

WITHOUT

ANY COMPENSATION

Labour Pains

Anyone running an industrial unit in India undergoes labour pains. The pain may be a bit misplaced compared to what women endure during childbirth.

I had formal training in Personnel Management while I was at NITIE. I never liked such subjects, as they were very unlike mathematics or physics. There is never a definitive answer. But then, in the real world, we have to deal with human beings, whose behavior is quite unpredictable.

At NITIE we went through case studies, theory X, Y, Z and so on. All such courses somehow failed to influence me enough to change my nature, especially with respect to dealing with people. For me, two plus two remains four. This probably is my biggest weakness and in spite of being aware of the same, I still choose to call a spade a spade.

I got involved with workmen, when I was employed with Steel Tubes (May1979- May1982). I had to take part in negotiations with union leaders. My interaction with workmen was considerable during that period as I was implementing various workmen related schemes. The workmen at Steel Tubes were first generation industrial workers and were fairly simple and amicable and as such I did not face any problems in dealing with them.

Once, on some issue the workers went on strike at Steel Tubes. I do not recollect the cause but do remember that the strike lasted a week to ten days.

The workmen had pitched a tent outside the factory gate and they sat there throughout the day, the numbers exponentially dwindling from morning to evening. Whenever any Director's car used to reach the gate, the workmen used to stand and start shouting slogans in unison. Similarly, when our Matador used to drop us at the main entrance, the workmen used to close-in, loudly shouting slogans like "Dutta Hai Hai", "Baheti Hai Hai" and so on. Baheti was the MD and Dutta was the

Works Director of Steel Tubes. I had joined Steel Tubes as an Industrial Engineer and was in the process of establishing the Industrial Engineering Department.

Probably on the second or the third day of the strike, they noticed me and the slogans started, "Joshiji[1*] Hai Hai", "Joshiji Hai Hai". The chant went on for a while until Aslam, their notorious leader, realised the mistake the masses were committing. I could hear him yelling "Joshiji Nahi – Joshi Hai Hai" and the "Ji" got truncated.

EPISODE II

When I was handling the affairs of Migma (1985-1989), I had to taste a bitter pill. Our factory was at Pithampur and the Company matador used to ferry the staff from Indore to Pithampur and back every day. Most of the days I used to go by car to Pithampur while occasionally I took the matador ride. Here, unlike at Steel Tubes, I was the Managing Director and was totally responsible for the performance of our unit.

Once, on a rainy day, while we were on our way to the factory, and were a few kilometers away from Indore on the Bombay-Agra highway, a calf suddenly appeared on the road, frolicking across quite unexpectedly. Our driver slammed the brakes, but the vehicle skidded on the wet road and hit the calf. I was sitting on the front seat next to the driver who happened to be a Muslim. He, for a moment, looked at me for instructions. I instantly said "Chalo, chalo" which made him press the accelerator. By the time we reached the factory we thought it was the end of the matter.

In the evening, on our way back, I was driving my car. Our seventy-year-old consultant was with me. The matador was following the car at a short distance. As we reached Pigdambar, a village where the morning accident had taken place, we were stopped by a mob of villagers. We all were pulled out of the vehicles and given a good thrashing, until we managed to settle the issue by offering compensation of five hundred bucks to the calf owner. The villagers spared only three members of the

---

[1*] One adds 'Ji' to the name to address someone with respect

team - Mr. Paranjpe, our consultant, probably for his age; our young female engineer Preeti, for her gender; and surprisingly our driver.

The reader may wonder as to what is so special about this incidence as to make me narrate it. Such things happen and are part of life but the main story comes later.

Had the villagers known that the driver was a Muslim, the story would have come to a sticky end, and my asking him to move on after the calf was hit, was to avoid any such complications.

A few months later this same driver resigned. He had probably had some grievance about his low pay. It is perfectly fine if someone resigns. However, just before he left, he messed up the vehicle by adding sugar in the diesel tank. The consequence: a lot of money spent on repairs and for hiring another vehicle as a stopgap arrangement.

This taught me a big lesson about human behavior. Until then, I always used to disagree with my colleagues at Migma, who would look at every action of any workmen with suspicion, while I would assert, "Damn it! We have a calling-by-first-name kind of relationship. Why the hell do you doubt that they are against us; ultimately, they also realise that they get paid from the tappets we sell".

EPISODE III

Then one day, we had to sack a workman for his perpetual absenteeism. Fortunately, or unfortunately, he was a Muslim youngster and was residing at a ghetto near Pithampur, quite notorious for its links with the underworld. Soon we were visited by "a Bhai" who asked us to re-employ the lad or else....

We certainly wanted no violence (Once bitten, twice shy) and at the same time did not want to reemploy the lad, to avoid setting a bad precedence. And so, we got into action. One of our vendors from Dhar, a near-by town, knew a Muslim "Dada". With his help we got the Molavi and some other elders of the ghetto to our factory. We explained the situation to them and proposed to them that we would re-employee the lad but then in future we will not employ any more Muslims. The wise men went back and peace reigned. Later we heard that the elders gave the lad a thrashing for earning a bad name for their community.

Other than these, there were no major labour problems at Migma. Nor even at Static. However, when I started writing this chapter, I had in mind a different case, which I narrate below.

THE MAIN EPISODE

When I took over Static, it had employed one Hemant Atre. He was the production supervisor, being paid a low salary of around 1600 rupees a month. He did not have any formal technical education and had just completed 5th standard. He joined Static in 1970, as a helper and had risen to the post of production supervisor over the period. He had a very good grasp of his work and a personality with leadership qualities.

During my first year at Static, I had increased the salaries of all staff to a reasonable level and as a result this chap started getting more than 2000 rupees per month, which later went up to Rs. 3100 per month by the end of 1993. Here, I must admit that I failed to judge the employed personnel at Static; or rather I took a long time to do so. By then the damage was done. By early 1994 I learnt that this chap was making money on the side. Moreover, he had grown too big for his shoes. I had other engineers in the organisation, and Hemant's interference with their work had grown beyond tolerance.

And so, by the end of that year we decided to sack him. We paid all his remuneration dues like gratuity, leave and notice pay etc. He got over Rs. 60000/- from us and that was a considerable sum. All this happened in December 1994, just two years after I had taken over Static.

Hemant took the cheque, but kept coming back to us asking us to reconsider our decision. He then asked us to pay him workmen's retrenchment compensation, which amounted to Rs. 40000/-. We flatly refused, reasoning that he was not a workman.

He then complained to the labour department (of the State Government) who served us a show cause notice.

At that point, I took the help of Mr. Bhatnagar, a retired assistant labour commissioner (who had worked with me at Migma) and sent a reply to the notice giving documentary evidence that Hemant was a supervisor and not a workman and hence not eligible for any retrenchment compensation. The evidence comprised of 30 odd annexures. These included photocopies of attendance registers; salary registers with computerised printouts with his designation and his signature. We had enclosed leave applications of workmen endorsed by him, instruction sheets issued to the workmen, which were prepared and signed by him, and many other relevant documents. All this did not satisfy the labour department and they called us for a hearing.

The hearings went on for twenty odd occasions spread over two years. Each time the Government officials insisted on working out a compromise, probably to improve their statistics. However, being extremely confident of our stand we did not yield. All this was a painful process and consumed considerable time. I could have considered paying him off to avoid these troublesome and torturous visits to the Labour Commissioner's office. But then, at Static, we employed fifty odd persons and every one could blackmail us by creating a situation, which would force us into sacking him and then subsequently paying the ransom.

Finally, after two years, the labour department gave a ruling that the case be dropped as Hemant Atre was a supervisor and not a workman and therefore not eligible for workmen's compensation. We were extremely pleased with the ruling not realising that we had only won the battle and not the war.

After about a month or two, we again got a letter from the Labour department, signed by the Labour Commissioner, stating that Hemant Atre's case was being referred to the Labour Court. We were surprised but helpless. We later learnt that Hemant Atre's lawyer had obliged Gupta, the then Labour Commissioner who was handling the case, and had in turn taken this favour.

In the course of my interaction with various Government officials and lawyers, I had learnt that if any official had given a ruling, he on his own was not authorised to change it. It had to be reviewed by his superior authority for any amendment, particularly a reversal. However, in this particular case, (our lawyer informed us) this principle would not be applicable, as the file had already moved to the Labour court.

The court case went on and on until the judgment was announced in January 2004 i.e., after eight years. This shows the difference between Englishmen and Indians. They say 'justice delayed is justice denied' while we believe in *'bhagwan ke ghar der hai andher nahi'*. [God's justice can be delayed, but never denied]

During the trial, we provided the court with all the documentary evidence. We had engaged Girish Patvardhan, the most renowned lawyer of Indore dealing with labour cases. Whenever we discussed the matter with him, he appeared to be sure that our side was strong, but at the end, he always added, "but then, we never know".

If I am not wrong, as per the Indian laws any employee getting more than Rs. 1600/- per month was deemed to be a non-workman at that time; and thus, not covered by labour laws. For years together the figure had not been revised and hence it was a defunct law. Girish would say, "The court will not take cognizance of it". The Judiciary can ask the Delhi Government to clean up Yamuna, but cannot clean up their Laws.

The uncertainties, therefore, continued for a few years until my turn for my statement in the court came sometime in 2003. Unfortunately, we could not find any letter or document in the office, which could prove that he was promoted as a supervisor. In my opinion the circumstantial evidence was good enough, though. Month after month no worker would sign, marking his attendance in the attendance register meant for supervisory staff, nor would any workman sign on the payslips where his name and designation was printed as XXX, Production Supervisor. However, I wanted to be doubly sure of our stand.

During this whole process, we had faced one more problem. We found that some papers from his personnel file were missing. We suspected that someone very loyal to Atre may be behind such happenings and so we had to keep all the papers secured at home, and bring the same on the day of the court hearing.

Our chaps had searched all the possible files to dig for any additional evidence. Finally, we came across a document with Hemant's signature as a supervisor. This document was different than all the previous ones.

Hemant Atre had gone to Garden Reach Shipbuilders & Engineers Ltd., Kolkata in January1992 to negotiate a contract for supply of transformers worth seven lacs. As a matter of fact, on my first day at Static i.e., on 6th January 1992, he was not at Indore but at Kolkata. There he had signed as supervisor on behalf of Static Transformers on the minutes of the meeting of TNC and also had taken part in commercial and price negotiations. A photocopy of these minutes was in the file. Since these meetings were attended by GRSE officials and two or three representatives of different Directorates of Indian Navy, as a matter of practice the original was kept by GRSE and photocopies were provided to others.

I immediately requested GRSE for the original document. Since that order was executed long back, GRSE had no difficulty in obliging us. During my statement in the court, I produced the same as additional documentary evidence. I argued that a small-scale company like ours could not possibly send a workman to negotiate an order worth seven lacs, which during that period made up 15% of our annual turnover. I am sure even Telco or L&T does not depute a workman for such work.

After maybe   six months or so, I was cross-examined by Atre's lawyer. The cross-examination could not be completed in one day and continued on another day, two months later. Girish's assistants who were present during the cross-examination were extremely excited and informed Girish later that I had given Pradhan (Atre's lawyer) a tough time.

Anyway, the proceeding went on and on and in January 2004 the court judgment was declared. Girish's assistant told us that it was in our favour. At last, we were relieved, in fact, elated.

In the game of Bridge there is a saying: "The Queen follows the Nine". In my life I would say, "Every good news is followed by two bad ones". When the judgment was made public a few days later, I went to Girish to pick up our copy. He informed me that there was a mistake in his information, "The court has held," he added, "Hemant was a workman and his dismissal had made him face financial hardships and therefore he should be compensated by payment as per The Workmen's Retrenchment Compensation Act." Girish said that court has not asked us for his reinstatement and to that extent gave us a relief.

I discussed the matter of moving the High Court. Girish, however discouraged me saying that the High Court will first ask us to deposit Rs. 40000/- with it and secondly, we have to pay court fees etc. Further the chances of the High Court reverting the labour court's decision were slim. Girish was a working partner of Sharad Patwardhan, a close family acquaintance of Nilesh. Girish therefore had not taken a penny from us till then. Moving the High Court would also have resulted in taxing him again.

We therefore decided to pay up. I called Atre to my office, gave him four cheques of 10000/- each, to be encashed at periodic intervals.

--xxx---

WHAT IF

THIS CHAPTER IS DEDICATED TO

MY NEPHEW APU

WHO HAS MORE ASIMOVS

TO HIS CREDIT

THAN I HAVE

What If?

I am a fan of Isaac Asimov, one of the greatest Science Fiction writers. I recollect one of his stories about a couple who get hold of a magic screen wherein one could simulate one's life story of the past. One could see, "What would have happened, had one done X instead of Y?" Hence the title of this short story: "WHAT IF?"

The husband wishes in front of the screen, "What would have happened if I had married Merry instead of my existing wife?" The screen ends up showing that after some quarrel with Merry at a party he would have spilled wine & spoiled her dress, and that would have led to their divorce followed by the second marriage with his present wife. In short, the moral of the story was: "One cannot change one's destiny." However, those in a situation like mine must have pondered a number of times on WHAT IF lines. It is not brooding over the past, but a sort of daydreaming in reverse.

Today is my third session of writing (this attempted kind of autobiography) and I thought that I should start from the beginning. One truly becomes an IITian when one graduates from one of the IITs, which I did in 1975. By the time I passed out, I already had a couple of job offers; one from Damodar Valley Corporation and one from Consolidated Pneumatics Ltd., Pune. I had also qualified for admission for the Post Graduate Programme in Industrial Engineering at NITIE, a coveted School for post-graduation in Industrial Engineering. Since I was keen on pursuing higher studies, I decided to join NITIE, which selected around 50 engineering graduates every year for its two-year PG Programme.

I was to join in July 1975 and hence had declined both the job offers. I was enjoying the last of my summer holidays and then in June the first wrong thing happened. I had gone for an evening walk with a friend of mine and that is when I came across a bullock cart carrying heavy steel girders stuck in the mud. We helped to get the bullock cart on the road. During the process I had to push with all my strength.

That night I felt some pain in my chest which persisted for a week and was accompanied by fever. My father, who was a doctor himself, did not take the matter very seriously for the first few days. However, by the end of the week he examined me. Within five seconds of auscultation of my chest, he became very tense. He pulled the stethoscope from his ears and flung it away as if it was a poisonous snake. He only uttered, "It is Pleurisy".

He immediately drove me down to the radiologist for screening and then with the X-ray film to a specialist doctor who confirmed the diagnosis as Traumatic Pleurisy, a kind of Tuberculosis. As a consequence, I was bedridden for three months and missed my admission at NITIE. This happened in June 1975. My elder sister who was pursuing her PhD at TIFR (Tata Institute of Fundamental Research at Mumbai) went over to NITIE and explained the situation to the NITIE officials with a request to permit me to join in October instead of July. The request, however, was turned down. Then she requested them to permit me to join the next year's session i.e., the one commencing in July 1976, but even that request was declined.

After three months and over a hundred injections later I was out of the bed and had recouped. Luckily for me, I spotted an advertisement of Gajra Gears Ltd. Dewas, a small town around 35 KM from Indore, for recruitment of Graduate Engineering Trainees. I applied and was immediately selected. I joined Gajra Gears in Oct 1975 at a stipend of Rs. 550/- per month, one third of what I would have received at Consolidated Pneumatics.

The next year I reappeared for the entrance examination for admission to NITIE and improved my rank to within the first 20 (It was fifty odd in my first attempt) and joined the PG programme in July 1976.

So, sometimes, I wish I had a WHAT IF screen where I could have asked, "What would I be had my body successfully fought the TB bacilli and I had joined NITIE in 1975 rather than working with Gajra Gears?"

MY DAYS WITH GAJRA GEARS

Within a week of my joining Gajra Gears, one day all the GETs (Graduate Engineer Trainees) were summoned by the Company's Personnel Officer. He asked everyone to fill up and sign a Three-Year Bond which meant that if one left the service within three years one would have to return all the salary earned till then. Since for me Gajra Gears was a stopgap arrangement as I had already made up my mind to go for post-Graduation by next academic year, I refused to sign the Bond.

I was then called by the Executive Director of the Company who, in no uncertain terms, asked me to sign the bond or quit. I learned from him that they got some subsidy from the Government for employing GETs and that the Government insisted on a three-year bond. My argument that we should have been told this before we accepted the job offer was futile. Owing to the TINA factor (There Is No Alternative) I signed the bond.

Later when I resigned from the Job, I had to go to Mumbai twice to some Government Office to get myself absolved from the bond on the grounds that I was leaving for higher education.

Except for the above, the time I spent with Gajra Gears was uneventful. As a Graduate Engineer Trainee in the Industrial Engineering Department, my job was limited to issuing time standards for any new machining operation. I used to complete my work in less than a few hours every day. The work at Gajra Gears was so compartmentalized that, in spite of my wish, I was not permitted to take up other assignments. However, I did learn a great deal about the application of Industrial Engineering and also about Automobile Gears, Machining Processes etc.

--xxx---

STATIC PROPOSES AND BHEL DISPOSES
(JUNE 1995)

THIS CHAPTER IS DEDICATED TO

THE VENDORS OF

OUR NAVRATNA PSUS

Static Proposes and Bhel Disposes
(June 1995)

One of our main concerns at Static Transformers was the lack of orders. Before I took over, the turnover of Static Transformers was around Rs 25 lacs (1991-92). During the process of evaluation of the unit I had asked the Company's Director, Mr. Moghe, to give me Market Projections. I had asked him if there was any scope to grow to the level of Rs. 1 crore in turnover with the existing clients and products and he had promptly provided such a list.

In reality, however, it was not an achievable target. Upon joining Static Transformers, I found that sales and marketing activities, particularly order procurement was nobody's responsibility. The enquiries received by post from various clients were attended to and Moghe visited various scientists at CAT (Center for Advanced Technology) twice a week to get petty orders, which included even supply of Fevicol. On the whole, it was a mess.

One of my first steps therefore, was recruitment of a Marketing Manager and a Marketing Officer. Accordingly, we advertised and selected Narendra Vishwaroop, an Aeronautical Engineer, and Quraishi to form the marketing team. We also prepared and printed the Company's Product Catalogue. All these efforts yielded positive results within a couple of years.

Sometime in 1993, we got a query for Electrical Power & Starter Panels for Trishul Missile Launcher, which was planned to be built by BHEL (Bharat Heavy Electricals Limited), Trichy. Promptly, Vishwaroop visited the prospective client, located some 2000 kilometers away. The Launcher Project was subsequently transferred to BHEL, Ranipet, a small town in Tamil Nadu, between Chennai and Bangalore. We learnt that this indigenous launcher was to be fitted on INS Brahmaputra, a warship under construction at Garden Reach Shipbuilders and Engineers Limited (GRSE), Kolkata. Three ships of this class were to be built (as on date i.e., in June 2004, the second one is undergoing sea trials).

We, therefore, were keen to bag the order, as it would very likely get repeated thrice. After a long procedure of tendering, a visit by BHEL officer to evaluate our technical capability, and many visits of Vishwaroop to Ranipet, we finally got the order worth ten lac rupees which had a material component of around five lacs.

We were to design, get the drawings approved, manufacture the Panels for the Trishul Missile Launcher, getting some components directly from BHEL; get the panels tested at our factory as well as at some test laboratories; and finally supply the product to BHEL.

When any new equipment is to be inducted for fitment onboard a warship, it has to clear a number of tests - especially environmental tests. These tests are called Type Tests. Such tests include satisfactory operation of the equipment at -30 °C or at +55° C, at 95% humidity, under specified shock and vibration conditions, and so on.

The gruelling process of drawing approval started. We cleared the first step of preparing the drawings & quality assurance plan (QAP) and getting the same approved by the client. If I recall correctly, it took us no less than five visits of our design engineer to Ranipet, and seven revisions of drawings and QAP before the same were finally accepted.

It was the period when this new gimmick of ISO 9000 had begun to spread in the country. Starting from Sulabh Sauchalaya to the most sophisticated DRDO laboratory every organisation was claiming that they were ISO 9000 certified. I am still not very clear about the numbering and its exact implication, but when anyone starts talking about ISO9000 – ISO9001 or even 10000 I get reminded of Howard 5000, Howard 10000, the beer brands. In my mind, they both had the same level of importance and significance!

The panels were manufactured and cleared after testing and inspection at our factory. During the manufacturing process a number of component failures occurred. The panels were then shipped to Bangalore for testing at various Government Test Laboratories. It took several months to get the required tests done and finally the panels were certified OK and shipped to Ranipet. I must add that we also had to get the electronic cards tested at DRDO's lab at Hyderabad for ensuring that our equipment would meet the requirements of EMI, EMC (Electro-magnetic interference and electro-magnetic compatibility) standards.

The panels were then used during building and testing of the launcher at Ranipet. Surprisingly, in spite of many checks from the drawing stage, the panels had to be rewired, and components replaced many times. For all this our team of engineers and technicians were visiting Ranipet very frequently.

We had already spent more than what we were to get paid. We were, all the time, counting only on the profit from the future supplies of the next two lots wherein we would get a good margin. Once the design is frozen, all these exercises would not be necessary during the supply of the future lots. We would not have to carry out all such testing and would not even have to visit the client.

By the time we cleared the project, it was already the year 1995. Initially I was not going into the depth of various technical matters but had delegated the job, as there was no complexity involved in the design of the panel. However, as the matter was lingering over a long time, I decided to get deeply involved.

I was quite upset at the frequent component failures, changes in the wiring, and for every such failure, we were getting the blame. The fact, however, was that functional requirements had not been correctly defined by the client. All this made me realise that there was a fallacy in the whole procedure and I wrote an article, which was published in The Free Press Journal. Readers can get the gist of the matter from this article, which I am reproducing below.

Quote * * * * *

ISO 9000: The magic wand

I am not even sure of the full form of ISO 9000. However, everybody who is somebody in the Indian Industry knows that it is the in-thing today.

A few weeks back a friend of mine, an MBA and all that (and I suspect he too does not know the full form) visited our factory, incidentally an SSI unit. Typical of the young manager, he talked of the great Dr. Manmohan Singh, globalisation, liberalization and of course, the need to explore the export market.

Presently, I told him that none of my employees was capable of writing ten sentences without making a mistake and that our unit was not yet ready for ISO9 leave alone ISO 9000! The wise man pitied me for my ignorance, lack of ambition & foresight and predicted that I would be pushed out into oblivion by some MNC soon. Though this was not going to give me sleepless nights, it made me put in all my efforts to change the topic to Madhuri Dixit or someone alike.

And then the other day, I was attending a dinner hosted by an industrialist in Bombay. He is also a friend of mine. The dinner was to celebrate (or to be precise, to advertise) his company's obtaining ISO9000 certification. Since I knew none of the guests, I spent time chatting with the hostess.

After she had had a couple of rounds of Campari, I was speechless (I can be a good listener if a lady is charming). Our conversation (or rather her monologue) became quite informal. This time she changed over from Madhuri Dixit to ISO 9000. She asked me if I knew anything about it and even before I could reply, saving me the embarrassment of my illiteracy of the topic, she continued, "God knows what it is; even after our Company received ISO 9000, our goods are exported, rejected and returned" None the wiser, I left the party amused.

This was the lighter side of my story and before coming to the hard facts you must know a little more about our factory. Well, we manufacture tailor-made electrical equipment for defence, NPC, BARC and many other large industries. Our turnover is probably less than the cost of bottle caps that Pepsi must be buying annually.

A few months back we received an order for some electrical panels from a very large ISO 9000 company. M/s Bhel Puri Limited (Hereafter referred to as BPL and not to be confused with the consumer durables manufacturer BPL) insisted on knowing each and every detail about our manufacturing practice right down to how we screw (the screws).

BPL asked for BOM, QAP, ATP (and many other three-lettered permutations) before we took up manufacturing. We submitted and got approved the engineering drawings, bill of materials, quality assurance plan etc. It took us three months to do all this and two months to manufacture the goods. But I was more than satisfied since having taken pains to produce the equipment in accordance with quality procedures approved by an ISO 9000 Company, I was sure that we would not face any problems as far as performance of our product was concerned.

Incidentally, we had used a number of MCCBs (molded case circuit breakers) in the equipment, which we had bought from another ISO 9000 Company, Prompt & Greaves (P&G). Being what they were, they had collected their payment promptly from us.

And then the day of the shop trial arrived. Three of 20 MCCBs refused to work in line with their TCs (Test Certificates furnished by P&G). Promptly, P&G representative provided us with statistical calculations to prove that it was one in a million chance and got the MCCBs replaced. In spite of this prompt service, we were aggrieved since the Bhel Puri Inspector had gone back in the meantime. This story continued for a few months and finally our equipment was shipped and installed at BPL who has not yet paid us since they are not sure if our equipment will perform and they will take a few more months before their other equipment arrives and they perform full load trials.

Unquote * * * * *

The story does not end here. One day we read in the papers that the Trishul Missile was successfully tested at INS Dronacharya. The photograph of the launcher was published in most of the newspapers.

"INS" is a short form for Indian Naval Ship. However, the general public may not know that INS Dronacharya is a Naval Base (On the ground) at Cochin and not a ship. Subsequently we learnt that the launcher built by BHEL was so heavy (true to their name) that it would sink Brahmaputra if installed onboard. So, Brahmaputra was floating on the sea without missiles (the matter got reported in the India Today under the caption "Tiger without teeth".)

Whether BHEL continued in the business and built further launchers is not known. But I guess they withdrew from the project. No one lost his job or salary at BHEL for the loss caused to the taxpayers. The only people who suffered were small-scale suppliers like us.

--xxx---

THE BIGGEST GAMBLE

THIS CHAPTER IS DEDICATED

TO

MR. NAPHADE & MR. TIWARI

OF

HAL, NASIK

FOR

BEING IMPARTIAL TO US

The Biggest Gamble – Part I

In December 2001, while on tour in Mumbai, my colleague noticed a tender advertisement for supply of 58 Self Propelled DC Ground Power Units (GPUs). The Advertisement was published by Hindustan Aeronautics Limited, Aircraft Division, Nasik. He informed me of the same over the telephone.

I immediately sent one of my officers to Nasik to buy the tender documents. On preliminary study of the technical specifications, we found that we could easily manufacture the GPUs. The project required integration of various readily available items like a battery-operated cart, engine-alternator, transformer rectifier, a little bit of control circuitry and bodybuilding of the vehicle.

The tender was due on February 21, 2002. We started our home work immediately as we thought if we could grab the order, it would take us out of the debt trap and that we could live "happily ever after" once we executed the order.

Our first priority, therefore, was to choose a battery-operated vehicle and also select a suitable engine-alternator (i.e., a generator). Once in June 2001, while I was in Mumbai at Air India for rectification / maintenance of our collaborator AXA Power's equipment, I had seen a number of battery-operated carts there. So, I went to Air India and got the address of the manufacturer of the vehicle. The manufacturer was Jost Engineering Ltd. of Thane. However, the Air India official gave me their Pune address and mistakenly informed me that they have their Works at Pune.

And so, from Mumbai I went to Pune and telephoned Jost's office only to learn that it was a Saturday and that they were about to close the office. I urged the Jost Marketing Engineer to meet me at the Hotel. He reluctantly visited the hotel and we discussed our requirements. He agreed to send the offer within a couple of days.

That day in the evening I went to my cousin Vikas who was a senior Officer in The Design Department of Kirloskar Oil Engines Ltd. Earlier, for our Indian Air Force Project we had done considerable study of engines manufactured by different companies and had found Kirloskar as the most suitable choice. And so, we planned to use the Kirloskar Engine for the GPU. Vikas and I had detailed technical discussions and more or less finalised the HA494 Kirloskar engine.

During our discussions, Vikas mentioned about one Wing Commander Wig, and casually said that Wig was most likely to get the order. Wg. Cdr. Wig was an Indian Air Force Officer who had joined HAL Nasik on deputation where he had risen to a very senior position before he finally retired from service. Reportedly he had made a lot of money and had obtained a plot of land allocated to him in a prime location in Pune where he had built a Bungalow and a workshop adjoining it.

Vikas told me that he was a very *'Chalu'* chap and had contacts in HAL at senior levels as well as in the higher echelons of the IAF. He also informed me that Wig had invited him to see the trolley (Self Peopled DC GPU), which he had already built in anticipation of getting the order. This information was too much for me to digest and I decided to visit Vikas on Sunday evening after his visit to Wig's Workshop. On Sunday Vikas described Wig's trolley and even drew a sketch of the GPU for me. Wig had boasted that he had every one "set" at HAL for getting the order.

From Pune I returned home via Ahmednagar where I visited Crompton Greaves to get a quotation from them for the required alternator. The offer I got was for list price less 50 %. One can realise how the Dealers / Distributors and Retailers fleece the ignorant public by selling the items at the Company's list price.

On my return we waited for Jost Engineering's quotation and received the same after considerable follow up with them. The cost of the trolley offered was around Rs. 2.50 lacs. After studying the Quote received from Jost's Pune Office we felt that the same was sent as a mere formality. And so, we contacted their head office at Thane and explained the importance of the Project to Jost's senior marketing people. Mr. Chawla, their

General Manager realised the future scope and decided to visit us. He visited us along with Nair, Jost's Baroda representative, and Manoj, their Indore dealer. The team stayed at Indore for two days. I informed them that the equipment to be supplied to HAL did not have much technical content and hence there would be many parties who would be participating in the bidding and the order would be placed on the lowest bidder. As per CVC (Central Vigilance Commission) guidelines to the Government Organisations / Departments and Government owned Companies, the order had to be placed with the lowest bidder. These guidelines were introduced a few years back during Mr. Vithal's Chairmanship of CVC. I told Jost team that our bid to HAL was indirectly their bid. They would get the order only if we got it and that we should consider it as our joint venture. Realising all this, the Jost team slashed the price from about Rs. 2.5 lacs to Rs. 1.4 lacs, and also made sure that their Mumbai/ Pune offices continued to quote their standard list price of Rs. 2.5 lacs to any one asking for 58 vehicles.

We had one more procurement to take care. It was the battery charger, which, as per specifications, was to be SMPS (Switch Mode Power Supply, a relatively new Technology then) based. Jost could not offer it.

Search for an Indian supplier on the Internet proved futile. We could not have developed it at such a short notice. Nair contacted all his offices across the Country and specially instructed Jost's Pune Office to search for a supplier. Since Wig had a trolley ready, I was sure he would have a source in Pune. And finally, we got the name of Mr. Abhyankar who was known to me as he hailed from Indore and was, at one time, my neighbour.

We contacted him and got his offer on phone and then, with all the available information, we could prepare our offer. We specified the engine / alternator / vehicle, etc.; enclosed all the catalogues; inserted a statement that we should be permitted to make a final selection of engine, alternator etc. without compromising the required performance parameters. The tender was due for submission on Feb 21st and was to be opened on the same day.

It was the evening of the 18th when we were taking the final prints of the tender documents. It was planned that one of our officers, Praveen, would leave with the tender on the 20th morning by bus so that he could reach Nasik the same night and he would go to HAL at Ojhar, about twenty kilometers from Nasik, on the 21st morning; deposit the tender before 1 PM which was the deadline for submission of tender. He could also have travelled by overnight luxury bus, which would reach Nasik by 7.30 or 8.00 A.M., but then we had to provide for possible traffic jams on the highway (or the bus could have a breakdown). We definitely did not want to miss the bus.

At 6.30 PM on Feb 18th, we got a call from HAL Nasik. Their Purchase Manager Mr. Naphade told us that there was an amendment in the required delivery schedule in the tender and that he was sending a Fax to us. The Fax arrived and it said: Please read: instead of existing entry under the column 'delivery period' "Prototype required within 15 days[2*] of the order i.e., by 31st March 2002 and bulk supply 10-15 per month July, Aug. 2002".

Though the language was a bit unclear it was evident that this was Wig's doing, clearly to dissuade other possible suppliers from bidding. Some months later, I was to learn that it was Mr. Bora, a very senior officer at HAL Nasik, who had this clause inserted. Bora had worked under Wig and was reportedly having very close relations with Wig. In our tender we simply wrote "we shall comply with the delivery terms provided the order is placed with us before 15th March 2002." **We were sure a Public Sector Company could never process an order so fast, and then our delivery commitment will not be called upon.**

THE D DAY ARRIVES

All this made us change our decision, and in addition I planned to join Praveen to attend the tender opening. Smita (my wife) and I left early in the morning on the 21st and drove to Nasik. At around 2.30 PM I rushed

---

[2*] For the benefit of readers with non-technical background I would like to explain that asking for the delivery of the Prototype within a short period of 15 days after ordering was like asking the supplier for the moon.

back to HAL from Nasik to attend the opening. There was a big crowd. More than ten parties had participated in the tender. As per HAL's practice, representatives of these parties were permitted to read every offer. After glancing through all the bids, I was sure only a few would be qualified. One party said that they would be mounting an imported unit on Jost battery cart. MAC Controls, another major player supplying GPUs to IAF, deviated on some technical grounds.

Now our task was to ensure that HAL did not throw us out of the race by finding our bid not as per the technical requirements. This was our first interaction with HAL, Nasik and somehow, we had to have some contact with a senior person who would be fair to us and not yield to Wig's pressure. So, on my way back from Ojhar to Nasik I called my cousin Air Commodore Jayanta Apte who then was AOC (Air Officer Commanding) of the Air Force Maintenance Command at Kanpur. He told me that he knew Mr. Mohan Nadgir, the GM of HAL Nasik, but not well enough to refer me to him. Instead, he suggested that I could meet A.Cmdr. Avinash Pandit, AOC of 11 BRD (Base and Repair Depot) This AF Station shares a common boundary wall with HAL Nasik and both use the same Runway. Since IAF is HAL's biggest customer, it was natural to expect the AOC of 11 BRD to have a good influence on the senior managers of HAL Nasik.

The same evening, I telephoned Pandit and fixed an appointment for the next day. I reached the AF station at the scheduled time. AC Pandit gave me a patient hearing and asked me the names of the people involved in the procurement. I told him that presently the technical scrutiny would take place and, if I knew correctly, one Mr. Bora was involved. "Oh! Wah to Badmash Hai" (Oh! He is a scoundrel), was Pandit's instant reaction. After a long pause he advised me to see Nadgir, GM of the concerned division and said, "Mr. Nadgir is a clean chap; Give him my reference and express your apprehensions to him. I can't think of any other person who would help you." The next day I met Nadgir and got a positive assurance that there would be a fair play.

Since HAL officials had given an indication that the requirement was very urgent, they would be calling us for TNC within a couple of days.

(TNC is the abbreviation of Technical Negotiation Committee. Primarily this committee is supposed to discuss and clarify all the Technical Requirements with the supplier so that no ambiguities remain.) We therefore decided to stay at Nasik for one more day. I had given my hotel's telephone numbers to the concerned officer so that he could inform me of the TNC schedule.

At Smita's suggestion, we spent the day window-shopping and, in the evening, we drove to Trimbakeshwar. Before we left for Trimbakeshwar I had informed the receptionist of the hotel to note down any incoming messages. At Trimbakeshwar there was a mile-long queue at the famous Shiva temple. The place was swarming with beggars and vendors who were trying to harass the visitors. We, therefore, returned without any *'Darshan'*.

On reaching the hotel the first thing I did was to enquire about any messages for me. The receptionist said "Yes, there was a phone call, but well I am not sure if it was for you; had it been for you the telephone attendant on duty would have left a written message. The person who attended the phones in the evening is off duty and has gone home". For the next half an hour we interviewed each and every staff member of the hotel and concluded that there was no call and so we decided to leave for Indore as scheduled the following day. I was only to learn later that there was a call from the Purchase Manager to inform me that TNC was scheduled two days later.

And so, the day after I reached Indore, I again headed for Nasik. This time, I travelled alone by an overnight bus.

The TNC was held as scheduled except for the fact that instead of 11 AM I was called in at 5 PM. Later, after I had become quite friendly with Mr. Naphade, the Purchase Manager at HAL, I remarked that HAL degrades all its visitors; HAL turns them into waiters.

Another problem faced by visitors to HAL was that one had to park one's vehicle at the gate and walk half a kilometer to the Administration Building and then stay seated in the reception room. There is nothing you can get to eat or drink except water. If one wants to have some snacks or a cup of tea, one has to walk to the gate and go another kilometer where one can find some roadside Thellas.

Representatives of most of the bidders were present and during this waiting period, we got to know each other. I got introduced to Wig's son, who was also present. When the hunger became unbearable and most of the HAL staff left for lunch for their homes in the nearby colony I decided to go out for some snacks. Parmender, Wig's son, offered to give me a ride. As we came out of the building, he ushered me to an Esteem parked in front of the entrance, where cars of all senior HAL Officials were parked. Visitors like us did not get such privileges. This only confirmed that even Wig's son had a lot of clout at HAL.

We drove to a nearby Dhaba and ordered some snacks. Just for the sake of starting a conversation, I asked him regarding his source for the NATO adapter. This adapter is used for supplying power to the aircrafts, helicopters etc. The requirement for such adopters in India is limited and hence there is no reputed manufacturer of these or similar items in the country. The cost of such an adapter, if imported, is phenomenally high. We had been buying such adopters from a tiny unit in Virar near Mumbai, owned by a retired Naval Commander. This source was not known to many. In reply, Parmender said that he manufactured the NATO adopter himself and would be glad to supply the same to us and that he would be sending a quote by email.

Finally, my turn for technical discussions came around 5 PM. A Jost Engineer had accompanied me for this meeting so that he could provide any clarification concerning the electric vehicle. Since we had done the homework quite well, I had no problem answering the technical queries. Surprisingly Bora came up with one more technical requirement he said that the sound level at three meters

should be 85 ± 3 db. Never during my past 25 years had I worked on sound levels. I referred to the Kirloskar catalogue, which mentioned that the engine's sound level was 96 db. at 1 M. I made a quick mental calculation and accepted Bora's condition.

Firstly, the sound level reduces if we measure it at 3 M instead of 1 M in some logarithmic scale; and secondly, I thought I could replace the panels and doors of the GPU with fiberglass rather than metal to absorb the sound. The only question I asked was why ±3db, it should rather have no negative tolerance[3*]. To which I was given some vague reply. It perhaps speaks of the general IQ levels of the technical people in Government Service.

The second question I was asked was about the design of the driver's cabin. I told them that we had not yet designed it. That was the end of their queries. It was my turn to ask questions and so I drew their attention to our offer and showed them a paragraph where we had mentioned, "As stated earlier we have selected HA494 Engine, Crompton Greaves Alternator and Jost Make Electric Vehicle. However, we should be permitted to make a final choice without affecting the performance required." To this I was told in no uncertain terms that we could not do that and I was asked to give an undertaking to that effect in writing. And so, I wrote down the confirmation.

PRICE BIDS OPEN

After a gap of about ten days, we were called for Price bid opening entailing another trip to Nasik. Many other Government Companies such as Mazagon Docks Limited, and Garden Reach Shipbuilders Ltd. are better than HAL in this respect. They call you for TNC/ PNC (PNC is Price Negotiation Committee) and finish off both the formalities in two days so that the outstation parties do not have to visit twice.

The price bids of four parties, which were technically cleared, were opened at 5 PM instead of 3 PM. One was a French company, another bidder was from Delhi, the third was Wig's firm and the fourth, of course, was us i.e., Static Transformers Pvt. Ltd. The price of TLD, the French company, was over Rs. 30 lacs without Customs duty & other taxes. The Delhi Company quoted Rs.7.19 lacs plus 16% Excise Duty and 4%

[3*] For the benefit of readers, I would like to clarify that this requirement in specification ensures that the noise created by the equipment, when in operation, is bearable. So, one should specify only the upper limit of the noise level. However, in this case an even lower limit of noise level was specified which means that the equipment must make some noise. Very funny!

Sales Tax; Wig's had offered a price of Rs. 6.19 lacs plus 16% ED & 13% Sales Tax, while we had quoted Rs. 5.18 lacs plus 9.6% ED and 10% CST. Clearly, we were the lowest. **IT WAS TIME TO CELEBRATE**.

It was later, sitting in front of Naphade during one of my Nasik visits, that I got an opportunity to read the notes from their file. Bora had written that only Wig and TLD, the French Company, were technically satisfactory. He had rejected the Delhi party on some grounds, and Static Transformers too, because we did not have the drawings for the driver's cabin ready. It was Naphade who informed me that we were included in the Qualified List of bidders at the insistence of Trivedi, HAL's Deputy Manager Finance.

I stayed back for a day at Nasik to check their procedure and to estimate the approximate time involved in the Order processing. I was told that a purchase proposal had to be sent to Bangalore to HAL's corporate office for approval and hence I should expect to get the order within a month or so. **Happy at last, I returned home**.

This Order was going to take us out of all our miseries as it would contribute over Rs. 70 Lacs in one year, which, along with the other orders with us, would liquidate most of our debts and other long overdue liabilities.

However, this once again turned out to be wishful thinking. While we were all waiting for the order, we received a fax from HAL informing us that their team would be visiting our factory to evaluate our technical capability to manufacture the GPUs, especially with regard to: - **a)** The availability of NATO adopter **b)** Availabilities of measuring instruments and **c)** Our manufacturing facilities. It was obvious that this "NATO adopter" business was added at Wig's instance as he thought that was one problem area for us.

In the meanwhile, we had started preparations for manufacturing the prototype. Immediately on my return from Nasik I went to Jost (Thane), Kirloskar (Pune) and Crompton Greaves (Ahmednagar) to finalise the order for the Electric Vehicle, Engine and alternator. While I was at

Kirloskar Oil Engines, with my discussions regarding the Engine with Vikas just about to be over, we spotted Wig walking towards him. Vikas immediately asked me to leave and I obliged.

That day in the evening I went to Vikas to check out what Wig had talked about. Wig in his bravado had told Vikas that he had arranged for a visit of HAL (Nasik) officials to our Works at Indore for technical evaluation and that he would get us out of the race by getting us technically disqualified.

On 3rd April, HAL's team of three officials arrived at our premises in Indore. The first things we showed them were three GPUs fully equipped with cables and NATO adopters. These were to go to HAL (Bangalore), for starting and servicing of ALH (Advanced Light Helicopters). During their two days' stay the team was fully convinced of our technical competence. Once the team left, we again started counting days. This time the wait was not long. We were called by HAL for PNC, which resulted in another visit to Nasik.

As usual, I had to spend a few hours in the reception area, waiting to be called for negotiations. There are a number of government organisations which do not hold any price negotiations. As per the rules, all Government organisations have to place their order on the lowest bidder who already quotes his lowest possible price in order to be the lowest amongst all the bidders so as to get the order. Knowing that he is bound to get the order, why should he reduce the price? The officials use all sorts of arguments to get the price reduced. One typical argument is: "It is my personal request" or "For the sake of my chair" and so on and so forth.

For three hours the HAL team of AGM, DGMs etc. persuaded me to give some discount and every time my answer was that we have quoted our lowest and that is how we are lower by one lac than the second lowest bidder. After 3 hours of haggling, when the HAL team realised that I was not going to budge, they gave up. I was asked to wait for collecting the order personally. HAL's working hours are from 9 AM to 5 PM. However, they have a culture of working late into the evening. As a result, I was handed over the Purchase Order at 8.30 PM on April 30th. I missed the overnight bus for Indore, which used to leave Nasik at the same time. **I informed everyone at Indore that we had won the war and that it was time to party. I returned home on May 2nd. It was only later that we realised that we had not even won the battle.**

THE EXECUTION

As per the terms of the order, the prototype was to be offered for inspection on 15th May. It was certainly more than an impossible task. We faced a number of hurdles in building the GPU. One big problem was getting the Sales Tax Forms, which were required for importing items from outside the State of Madhya Pradesh. The MP Government had just introduced a new system under which the importer had to send four copies of a form called Form-75 to the supplier who was then supposed to send two copies of the same back, along with the material. One copy of the form would be verified and retained at the Sales Tax Barrier at the state border.

The first problem was to get the forms from the ST office, which was always swarmed by traders / manufacturers for getting the forms issued. It was a Herculean task to even reach the counter issuing the forms. Our peon failed to get the forms on two successive days. On the third day when he was to leave at 8 PM for Ahmednagar to collect the Alternator from Crompton Greaves, Uday succeeded in getting the forms issued out of turn by bribing the office peon Rs. 200. I was waiting in the car along with our peon when Uday came down from the S Tax office at 6.30 PM. I drove to the Bus Station immediately and reached my destination just in time. Our peon managed to board the Ahmednagar bus. Two days later, he returned with the alternator. He had loaded the 250 kg box on top of the overnight passenger bus. The passengers were quite unaware of the risk they carried on their heads that night.

Similarly, Nilesh had gone to Pune and camped there for a week until he got the Kirloskar engine dispatched. All these efforts were put in to meet the delivery deadline, which we knew was impossible to beat. However, we wanted to deviate as little as possible. Our entire team worked day and night. Those days my routine had changed. I used to get up at five in the morning and drive down to the factory. I would evaluate the progress of work and plan for that day's work. There were no readymade drawings available with us. I had to constantly think of further design aspects and plan for the day's work. After half an hour to forty-five minutes I used to return home only to go back by 9 AM. Except for a brief lunch break I used to be fully involved in the work till 10 pm. Our workers used to work from nine in the morning till midnight.

By 20th May the GPU under construction had taken some shape. We were contacted by HAL's Purchase department on May 16th. They wanted to visit us for inspection and in spite of our GPU not being ready, HAL sent a team of two officers on 22nd May to check the progress. After assessing the progress, they reported that the GPU was not ready fully; however, 80% progress was achieved.

SETBACKS

Soon after we started taking trials of the GPU, we had a major setback. The Crompton alternator purchased by us had a special provision. We could adjust it such that its output voltage would increase as the load increased. Our testing revealed that it was not increasing sufficiently. So, we adjusted the same, however this did not yield the desired level of increase in voltage. Over the phone, we checked with Crompton's Head Office at Ahmednagar. Their Marketing Persons were not even aware that this feature existed, leave alone how it worked. They referred us to their technical expert. After a number of calls he asked us to continue increasing the feedback setting further. From our discussions I got the impression that he was also not fully conversant with this feature. Probably only the French designers of the Automatic Voltage Regulator were knowledgeable in the matter. However, we had to believe in and use the local expertise.

We therefore continued taking trials with increased feedback. It was truly a TRIAL & ERROR method. Each TRIAL resulted in a serious ERROR. The AVR (Automatic Voltage Regulator) burnt and the alternator burst. It became operational only after a week, during which we must have spent thousands of rupees on STD calls to Crompton to pressurise them to send their service engineer and also had to agree to pay additional Rs. 15000/- for the AVR, though in principle it had burnt during the guarantee period and certainly due to lack of knowledge about its working, which was their shortcoming.

Similarly, one day, the SMPS Battery Charger blew up while in operation and Desai had to carry it to Pune for getting it rectified. Typically, Abhyankar took no responsibility and refused to send his technician for repair.

The HAL team revisited us for inspection on 1st June by which time our GPU was ready. They carried out thorough inspection for four days. I recollect the events of the day on which the 25 Kms road test was carried out. We could not locate a relatively empty stretch of road without big potholes within the city where we could carry out the road trials. We shifted our venue to a large playground. The trials started. However, before a round was completed the GPU got stuck in the mud. Finally, we decided to go to the highway and accordingly got the GPU towed out of the city by an ambassador car/ taxi. From five to ten in the evening I drove the vehicle nonstop in heavy rain. The GPU had no wipers and its headlights were hardly luminous as compared to those of approaching trucks and other vehicles.

FAILURES

The GPU passed all tests except the most vital requirement. When the aircraft starting was simulated, the engine rpm (Speed) came down drastically and, when the vehicle battery was tested for its capacity, it fell short by thirty minutes during the five-hour test. The battery charger blew up once again in front of the inspection team.

After the inspection team returned, we took up the matter with Kirloskar and the Battery supplier who informed us of the remedial action. Primarily our engine setting was to be corrected and the acid concentration of the battery was to be changed. Equipped with this information I visited Nasik where a meeting was held with the inspecting agency of the Air Force and HAL officials. They told me that they would give us one more chance and accordingly sent the inspectors for final inspection on 24th of June.

LAST BUT ONE INSPECTION

The inspection this time went smoothly but for the fact that we were badly squeezed for time. The last test of battery capacity was carried out on the last day from midnight till five o'clock the next morning. If there was a method of counting the mosquito bites, the count would have made it to the Guinness Book of Records. The load test was about to be over when the electrodes caught fire. Barring this mini-incidence, the last but one final inspection was successfully completed.

THE CUSTOMER IS ALWAYS RIGHT

As per the order, the GPU was to go for field trials to the Air Force station and we started our wait for the "Task Directive" from the IAF. We kept following with HAL and they informed us on 8th of August that the Air Force, who was the final user, wanted some modifications to be incorporated in the GPU and that it was not acceptable to the Air Force in its present form.

The Air Force wanted the GPU to have four wheels rather than three (Asking for a Maruti 800 instead of an auto rickshaw); they wanted the power to be enhanced so that the GPUs could work at Leh (asking for Maruti Esteem instead of Maruti 800). There were many other minor additional requirements. All this not only would add to our costs but also render the existing GPU useless, as every subassembly would have to be changed to one with higher capacity.

Earlier our arithmetic was very simple. Every GPU would give us a contribution (i.e., Selling price less cost of material, transportation etc.) of over rupees one lac twenty thousand, and thus fifty-eight GPUs would give around seventy lacs. We had of course spent much more than the selling price of the first unit till then in manufacturing the prototype, but it is a part of the game in such business.

It was however, impossible to maintain the price and we therefore informed HAL that this would mean Rs.100000/- increase in the cost which would still keep our offer lower than the other bidders. However, we started sensing that some forces were acting to ensure that the order got cancelled and requirements re-tendered.

DEADLOCK

IAF was not ready to change the specifications, and HAL was not willing to give us a price increase though technically it was not irregular in such orders. But someone at the top at HAL was very keen to get the tender re-issued.

The junior HAL officials were not taking any decision to resolve the deadlock. My visits to Nasik were yielding no result. During one such visit, I tried to meet the M.D. but was refused any appointment. I, therefore, called him at his residence from Indore. (My calls to him at the office were always blocked by his PA).

I tried to explain the situation on the phone; he however refused to listen. He said he dealt with a number of larger issues and was not aware of the case. He snubbed me for calling him at home and asked me to meet him in the office.

I once again travelled to Nasik for the meeting and returned with a typical promise: "I will look into the matter". A month later I met him again but the meeting proved futile. During that visit I also learnt from junior officers that the file was being sent to their Corporate Office at Bangalore for decision. The Government babus will do wonders at Wimbledon. They are masters at pushing the ball on to the other's court.

It was time to lobby our case at Bangalore. Phone calls to various directors were getting us nowhere and so we decided to approach Mr. Mohanti, the chairman of HAL. Getting through to him on the telephone was impossible, leave aside a face-to-face meeting.

I, therefore, took the help of Milind Mahajan, son of Mrs. Sumitra Mahajan, M.P. from Indore, who during those days was State minister of Communications. Milind, with the help of his mother's office, got me the telephone number of Mrs. Laxmi Subramanyam who was the M.D. of a Bangalore based PSU directly under the Communication ministry. When I spoke to her, she had already been briefed and immediately fixed up my appointment with Mohanty, the chairman and MD of HAL at Delhi.

Mohanti gave me a patient hearing, asked me to provide the case history on a piece of paper which I promptly did. The meeting ended with another assurance of "I will look into the matter".

After about two or three weeks and a number of calls to Mohanti, we realised that his "looking into the matter" was not going to give us justice. Had I been in his place, I would have simply written "If what Static claims is true, I find no reason for not accepting the GPU and for not giving them the Bulk production clearance at enhanced price." No CAG, CVC, Court could object to it. However, I started believing that "only spineless person can become successful chairman of a PSU".

INSHA ALLAH [God Willing]

It was time to approach higher ups. During those days, BJP was in power and Mr. Haren Pathak was the minister for defence production and supplies. Since Mrs. Mahajan commanded a lot of respect in the higher echelon of BJP and since she knew my background, she wanted to help me. I got an appointment with Haren Pathak on 10th December.

I was under severe financial pressure; my woes were increasing day by day. My well-wishers and close relatives were blaming me for being a non-believer, particularly my sister, Vinaya (Nilesh's Mother) who felt that the root cause of all our problems was my being atheist. My argument was that, as I was honest and didn't try to harm anyone God should be good to me, was not acceptable to her and so I gave in to my family members' wishes and agreed to carry out Satyanarayana Puja (a religious ritual to ward off evils, or for 'thanksgiving') in the factory.

Our workers, who were not paid for months, were also relieved by the knowledge of my change of heart. Shantanu, my younger son carried out the Puja on a Sunday in December 2002. That night everyone; our workmen, staffers and my sister must have slept peacefully, now that we had lord Satyanarayan on their side.

I continued to take more worldly steps and left for Delhi the next day for my meeting with Haren Pathak. I had the appointment at 11 A.M. and I left my hotel at 10 A.M. I took an auto to the south block. As the auto started to climb up the Safdarjung over-bridge, a speeding Maruti joined the road from the side lane, I panicked and shouted. However, before the sound waves of my shout could reach the auto-driver, the car hit the auto. The dynamics of our motion was beyond my comprehension. My memory cells could not record the happenings during those few milliseconds, though the frames of before and after the main event are quite vivid in my mind.

After the big bang, our mangled auto rickshaw had turtled and was standing in the middle of the road. Luckily no vehicle was following us closely else it would have surely hit us. Some people stopped by and helped me out. The driver was still trapped in the auto and was bleeding profusely.

I realised that my well ironed clean shirt was torn at many places and the left sleeve was stained with blood. Not bothering my totally deranged appearance, I collected my briefcase, walked to the curb, stopped the next vacant auto and moved on. I was at the security gate at fifteen minutes to eleven.

Since I had met Haren Pathak before in some other connection (during his earlier stint as Minister for Defence Production and Supplies), I thought I knew the location of his office and I had no difficulty in reaching that office. I informed the officer, presumably the Minister's PA/PS of my appointment at 11 A.M. I was asked to wait in the neighbouring room.

For the next one hour I waited, periodically checking with the staff to learn that the minister was busy. My mind was working at maybe one Hz instead of its usual Mega Hz speed. After about an hour and a half a peon informed me that the Minister had left for lunch. When I told him that I had an appointment with Mr. Pathak, he looked surprised. He said *"Ye to unka office nahi hai."* (This is not his office) It was my turn to look surprised. Taking directions from the peon, I rushed to the right office and managed to explain the delay in my arrival to Haren Pathak's PS.

Finally, I could meet Haren Pathak just before lunch. Had my mind been alert, all this could have been avoided. The believers have a nice explanation for God's grace; "It was to be a more severe accident, but lord Satyanarayana saved my life and let me off with minor injuries, and one good shirt torn to shreds."

YES MINISTER

Haren Pathak listened to my story and instructed his PS to call Mohanti from Bangalore. Within minutes his PS confirmed that Mohanti would visit a few days later. I was quite impressed by the power the minister enjoyed. Greatly relieved, I thanked him before leaving his office.

After about ten days, we learnt that HAL had decided to re-tender the order. The bureaucracy had won. I was not to give up, and fixed up another meeting with Haren Pathak. This time Milind Mahajan who was in Delhi accompanied me.

The minister pacified me and said, "I have made Mohanti agree to buy the prototype manufactured by you. You see, the poor fellow is waiting for his retirement. He is not a strong man. His deputies are not permitting him to go his way."

I continued my protest. He consoled me further, HAL's board has decided to re-tender the order, and they are going to invite bids only from the parties who had qualified technically. So, don't worry, I assure you that you will get the Order. I will help you get it. I know HAL has been unfair to you. But you know how all these chaps are? I suggest you go to the court, if they cancel the order and sue them. I will back you up."

Milind and I left his office while I mumbled, **"YES MINISTER."**

WINDING UP

To cut the further story short, HAL cancelled the order; sent a team for inspection of GPU as a necessary formality; gave a dispatch clearance; paid us for the first prototype after the usual delay and re-floated the tender for 58 pieces. More than a year of effort was wasted, resulting in a huge loss to us. Had I succeeded in executing the order it would have been another story. But as things went, I am forced to call the happenings, "THE BIGGEST GAMBLE."

THE BIGGEST GAMBLE PART II

On my return to Indore, we all discussed the matter and concluded that we could not depend on the minister's promise. We even consulted some good / renowned lawyers to examine the possibility of moving the court. We were advised that we could certainly go ahead, but it would have to be at Nasik court and then at Bombay high court. The compensation would have to be paid by HAL, but it would come through only when our great grandchildren had themselves become great grandfathers, and in the process we would all lose our shirts.

We had also realized that our friend from Pune had great influence with HAL officials as well as with the concerned IAF officials. Further, by that time, our costing and GPU details were easily available to him. The bidding in the tender would be so cut-throat that even if we got the order, the margins would shrink so much that it would probably not be worth the effort.

I, therefore, suggested a seemingly impossible alternative. I said, "Let us join them if we cannot fight them".

BUILDING THE BRIDGE

Rightly or wrongly, I hate middlemen. I know the readers will consider this as my having double standards as I myself have played (or tried to play) that role. But then I too am a human being.

The best bet who could play the role of a middleman was Bora who had by that time retired from service. I got his telephone number from a HAL employee and called him. He was quite amicable on the phone. During my meeting with him I narrated the whole story (which he knew, but from the other side of the table); and then concluded by asking, "What if we work together?"

That would end the rat race (rather race with the rat). Bora showed keen interest in my proposal and why not? In such an eventuality he would be getting 'cuts' from Wig as well as from us (we Indians like to call it, more honourably, consultancy charges).

Bora informed me that HAL's budgetary cost was around eight lacs forty thousand per GPU and thus there were enough margins for all. We, therefore, made a basic framework. I proposed that we could take the order and buy the battery cart from Wig at an inflated price so that his returns were guaranteed; alternatively, he could take the order and buy the transformer rectifiers from us at our price. It would be a win – win situation. Both would cover Bora for his service.

At least sixty rounds of tele-discussions between Bora and me on the one hand and between Wig and Bora on the other took place. I never spoke to Wig directly. Nothing was concluded between us as Wig was vacillating. His son was totally against the idea of joining hands with their staunch enemy (i.e., us), and at the same time Wig saw some merit in our proposal. Secondly, it was extremely difficult for Wig to trust us (as he told me later).

THE SECOND D-DAY ARRIVES

As we had not joined hands with Wig, we filled the tender and offered such a low price that had we got the order at that price, we would have lost heavily. It was a big gamble. We were betting not only on Wig's getting convinced to join hands, but also on our being able to change the price over the tendering process, before the price bid opened, in the event we did not join hands.

A day before the due date of opening of the tender, I started from Indore to Nasik with the documents. Visits to Nasik had become so routine that it was as if I was visiting my own backyard. I had planned to leave by car in the morning so as to reach Nasik one day earlier. However, I got delayed due to some trivial jobs at the factory and was only able to leave by two in the afternoon. Smita accompanied me on the tour. Around seven in the evening we were at Dhulia. We decided to have a night halt there and leave for Ojhar early next morning. Ojhar was only about a hundred kilometers from there.

THE GREAT PERIL

In spite of extremely slow service at the hotel, we got ready and started sharp at 7.A.M i.e., six hours prior to the closing time of the tender. After we logged around twenty kilometers in about twenty minutes on the four-lane highway, I had to slow down and finally stop, as there was a traffic jam on the highway. NH-3 i.e., the Bombay-Agra highway is quite notorious for traffic jams but that was for the part in MP, and not the part in Maharashtra, where the highway was pothole-less.

For the next one hour, we were stand still. No vehicles were coming from the other side either. At around eight thirty a few cars coming from the other side crossed us. That raised some hope that the jam was getting cleared.

I spotted one MSRTC (Maharashtra State Road Transport Corporation) bus coming towards us from the opposite side at a snail's pace. I got down from the car and signalled at the driver to stop. I asked him about the cause of the jam and when one could expect it to get cleared; I had to reach Ojhar by noon, I mentioned to him.

He informed us that an accident had taken place around ten kilometers ahead. Two trucks had collided and gone turtle, blocking the road completely. He said he had crossed the distance in over five hours and that there was no chance of the jam getting cleared by evening and that I could not reach Ojhar at all if I waited there. He then advised me to go back to Dhulia and reach Ojhar by another route through some villages.

Smita and I discussed the possibilities. We were panicking. The jam was taking away the possibility of having cheese in spite of no one having moved it. Within minutes, we decided to take a U-turn as advised by the MSRTC driver. We reached Dhulia and took the alternate route to a town called Chandwad, only around fifty kilometers from Dhulia.

The road (if we could call it that) was in such a state that I could hardly make ten kilometers an hour. I covered thirty kilometers in three hours to reach the highway again, thus circumventing the ten kilometers jam. Right till we joined the highway we were quite certain that the car would give away. Driving on that stretch full of foot deep potholes with innumerable pointed stones was an ordeal. But thanks to Suzuki we managed to reach Ojhar and drop the tender documents by midday, an hour ahead of the deadline.

TOM & JERRY SHOW

Having completed the tender submission, I dropped Smita at a hotel in Nasik and returned to the arena after a quick lunch.

One of the causes of Wig's hesitation was also the possibility of another party quoting low and taking away the order. At 3 P.M. when the tenders were opened, I got a pleasant surprise. Only three parties had quoted - Wig's, Static, and a French company. Since the French offer was around six times our offer (in the earlier tender), their bid was a mere formality.

The competition was only between the two of us. It was going to be a Tom & Jerry show. That was all we learnt that day.

THE TECHNICAL CLARIFICATIONS

After a couple of weeks, sometime in early March, we were called for technical clarifications. It was going to be a mere formality. HAL had called an IAF representative so as to avoid further amendments to the technical requirement as had happened previously.

During our discussions the IAF representative, a wing commander, sprang a surprise. He said IAF wanted the GPUS to operate at 3500 meters altitude instead of 2500 meters. He appeared drunk and was in a hurry to end the discussions, as he was to go to Shirdi (obviously at the cost of HAL) for *'Darshan'*.

Anyway, till that day our peace talks with Wig had not reached any conclusive state. He was still playing blow hot blow cold. I therefore took the opportunity to prolong the opening of the price bid by saying "Sure, we can supply GPUs which would operate at 3500 meters. However, that will change our cost and we would like to revise our price bid". Everyone promptly agreed and HAL gave us a week's time for submitting the revised price.

That evening I spent a couple of hours with Bora. We discussed our strategy, which would build Wig's confidence in our proposal. At Bora's instance, I spoke to Wig for the first time from Nasik. This was to indicate our seriousness in the matter.

THE PUNE SUMMIT

Over the next few days, we continued communications twice a day. Finally, we all agreed to meet face to face at Pune two days prior to the last day of submission of revised prices.

I hired a cab and went over to Nasik traveling overnight. We (Bora and I) left for Pune immediately and managed to reach there by lunchtime. Wig had booked us in a hotel. He and his son arrived soon after we checked in. He was very hospitable. After a sumptuous lunch, we started the shop talk.

Our discussions went on and on and even after spending three hours together, I saw no agreement forthcoming. Right from the beginning, I kept saying that both parties should quote independently and if we turned out to be lower, we would buy the battery cart from Wig at a pre-decided price; and if he won the order, he should buy the transformer rectifier from us, which would give us a reasonable profit. I brought the endless discussions to a close by making a firm "Take it or leave it" statement. The Wigs excused themselves after agreeing to come back the next day with a decision.

That night we wined and dined at Wig's lavish bungalow. Slightly tipsy, Wig's vocal cords became overactive. He went all out to praise me making statement like, "I know Mr. Joshi, you are an IITian and are very intelligent." Who in the world doesn't feel pleased to hear such words even with the full knowledge that the speaker is saying it only to please the listener.

He then added, "You have taken great efforts and have worked really hard". I was going sky high with twenty milliliters of scotch already down the throat and such remarks kept coming from our business rival. But then, from the summit, I came back to the ground when Wig elaborated on his statement. By "my hard work" he meant "my meeting the MD and the Chairman of HAL and my two meetings with the minister," "Quite a lot of running around", he quipped.

By the next day wisdom had dawned on him and he agreed to my proposal. We returned to Nasik soon after shaking hands.

NASIK SUMMIT

Junior Wig came over to Nasik the next day and we worked out a formal agreement and before going to HAL for dropping our final price bids, exchanged cheques worth around thirty-four lacs. All post-dated over a period of one year.

The same day the bids were opened in the afternoon. The result surprised the HAL officials, but not us. The French had maintained the price at Rs. 30 Lacs, Wig had quoted eight lacs ten thousand and we had filled in nine lacs. Why work hard and earn, if you can make easy money. (I hated to write the last sentence but then my experience in working with IAF, and other Indian Government agencies has taught me the bitter facts of life. One cannot fill one's tummy eating principles.)

Back home, my well-wishers and advisors would have called me a stupid fool to have played the gamble, especially giving Wig cheques of equal amount.

Even Smita and other family members who knew the history well would have considered my business acumen to be negative. I therefore kept them only half informed. My giving him cheques of equal amount, one for one, was known only to Nilesh and Uday. I had played the gamble (as I call it now).

There were hundred legal ways in which Wig could wriggle out and avoid payments to me. He could have made an extra profit of twenty odd lacs. Moreover, my giving him an offer that I would pay him the money in the event I got the order was bogus. Our financial condition was so precarious that I could not even dream of paying five thousand rupees leave aside five lacs which I would have to pay on receipt of the order from HAL

The cheques given to him were of Maharashtra Brahman Sahakari Bank where our account was frozen and the bank had already obtained court order for recovery of Forty-Six Lacs from us. Anyway, my showmanship had worked well.

THE HICK-UPS IN PAYMENTS (JUNE 2005)

I had started writing this chapter about seven years ago and had stopped after scribbling a few pages, primarily because it was an on-line kind of a situation then. Part-1 of the story was complete. Part-2 of the story was going on. Hence, I could not have continued writing and or completed the chapter; but I hope I do it today.

Wig paid Rs. 5 Lacs in six months as advance. That was far beyond the agreed schedule. Through my HAL friends I kept track of his progress on execution of the order. He was quite behind schedule and in spite of his PR he took much longer time in getting his prototype approved & field tried. The cheques with me were not to be deposited as the payment beyond five lacs was linked to the milestones of the project, i.e., receipt of order, approval of prototype etc.

He paid but not before a lot of follow up and delays. Towards the end he cut off communication with us while he still owed us around 2 lacs.

It was precisely a week before the validity of last cheques (his and ours), that I decided to call the shots & deposited his cheque in such a way that it would be presented in his bank on the last valid date. Our trouble shooter Praveen carried the cheque to Pune and as expected the cheque bounced. Praveen returned with the bounced cheque.

Bouncing of cheques had become a criminal offence by that time. As a result, Wig was badly shaken. He requested me to visit Pune to settle the issue which I did, accompanied by Bora. I got a valid cheque in lieu of the bounced cheque and I returned to Indore with it. The gamble had paid off but the amount of gains, less expenses, were considerably lower.

--xxx---

UNTIL THINGS DID NOT GO WRONG

THIS CHAPTER IS DEDICATED TO

SIDDHARTH

MY ELDER SON

WHO CRACKED JEE

WITHOUT THE HELP OF THE COACHING CLASSES

HIS AIR (ALL INDIA RANK) WAS THE SAME AS MINE

AND

HE WENT ON TO EXCEL AT IIT, KHARAGPUR

Until Things Did Not Go Wrong

Until I passed out of IIT at the age of twenty-two, nothing drastic had gone wrong with me.

THE PRE IIT-DAYS

I studied in Marathi medium schools till Standard 8 and then in a Hindi Medium school till the 11th. I could not get admission to an engineering college nor could I appear for the JEE due to the lower age limit of sixteen years during those days. I therefore secured admission for graduation in science, by default. During those days, at Indore, there were no coaching classes for competitive exams like JEE. Hardly one or two students would get into IITs from the city. Of course, there were only five IITs then, with less than 1500 seats for the B.Tech. programme. The JEE used to take place in the first weekend of May every year. There were four papers - Physics, Chemistry, Mathematics and English, three hours in duration each. I appeared for JEE as a mere formality. The only preparation I had done was going through the solved papers with Shrikant Chendke.

At that time, I had made a small prediction. I had told my friends that from amongst our known batch mates that if one person got into IIT, it would be Vishwanath Krishnan, a college mate of mine; if two got selected, I would be the second one. And if more got in, then the others stood some chance. One day in June, I received a brown envelope by registered post. It contained the interview call for admission. My All-India Rank (AIR) was 1260. My prediction had come true. Vishwanath Krishnan's AIR was 230 and we were the only two to make it from Indore.

For the interview, I went to Mumbai. A senior friend accompanied me to Ratlam junction from where I boarded the Frontier Mail for Mumbai. A distant uncle, with whom I stayed at Mumbai, accompanied me to IIT, Powai for an interview.

Before I left for Mumbai, my father had advised me not to opt for IIT Kharagpur or Madras (now Chennai). Kharagpur was facing Naxalite trouble during those days and Madras was farthest from Indore. When my turn came, admission was open to the Electronics / Electrical branch at IIT Kharagpur. Mechanical Engineering seats were vacant at IIT Kanpur, Madras as well as Kharagpur. My choice was obvious, Mechanical Engineering at IIT Kanpur. Luckily Vishwanath Krishnan had also opted for IIT Kanpur. He of course deservedly got into a more prestigious Electrical branch.

Those days the admission procedure was spread over a week to ten days. Every evening the IITs exchanged telegrams so that all the five centers were updated of the status of vacancies in all the branches. Kanpur used to admit 300 students every year. However, in our batch more than 420 were given admission.

From the grapevine I later learnt that an influential industrialist, who was on the Board of Governors of IIT Kanpur had purposely arranged to send wrong information of balance vacant seats to other IITs so that his grandson with much higher AIR could make it to IIT Kanpur. For better or for worse, my life would have been different had this trick not been played.......

THE JOURNEY BEGINS

Vishwanath Krishnan and I started our first journey to IIT Kanpur, which I was to repeat twenty-one times over the next five years. Our parents bid us good-bye at the Indore Railway Station in the afternoon and from then on, we were on our own. We reached Bhopal at night and stayed over in the waiting room. Next morning, we were to catch the Punjab Mail. Vishwanath Krishnan's father was a High Court Judge and hence we had two police constables to help us board the train at Bhopal. They literally shoved us in the unreserved bogie of the mail along with all our luggage. I am sure that the physicist who invented the closest packing structure had never seen such a crowd in one railway bogie; otherwise, I am sure he would have formulated a different theory.

THE FIRST GLIMPSE

By noon we were at Jhansi where we shifted to another train going to Kanpur. While we waited for the train's departure, we found a beeline of ten to fifteen city-bred youngsters imitating a train on the platform, like the kids of kindergarten would do. It was a ludicrous scene. VK immediately realised that these were all freshers like us coming from Mumbai. The seniors who were on the same train were ragging them. That was the first glimpse of ragging, which I faced for the next month or so until the freshers' night. During the journey, however, our presence remained inconspicuous to the seniors as we were in an unreserved bogie.

Ragging at IIT Kanpur had its own code of conduct. No fresher was physically harmed. There was no stripping beyond decency. Mental harassment was tolerable. It would help the fresher to shed shyness. Personally, I believe I got tremendously benefited by getting ragged. I was a typically shy villager compared to the English medium educated, cosmopolitan crowd.

Finally, in the evening we reached Kanpur and took a tempo ride to IIT, which is about fourteen kilometers from the station.

THE BEGINNING

The ragging, intense academics, atrocious quality of food and cultural shock resulted in frequent pangs of homesickness. It was like getting into an alien environment. The only means of communication with my parents was through letters, which took a week to make a one-way journey. I only wonder as to how I did not break down, or how I managed to avoid depression. If I remember correctly, during my ten semesters stay at IIT, there were at least ten cases of suicides and an equal number of cases of nervous breakdowns. In addition, there were cases of students taking to drugs like charas and marijuana.

During the initial days, a batchmate from Mumbai used to go to the post office two kilometers from the hostel at night and sleep there in the verandah to avoid ragging. Another batchmate, Wagle, also from Mumbai, had insomnia as it was too quiet for him to fall asleep. Nevertheless, life went on and I became part of the system.

THE FIRST SEMESTER

We had five subjects: - Physics, Chemistry, Mathematics, Technical Arts (TA) and English. I had no difficulty with Physics and Mathematics. The Professor in charge of Chemistry 101, Dr. Davenport, was an American. He used to deliver lectures in L-7 (Lecture Hall seven) to 400 odd students. His accent was beyond my comprehension and I could understand hardly ten percent of what he said. TA was basically engineering drawing. My doing well in the subject was out of question as I could not draw a straight line even with a ruler.

The worst was English 101. With my background, my knowledge of English was extremely poor; my vocabulary probably consisted of less than 1500 words. I remember that in the final exam of Physics 101, in which there were no optional questions and one had to attempt all the problems, I had to leave one problem unsolved as it was about an escalator. I did not know the meaning of the word and was too ashamed to ask the Professor. On another occasion, a professor snubbed me for spelling Kanpur wrongly. I recollect not understanding the meaning of notices, which had words like agenda, quorum etc. Once during a chit-chat session, I scribbled the name of Rajeev Bhagwat, a batchmate from Pune, with wrong spelling. All the seven or eight colleagues present laughed at me.

Our batch was divided into thirteen sections on the basis of our marks in the English paper of JEE. Obviously, I was in A-13. English 101 was taught to us by one Mrs. Guha. She had prescribed "School of Scandals" as one of the text books. I got a copy issued from the library and started with the first chapter. Typically, it started from the center of the page. On the first page, there were thirteen words I did not know the meaning of. In spite of having complete autonomy, Mrs. Guha did not budge when all the students approached her with a request to prescribe a simpler book. On account of this my life became miserable and I struggled hard.

FROM THE FRYING PAN TO THE FIRE

Only thirteen out of about 30 students of our section had passed English 101 and most with D grade. As a result, the section was disbanded. As luck would have it, I was shifted to A-1 which was full of masters of the language. I was the only black sheep as far as English 102 was concerned, which was conducted by the pretty Ms. Raina. She used to scold me every day in the class. A pretty woman admonishing me publicly was extremely agonizing.

Once she called me to her room and gave me an extra assignment. She handed over a 200-page novel and asked me to write a synopsis within a week's time. It was an impossible task (I did not know what "synopsis" meant).

I had befriended Rahul Gautam, (The owner of Sheela Foam, manufacturer of Sleep Well mattresses), a handsome and polished student. He was amongst the few who did not belittle me for my lack of literary skills. That night I went to his room and told him of my plight. Within days he gave me a two page write up which I submitted in my handwriting, deliberately introducing a few spelling mistakes.

The second semester went by. By this time, I had improved to 8.0 points with an A grade in Maths and Tech. Arts, D in English and B in others.

PROVING MYSELF

I was greatly relieved that English was no more a subject of study in the second year. However, we had to choose one elective, offered by the Department of Humanities and Social Sciences, and I went for Economics.

In that semester I scored three As and two Bs in Maths & economics, scoring a SPI (Semester Performance Index) of 9.2 which was quite a respectable figure. I should have got an A in economics. The professor, however, had not given me full marks for one question. The question was simple, "Prove that the average cost of manufacturing is lowest when it is equal to marginal cost." I had proved it using calculus. He however wanted the students to give examples and explain the matter subjectively. Anyway, I had proven myself.

In the next year and a half, I shared the room with Rahul Gautam. My routine changed completely. I used to wake up at 11.30 AM directly for lunch, missing all the morning lectures. Then I attended the labs or tutorials if absolutely necessary. I used to spend time in the canteen till midnight or even later.

A few days before the exams, I used to study using Rahul's lecture notes (after he went to sleep), or from the prescribed text books. Sometimes when I was not prepared, I would leave the question papers blank. Obviously, my score plummeted.

MOMENTS OF TRIUMPH

But then there were moments of triumph. During the third year, we had one course on Fluid Mechanics. It was supposed to be a very tough course. One day after the mid-semester examinations, Rahul came back after the morning lectures and banged the door which woke me up. He said "You *******! You are amongst the top ten to have done well in the exam. The Prof has displayed your roll number 70323 on the blackboard. How can you do it by studying my lecture Notes?"

Another incident took place when I was in the fourth year. We were eighty students in Mechanical Engineering. One evening I was having coffee in the lawn near the canteen when a group of my batchmates approached me. Mohan Shetye, the topper of our department was leading them. He told me that the professor of our "Heat Transfer" course had taught something during the lecture which appeared to be wrong, and asked me to check.

After going through the matter, I confirmed that the prof had erred. The group then urged me to attend the lecture the next day; they even offered to wake me up in time, so that the Prof. could be taken to task.

MOMENTS OF DEJECTION

I failed in two humanity courses. One was 'Contemporary India' and another was 'Demography'. As a matter of fact, I had skipped the exams, as I knew that I would fail. I had to, therefore, stay back in the summer after the 4th year and make up by taking up two other courses.

This was not the greatest dejection. In the 5th year, a team from L&T came for campus interview. After screening 300 odd students, they rejected a handful, which included me.

Barring such mini episodes, I passed out on schedule. in April 1975, with a not so bad a score of 7.3. My personality, especially my confidence level, had probably gone up to the highest possible level.

--xxx---

OLDIE'S DAY OUT OR '*YE MERA INDIA*' (NOV 2004)

THIS CHAPTER IS DEDICATED TO

MR. RAGHUPATHY NARAYANMURTHY,

MY NITIE CLASSMATE

WHO

EDITED THIS BOOK.

Oldie's Day Out Or *'Ye Mera India'* (This Is My India) (Nov 2004)

The time is 2.50 pm on Monday, November 1, 2004; I am writing this, sitting in a hotel room in Secunderabad. Today, my plan of work was quite simple. Yesterday, Uday, our accounts officer, had called me from Indore and confirmed that he had sent a DD in the name of Vardharajalu, a scientist working at DRDL, by DHL on Saturday. The envelope was addressed to my name, c/o DHL office.

Uday had given me DHL's Secunderabad office address and phone number. The address included a landmark, which was, "Near Anand Cinema ". I had spotted the Movie Hall the day before, while I was going to the Airport. The landmark (cinema) happened to be quite close to my hotel.

And so, my plan for the day was simple: Call up the courier to confirm that the envelope had arrived from Indore. Go to their office and collect the same. Call Vardharajalu to the hotel and hand over the DD in exchange for cash. Then go to the electronic components market; buy the required components and head to the Airport. I was to reach Air Deccan's office at 2.30 pm for commissioning the GPU (ground power unit) supplied to them and needed some electronic components for that purpose. In the meantime, I was to get some faxes from Indore to help me locate the components to be replaced in the GPU. There was nothing unmanageable about this whole exercise.

Having nothing to do till 11 AM, I wrote out a chapter of my diary (Miraculous Memory). Sharp at 11AM I called DHL. The person who attended the phone told me that for deliveries I had to call another number. For the next 30 minutes I tried calling that number; however, the call could not go through.

THE FULL CIRCLE

And so, I skipped my "telephoning" part and walked to the Anand theatre. I reached across the Cinema Hall, which was on the other side of the road. There was such a heavy traffic that crossing the road was impossible. I, therefore, scanned the name boards. AFL courier, DTDC and some other courier services had their offices across the road. However, I could not spot DHL.

I therefore asked a passerby for directions. From his uniform and the rucksack, he was carrying, he looked like he himself was a delivery boy of some courier company. He asked me to walk further ahead and informed me that DHL's office was on the same side of the road as I was on.

I must have walked about half a kilometer, but found no trace of DHL's office. However, I came across FEDEX couriers. I entered their office. The receptionist there told me that DHL was a kilometer ahead at the Airport Road crossing.

I took an Auto and reached the crossing where I saw prominent boards of DHL & BLUE DART Couriers hanging from the second floor of the corner building. I climbed up to the second floor to find only 'BLUE DART's office there. I had no choice but to enquire at the Blue Dart's office about their rival's location.

The lady at the counter was busy attending to some clients. After a wait of ten odd minutes, when I could get her attention, she informed me that I had left DHL's office four buildings behind. No explanation for DHL's board hanging outside this building.

Anyway, customers are not choosers in India. I walked back four buildings, backtracking my path. As I was walking back, I thought, "Maybe BLUE DART has bought over DHL and has taken over its operations while they have left DHL's board as it is, maybe they will obliterate DHL's identity over a period."

At last, I found a DHL office. The front desk had three attendants, all busy with customers, filling up forms, taking envelopes from clients and writing out receipts. I noticed one client paid two thousand rupees for a small packet, which was quite odd, but then it was none of my business.

I was waiting for my turn with a piece of paper in my hand on which I had scribbled the airway bill number of the envelope sent from Indore. Sometime later, one attendant took pity on me and took the paper from me. After a minute or so, he loudly counted the number of digits of the airway bill number. Handing back the precious paper to me, he curtly said, "We do not have twelve-digit numbers. We use ten digits. This is not our number."

That was very odd. I called my office and got a reconfirmation of the twelve-digit number. Our people at Indore also checked other DHL receipts they had in the office and told me that every DHL receipt had a dozen digits. I told the attendant that maybe DHL's Indore office added two extra digits and therefore he should check the first ten or last ten in the computer.

However, he had already got busy with another client. Then a young girl (one of the three attendants) who had heard my pleas took the chit and after glancing at the figures asked me about the originating station. I told her that the envelope was to come from Indore.

She clarified the mystery. This was the DHL office for handling international services. She informed me that AFL Courier, who had the office next to the Anand theatre, handled the inland deliveries of DHL.

Yet another Auto Ride... I took a U-turn from the Airport Road crossing and came back practically to the starting point except that I was on the other side of the road.

TANGENT TO THE CIRCLE

At the AFL's office, the attendant said, "Yes, I believe there was an envelope from Indore." He took the chit from me and punched the dozen digits into the computer. Turning to me he said, "The envelope has been handed over to the delivery boy".

"Where will he take it to? The address says S. A. Joshi, care of DHL Office"; was my obvious query.

Then the attendant's colleague came to my rescue. He had heard the entire conversation. He told me that the delivery boy carried a mobile and that he would contact him. And so, he called up and instructed the courier to deliver the envelope to my hotel. Another auto ride in a direction tangential to the circle I had just completed!

On my return journey from Hyderabad to Indore I was wondering about the wild goose chase I had to go through. Maybe, I thought, BLUE DART or AFL had bought over "DHL" and that way, over a period of time they would obliterate DHL's identity. In today's business environment of acquisitions and mergers, such things are quite possible and aggressively practised.

On the flight from Bombay to Indore, after I finished 'Indian Express' and 'Asian Age', I picked up The Economic Times. It was dated Nov. 5, 2004. The bold headline of a news column was really amusing. It read, **"DHL BUYS OFF MAJORITY SHARES OF BLUE DART"**

THE REST OF THE DAY - IN THE AGE OF IT

To continue my story and ordeal, back at the hotel, I had to climb up to the third floor as the lift was under servicing. I called the reception from my room to check if any FAX was received from Indore. The receptionist informed me that their FAX machine was out of order.

I, therefore, skipped the tea, which I had ordered; and walked down & out of the hotel. The first shop with the yellow board I spotted on the road was locked. I saw another board two buildings away. I entered the shop and enquired, only to learn that they had switched to the Internet.

The third shop was just across the road. It had a glass door through which I could see a lot of telephone instruments. I reached the shop and tried to open the door. I tried all techniques, PUSH, PULL, and SLIDE. Nothing worked. I was about to utter "OPEN SESAME", when a person standing in the vicinity told me that the shopkeeper had locked the door and gone out for some personal work.

I could not find any other shop with a yellow board nearby and so I decided to go to the electronics market. I had taken directions from the hotel receptionist. It was supposed to be quite nearby. Around ten minutes walk away. And so, I walked as directed only to find TV, VCR, and VCD shops. It was an Electronic Goods Market.

One of the shopkeepers told me that the Electronics Component Market was on a road parallel to the one where I stood. He asked me to cross through the maze of buildings by a narrow lane. I moved on and on, as directed, and what (as I was told) was to take only ten minutes turned out to be more than forty minutes.

At last, I bought the components and after tying up with an electrician for the Airport job returned to the hotel. Near the hotel I finally found a FAX center, which was open. The young girl gave me the telephone number and told me that her machine will be operational after about an hour. Reason: It was out of paper and she did not know as to how the paper role was inserted. I helped her do the job. Then I called up my office, got the fax transmitted, and went back to the hotel. Again, I had to climb up to my room.

It was almost 2.30 PM when I returned to the room. Vardharajalu came at 3PM. After he left at 3.30 PM, I had some biscuits for lunch and left for the Airport at 4PM. From time to time, I was re-estimating my Expected Time of Arrival at the airport and had informed the Airport Manager of Deccan that I would be reaching at 4.30 PM instead of 2.30 PM.

I reached the Airport at 4.15 pm and telephoned the Airport Manager of my arrival. He was to send a pass to me to enable me to enter the restricted area. Danzal, Deccan's Airport Manager, asked me to wait outside. He told me that he had just sent a person to the concerned authority to get the pass signed.

The wait started. I called Danzal every 20 minutes only to hear "Ya! Ya! Mr. Joshi, my chap is on the job". Finally, two coffees & six Sprints later, the pass arrived at 6.45 PM. From that time till I returned to the hotel, it was work, work and work.

The only pleasing moment during that day was when I heard Danzal's remark about the Self-propelled Aircraft Starting Trolley which we had supplied to Air Deccan. He said, "Aesthetically it is quite nice, it looks like a real life-size LEGO toy. I now have to get the vehicle registered with the RTO". This made me comment, "Thank You! You have equated me with Ratan Tata."

Only at 11 PM did the rest of the day end and the rest for the night start.

--xxx---

THE THUGS OF DELHI AND THE GULLIBLE INDIANS

(1996)

THIS CHAPTER IS DEDICATED TO

MY FRIEND, ASHOK PATANKAR

WHO LISTENED TO MY NARRATIONS

AND

PROVIDED HEALTHY CRITICISM

WITH KEEN INTEREST

The Thugs of Delhi and the Gullible Indians (1996)

I am not sure if statistics can support the statement that the percentage of thugs is more in Delhi than, say, in Chennai or Bangalore. However, it is common knowledge that as a visitor to Delhi, one stands a good chance of being cheated. Vishwanath Krishnan, my IIT batch-mate from Indore and now settled in the US, very categorically says that he divides India into two parts; Vindhyachal Range being the dividing line. The part below Vidhyas is the civilised half.

There are a number of cases which one hears about from people who have travelled to Delhi. Anil Dutta, who was my boss at Steel Tubes, tells an amusing story. He went to Delhi on a tour and from the Airport he went straight to Hotel Akbar in Chanakyapuri. That was before the days of TV. Being fond of English movies, he checked the newspaper and decided to watch the evening show at Chanakya Theatre nearby. And so, he went out, got into a taxi and asked the cab driver to take him to Chanakya Theatre. The taxi driver turned the meter down and started driving the taxi. After about half an hour's drive, he dropped Anil at Chankya. Anil Dutta paid the correct meter fare of Rs. 100/- and got into the theatre. After the movie, he went to the taxi stand at the theatre and asked a taxi driver to take him back to Hotel Akbar. This taxi driver was not as clever or cunning as the previous one. He looked at Anil Dutta with a bemused expression, and pointed to the ten-storied building just across the road. The bright neon sign of Akbar Hotel was glowing very conspicuously in the dark of the night.

Similar stories concerning the auto rickshaw walas of Delhi are told by people. Whether true or not, when I narrate Dutta's taxi episode, the listener comes back with the story of a Delhi auto fellow who took his client on a ride by taking him on a forty kilometers round trip from place A to place B, just a couple of kilometers from each other, by driving in the opposite direction on the ring road.

I too visit Delhi frequently and have to ward off hoards of auto and taxi drivers who gherao the prospective victim at the Nizamuddin station. I try my best to spot a relatively honest auto / taxi driver, not necessarily succeeding every time. Sometimes these auto chaps come up with ingenious methods to make their customers, especially the tourists, fall into a trap and check into a hotel where these bandits get hefty commissions.

Once, I reached Nizamuddin from Indore and took an auto. I asked the driver to take me to South Extension. On the way, the autowala asked me as to which hotel I was going to. On my reply, he reacted with a big surprise, "Sir! Don't you know? There was a police raid two days back there. They found some flesh business going on. They have sealed the hotel". On some other occasion, another autowala came up with, "The owner died yesterday and so the hotel is temporarily closed". But the best one was by an auto driver who took me to an office and said that due to security reasons all outside visitors have to register at this office. I played along. The office person called up my hotel and mocked a conversation. He came back, "Sir! There is no vacancy there."

Thank God, I am not so gullible as to get trapped.

THE MAIN EPISODE

The main episode that I now intend to narrate reminds me of stories from Malgudi Days, authored by R.K.Narayan. One day we got a letter from an NGO called 'INDIAN NATIONAL ECONOMIC FORUM'. It said that Static Transformers Pvt. Ltd. was selected in the preliminary screening as an organisation to receive the Best Entrepreneur Award for year 1995-96 and that we should send details of our Company to them, and include the resume of the Promoters.

Earlier we used to receive such letters from similar NGOs, which used to rightfully land in the dustbin. However, this time we sent a response. There was no harm, as long as we spent only on postage. We got a prompt reply stating that we would be informed about the result soon. An eminent panel of Delhi's "Who's Who" would be reviewing all the eligible candidates / firms. And finally, the selected candidates would be awarded the reward at a function to be held in The Taj Hotel on such and such date, by the Honourable (?) Minister, Mr. Jagdish Tytelor.

During that period, I used to visit Delhi often, and during one of these visits I went over to the office of this so-called NGO. It was situated in a posh locality of South Delhi. The office address was common to that of a college office, which used to award diplomas in Management etc. in collaboration with a British University. The office walls were decorated with photographs of a number of Cabinet Ministers handing over trophies to people at some functions. I talked to the person who had signed the letter sent to us. He was a young Sardar.

After the preliminaries, I asked him as to why this NGO had selected us and who gave them our address etc. He informed me that various Government Departments recommend the names to them. Though I could sense that something was fishy, I was unable to disbelieve him as until then I had not been asked for money or any other favour. In order to further investigate into the genuineness of the matter, I bluffed that I had plans to go abroad and I might not be able to attend the scheduled function, and secondly, I said, 'It is better, therefore, if I knew if my selection is final or not, at the earliest'

He immediately took out a fat file and looked into the papers, holding it in such a way that I could not even get a glimpse of the contents. Closing the file and keeping it down, he assured me that my selection was certain and as a result I should postpone my visit abroad. He then took out a glossy magazine printed as a souvenir of some earlier, similar function. The quality of printing was comparable to "Namaste" or other publications printed by Airlines for in-flight reading. It contained a lot of photographs of people receiving trophies from cabinet ministers. The Sardar also informed me that the programme would be televised on Doordarshan.

Then came the expected surprise. The Sardar said, "You see, we print this souvenir with your photograph and you have to contribute by sponsoring an advertisement". He handed over the paper giving advertisement rates, which ranged from Rs. 5000/- to Rs. 25000/-. I mumbled "OK" and walked out.

Soon after my return to Indore I received a letter from this NGO confirming my selection. The letter also urged for placement of advertisement.

To attend the scheduled programme I reached Delhi, accompanied by my wife Smita early in the morning on 7th March 1996, and checked into a three-star hotel. I went to the Sardar's office in the morning to inform him that I would be there for the function. He immediately came to the point and asked me to pay; else he would cut off my name from the list. I told him that I had instructed my office to send a DD and the same should reach him on that day itself.

I reached the Taj with Smita and went over to the hall where the function was to take place. There must have been around two to three hundred people in the audience. The colourful gathering of well-dressed people represented practically the entire nation. The podium was occupied by the officers of the NGO. The young Sardar was sitting with an assistant behind a curtain surrounded by a gathering. The assistant had a first-generation mechanical machine, which was used to print the credit card payment vouchers. One by one, those who had not made payment till then were signing the credit card vouchers.

The programme had already started. There appeared to be a last-minute change in the chief guest. Ambika Soni and K. C. Pant (then a cabinet minister of something) were on the stage. I do not recollect (since I never paid any attention to them) as to what was being said in the speeches, I was more concerned with the young Sardar who was ticking off names in his list.

The Sardar noticed me and waved, summoning me. The game plan of this NGO was very clear to me; get hold of say fifty odd suckers and make them cough up around ten thousand bucks on an average, spend maybe a lac or two for the function and pocket the balance. Those who come over from far away, spending money for the journey, would not return without the trophy, saving them from potential embarrassment back home. Some would not bother about such minor expenditure and get their photographs published in the local newspapers to gain publicity. And so, when I approached the Sardar, he warned me that he would cut off my name from the list of "The Best Entrepreneur for the year 1995-96" unless I paid up as he had not received any DD by then. I took out a cheque book, wrote out a cheque and handed it over to him (during those days bouncing of a cheque was not considered a serious offence). I told him that he should wait for a couple of days and deposit the cheque only in the event he did not receive the DD sent by my office.

I received the shining trophy for THE BEST ENTREPRENEUR FOR THE YEAR 1995-96 with my name engraved on it, from K C Pant. It must have cost the NGO at least 500 rupees to get the trophy made. Smita and I could hardly get anything to eat at the tea party that followed. People who had paid up probably wanted to get whatever returns they could and so they were grabbing the pastries, biscuits and whatever else they could snatch from the trays as soon as the waiters replenished them.

The next day was spent in meeting our friends and acquaintances in Delhi. Just for the sake of it, I collected my photograph receiving the trophy, from the photographer, paying him thrice the normal cost and took the night train to Indore.

I had issued the cheque on one of my defunct accounts, which had a balance of only 100 rupees. My accountant kept checking with the bank for a month or so. The cheque never came for collection. The young Sardar had intelligently guessed that the cheque would not be honoured, and if he deposited the same, he would probably end up paying collection charges to his bank. It was a case of Tit for Tat. My travel expenses were worth the experience.

With the silver polish worn off, the trophy still sits on top of the filing cabinet in my office.

--xxx---

HEADS YOU WIN - TAILS I LOSE OR THE POWER OF ZERO

(1998-99)

THIS CHAPTER IS DEDICATED TO

THE GREAT ARYABHATTA

WHO INVENTED "ZERO"

Heads You Win - Tails I Lose or the Power of Zero
(1998-99)

During the Ganesh Festival in 1966, an extempore speech competition was held in our colony. I was in the ninth standard then. I participated in the competition. As I reached the podium, I was given the topic for my speech. I unfolded the chit and read the title. It was 'ZERO', 'SHOONYA' in Marathi (probably in Hindi and Sanskrit too). 'SHOONYA' also means empty space of the universe. I recollect my opening remarks. I said, "I am to speak on SHOONYA. Please do not underestimate it, as it means NOTHING. It is as big as the entire universe." I do not recollect what I spoke for the rest of the three minutes.

This zero plays havoc if it gets misplaced. It can enhance the value tenfold or diminish it ten times if shifted beyond a (decimal) point. I have been a prey to this menace a couple of times.

It was around 1993 when we, at Static Transformers, had Quraishi, a young lad working in our Marketing Section. He used to prepare offers (quotations) for our clients. We used to get a large number of enquiries from various Naval Organisations. There was one establishment called "Materials Organisation " (MO) at Ghatkopar, Mumbai. This establishment procured material for the Indian Navy's Western fleet. As a matter of practice, MS sent the requirement of spares to the OEMs (Original Equipment Manufacturers).

We received a small enquiry for supply of a few tiny transformers which were spares required for some equipment supplied by Static Transformers in the past. Quraishi prepared and posted the offer. Soon, I was reviewing the quotations and found that Quraishi had submitted a price of Rs. 43000/- each for the transformer which was to cost us not more than a thousand bucks. I asked Quraishi about it. Quraishi too realized his mistake and admitted that he had goofed up and written 43000/- instead of Rs. 4300/-.

I recollect reacting sharply. "Look, Quraishi" I said, "Do you want to fleece your clients? Do you think we will get the order at such a price?" On my advice, he immediately sent a correction letter to CPRO by post. (Controller of Procurement: Officer, heading the purchase at Materials Organisation). Just two days later we got a surprise. We received an order for ten transformers at Rs. 43000/- each. The transformers were produced in a jiffy and were about to be dispatched to Mumbai. These were to give us a bonus of Rs. 420000/-. But then we were in for another surprise. We received an Order Amendment from CPRO, which said, "Read the unit rate as Rs. 4300/- instead of Rs. 43000/."

THE JACKPOT WAS GONE. IT WAS OUR OWN (UN)DOING.

A similar episode took place a few years later. Though similar in nature, it was rather a kind of mirror image. CPRO sent us a requirement for a large number of spares. There were 25 odd items in the list. This time the quotation was prepared by Nilesh who was very meticulous with figures. We had not graduated to using PCs by then and so the quotation was typed out. One of the items in the list was a Contactor, which Nilesh had priced at Rs. 33350/. The same got typed as Rs. 3335/- each. The mistake went unnoticed when the offer was sent.

A month or two later we received the order worth a few lacs, it included two contactors to be supplied at Rs. 3335/-. Nilesh did write to CPRO immediately explaining the typographical error. He even met CPRO representatives during his visits to Mumbai but to no avail. **It was therefore: heads you win tails I lose.**

YET ANOTHER MISTAKE

Static Transformers represented AXA POWER, in India. AXA Power was a Danish Company, which manufactured and sold power supplies required by the Aviation Industry all around the world. They were (and still are) number one in the world in terms of the volume of such supplies. Initially the Company was owned by one Mr. Ackerman, a Danish National, who was a nice person to deal with. He, however, later sold the Company to a very large American company.

Earlier, AXA Power had supplied three Power Supplies to Air India. Our quotation to Air India on behalf of AXA Power was submitted some time in 1994 and the order had materialised in 1998, after a gap of four years. Reportedly their project had been delayed due to the collapse of a hanger during construction.

Typically, when the Power Supplies were ready to be shipped, Air India's team visited Denmark for inspection and familiarisation. Static's role in this whole deal was to get the order, commission the equipment and train the user staff. It was therefore necessary for us to get acquainted with the functioning of the equipment ourselves. That would call for a visit to Denmark and expenditure worth Rs. 80000/-. We were severely cash strapped (a permanent feature for us). Secondly, we had already spent more than one lac rupees during the past four years on this project and so we proposed to Ackerman to subsidize the visit by 50%, which he readily agreed to.

I therefore joined the AI team at Delhi Airport for proceeding to Copenhagen. The team comprised a GM on the verge of retirement, and a young lady who was an Electrical Engineer by vocation. I travelled in the economy class on the SAS flight to Copenhagen while the AI team was in the Executive Section. Being employed by an Airline, they had this privilege. However, as their luck would have it, on the return journey they were deplaned at Copenhagen for lack of empty seats.

Subsequently, everything went well until the units arrived and we commissioned three of the four units. The fourth developed a snag. It being a part of the game, I do not wish to detail the events except to hint at the fact that the payments got delayed.

Internationally, the normal practice is to supply the material only against LC[4*] (Letter of Credit). Air India was not willing to open any LC but had agreed to pay immediately on commissioning of the units. Ackerman, on my personal assurance, had accepted the Order. The payment however did not come through for about three months after commissioning. We sent letters / faxes, talked to the concerned people

---

[4*] A letter from the bank, which assures the supplier of payment and ensures that it is made as agreed.

and finally approached the Finance Director who very apologetically stated that AI was having severe finance problems. Finally, after considerable follow up for another three months, a cheque was received by AXA Power and the same took an extra month for clearing. Our commission of Rs 2.5 lacs was credited to our account by AXA Power in just another two days through SWIFT Transfer.

Readers will wonder as to why I have narrated all these fairly routine happenings in the Indian Industry. The purpose was to provide a background for the blundering episode, which took place a few years later.

Air India floated another tender for four more units and we submitted the papers on behalf of AXA Power. About nine months later (at Air India, except for its aircrafts, everything moves at snail's speed), during my routine follow up visit, the concerned GM told me that AXA Power's offer price was the lowest and AI would soon be placing the order.

However, for months together we did not hear anything from AI. At last, after another four months or so, we got a letter asking us for confirmation on some commercial matters and also requesting us to offer an additional discount.

I dictated a reply, which apart from commercial confirmations, included a statement that we could not reduce the price any further. Later in the letter, I also stated that the price per unit would remain at USD 23,395. This was a misprint or typographical error. The correct figure was 23,995 per unit. This mistake went unnoticed even when Nilesh, who is otherwise quite thorough with paperwork, checked the letter before it was dispatched.

In spite of our taking up the matter of this typographical error with AI, the Order got placed at the lower price; and the units got supplied. Net result was that our commission on four units was reduced from Rs 3.5 lacs to less than Rs. 2.5 lacs. Had Ackerman been still the owner of AXA Power, he would have shared the loss but, as I said earlier, Americans owned the Company by then.

We paid a very high price for an oversight. **WAS IT A SILLY MISTAKE OR A BLUNDER?**

--xxx---

MIRACULOUS MEMORY (2004)

THIS CHAPTER IS DEDICATED TO

AIR MARSHAL DESAI

FOR

GIVING ME A PATIENT HEARING

AND

TRYING TO HELP US GET OUR PAYMENT EARLIER

Miraculous Memory (2004)

I have an extremely poor memory and that is an understatement. I have an excellent memory and I am being very modest in saying so. Do not get confused. I cannot remember faces, names of people, dates and spellings of words among many other things. However, I can very well recollect events and remember physics and mathematics I learnt in school and college.

Many a times when Smita and I watch a movie on TV, I ask her, "Who is this heroine?" And I get a reply, "Kaaay He? (What is this?) She is Madhuri Dixit / Aishwarya Rai / Karisma Kapoor." Those who are TV regulars must have watched a TV ad in which Juhi Chawla dresses up like Jassi. I thought that she was Jassi and failed to understand the ad. Only recently, Shantanu, my younger son, clarified the matter.

On a number of occasions this makes me face embarrassment. I would come across someone who would smile at me and start a conversation. Soon he/she would realise that though I had returned his/her smile, I have not been able to recognize him/her. Then I would be asked the most embarrassing question, "You do not seem to recollect who I am?" In the meantime, my brain would be scanning my memory cells without any fruitful result. Sometimes, from the conversation, I would get some clue and recollect his/her name just in time to save the situation.

This poor memory of mine made me hate history, languages, chemistry and similar subjects. Organic chemistry was the worst, you change 'e' to 'a' and the compound would change all its properties. I could never remember the vast variety of hydrocarbons when I studied the subject during the first year of B.Sc. But I will never forget that I scored seventeen out of fifty in the final exams and that was the threshold for passing.

DR. JEKYLL

Just to give an example of the better half of my memory, I am narrating an event which took place only a few weeks ago. My maternal aunt, who is eighty not out, visited us accompanied by her three daughters. We do not meet frequently. During the course of the conversation one of them referred to my visit along with my parents to their home nearly forty years ago. "Do you remember you visited us at Tikamgarh?"

"Yes! Though I was a kid then, I remember many things including the twin latrine," I replied. It was a very funny, first-generation latrine with two seats in one room having two doors. Probably, the builder of the Government bungalow had conveniently forgotten to build a wall in between. Or maybe it was a fashion to use it in pairs. In spite of such an oddity, none of my cousins who had stayed in that house for two to three years could remember it. My aunt, however, confirmed my statement.

Here is another example of my ability to recollect events which took place long ago. Last year during a bull session when my three elder sisters were visiting us, we started talking about the Good Old Days.

I narrated the event which had taken place more than forty-two years ago. My father had bought a secondhand car for 3000 rupees. We had gone to Mumbai and Pune on a family excursion. When we were travelling from Mumbai to Pune, at Panvel where the Ghats start, the brakes of our car failed. The driver found that the pipe carrying the brake-fluid was leaking. He bought a new pipe from a nearby shop, but could not get the brake oil. It was therefore necessary to conserve the oil. He cut the pipe from the leaking point; bent the tube and held a tumbler under the open end. The oil however refused to come out due to viscosity and atmospheric pressure. For a minute or so the driver and my father were puzzled and were trying to find a solution. I suggested that I will pump the brake paddle while the driver collected the oil. Forget the details; my sisters did not even remember the journey.

BACKGROUND FOR THE MAIN STORY

This incident took place a few months back, in July 2004 to be precise. In order that the readers appreciate it, I must provide the necessary background information.

I joined NITIE in July 1976 and graduated in May 1978. During that period the Indian Air Force used to sponsor one officer for the two-year

Post Graduation Course. He used to stay in our hostel with family. We had Squadron Leader Kumar with us in our batch. In our senior batch we had Squadron Leader Arora. The batch junior to us had no one from the IAF.

In 1996 I went to Delhi in connection with the introduction of a new product in IAF. I met my cousin Group Captain Jayanta Apte. He introduced me to his boss in the Western Air Command in Delhi, Air Commodore Arora. We held a fruitful technical discussion for about fifteen minutes.

A year later, I went to Jayanta's house. During our casual conversation I enquired about the whereabouts of A.Cmdr. Arora. He told me that Arora had retired and had started some horticulture business. He also casually mentioned that Arora had done Post Graduation from NITIE.

My God! Neither of us had recognised each other during our meeting. This was in spite of the fact that we had been together in the same hostel for one full year and must have interacted with each other on more than hundred occasions. Of course, we had met after around twenty years.

THE MAIN STORY

Our company had developed and supplied critical equipment to IAF. Payment however was held up for a long time for some frivolous reason. In July 2004, I went to Delhi with a determination to speed up the processing of payment pending against our year-old supply. It is yet another story that in spite of logging 1000 hours without any breakdown, and being judged as far superior equipment than the ones supplied by our competitors, the payment was held up due to 'red-tapeism'.

Even after a week's stay at Delhi, I saw no signs of progress, I thought of meeting the AOM. Air Officer Maintenance is the highest post among technical officers at Air Headquarters at Vayu Bhavan. I knew that one Air Marshal Desai had taken up the position a few weeks back.

I therefore telephoned his staff officer for an appointment. He, however, flatly refused saying that Desai was very busy. He asked me to meet his Junior ACS Eng. (A); I met him and gave him the case history. Though he promised to help me (and later I learnt that he did try to push the payment), I did not see much hope. Next day, which happened to be a Thursday, I again called the AOM's Staff Officer (SO) and pleaded for an appointment. Though he gave me a patient hearing on phone, he declined to oblige on the grounds that the AOM had taken up the post only fifteen days ago and that he was tied up throughout the day. At my request he however agreed to inform AOM and ask him for sparing some time for me on Friday, the last working day of the week. In the same breath he added that he did not think a meeting was feasible.

To check the outcome of my request, I called the SO at around 4.30 PM and got the expected negative reply. Since my mobile was not working, I had called him from a PCO. After replacing the receiver, I turned around to come out of the booth, but continued to turn the full circle; I picked up the receiver and hit the redial button. I asked for SO again and when he came on line. I asked him, "Just one thing, Sir. Was Air Marshal Desai in Bombay between 1975 to1978 at NITIE?" I could hear him enquiring with his colleagues and then he answered, "Affirmative".

I shot back, "In that case I am his classmate and you should therefore permit me to meet him." He then gave me the telephone number of IAF'S VIP Guest House where Desai was staying and asked me to call him at seven in the evening.

At seven sharp I called him and after exchanging pleasantries, told him that I was also in NITIE. He sounded curious and puzzled. He said, "But Mr. Joshi, I do not recollect having any Joshi in our batch. When were you in NITIE?"

"Between 76 to 78", I informed.

"How could you have met me? I left in May '76 and you Joined NITIE in July '76. Maybe you met me during the convocation." Desai's memory was weaker than mine. There was no convocation during my stay at NITIE. Anyway, I got the appointment for the next day.

For the next three days, until I reached Indore, I kept wondering as to what made me ask AOM's SO if Desai was in NITIE and that too between 1975 to 1978 while I was there only between 1976 and1978.

Secondly, I was aware that Arora had retired and only Kumar could possibly be in active service.

Then like a hazy, blurred picture slowly got clear, my memory focused on to a small happening in 1976. I was having a stroll with Bala, a year senior to me. On our way to Vihar Lake, Arora crossed us on Scooter. I happened to tell Bala, "This chap's kids are very naughty."

To which Bala replied, "You have not met Squadron Leader Desai. He was our senior. His son was a Devil." And there the matter ended.

The walk continued. The conversation drifted to some other topic. The information got stored in my memory cells. Zipped. For the next 28 years i.e., from July '76 to July '04, I neither heard of nor talked about Desai of IAF.

On that day in July 2004, the IAF – Desai got unzipped from memory and restructured and prompted me to call the SO. Google would probably search Squadron Leader Desai - IAF record in two seconds and provide the result saying, "Did you mean Air Marshal Desai"? For this search my brain took all of two days, but then I am not a computer operating at 53 Gigahertz but a '1953 model' human being.

--xxx---

GERMAN THIEVES V/S DANISH HONESTY (1998)

THIS CHAPTER IS DEDICATED TO

MEMBERS OF AXA POWER

OF

DENMARK

German Thieves V/S Danish Honesty

Shrikant Chendke & Ashok Patankar are my close friends since my primary school days. They have been acting as my sounding boards. More than proof reading of what I write, they are a source of motivation to me as they read with genuine interest and suggest improvements. A few days back Shrikant visited Indore. By then I had written one more chapter. So, when he completed reading the chapter, I asked him if he found it monotonous because I had included too many anecdotes related to travelling. When he said he did not, I decided to include this chapter.

I have been abroad a number of times. With each trip, my experience has grown richer. I have undergone unique experiences, some sweet, some sour, and a few bitter. I am covering some of these in this chapter.

TIT-BITS

In 1995, I visited Germany to attend the Hannover Messe (An Industrial Exhibition) and from there proceeded to Denmark. I reached Frankfurt railway station on a Sunday morning. To save on the hotel expenses, I decided to take an overnight train to Odense (Denmark) and accordingly booked my ticket for a 10 O'clock train. I kept my bags in the locker and killed time doing nothing, repenting on my failure to keep some reading material with me. Being a Sunday, there was no point in going around the downtown area as all the shops were closed and moreover it was snowing on and off.

During that visit, and even earlier, I had transited through Frankfurt railway station many times. When one has to use a handcart, one has to put a coin in the slot of the handle and the trolley gets disengaged from the stack for use. The chain of the trolley gets released from the next trolley in the stack. This system exists in many airports and railway stations all around the world.

However, there is a small difference at Frankfurt railway station. There the trolleys have two slots, one on each side of the handle. One slot is marked 'One Mark' and the other 'Two Marks'. During those days the Mark used to cost around twenty-two rupees. I must have used the trolley at least ten times as I had frequently transited via Frankfurt. Every time I would use a one-Mark coin and so while I was sitting idle, I thought, "How clever of me, I have saved 220 rupees ".

That evening a few minutes before the train's departure, a passenger came to the platform with his luggage. He unloaded it from the cart, pushed the empty trolley to the nearest trolley station, dovetailed the trolley into the stack, attached the hanging chain of his trolley to the next, and pocketed the coin, which popped out of the slot. It was a neat idea to motivate people to park the empty trolleys at the designated places. I boarded the train realising that I had not saved but wasted over 220 rupees. **I was not clever but too clever by half.**

FRANKFURT MAINS

On that Sunday evening, I took out my bags from the locker and was loitering on the platform. I had some pizza and at a shop spotted water bottles (rather bottled water). For a moment I left my cart unguarded and moved inside the shop. My suitcase and a brand new briefcase worth Rs. 5000/- were on the trolley.

Even before I bought the bottle, I realised that I had made a mistake and I turned around and took quick steps towards my bags. I am sure I was not away from my bags for more than 10 seconds; in the meantime my briefcase had been lifted. Luckily or wisely, I had kept tickets, passport and money in my inside breast pocket, which saved my skin. I went to the police station at one end of the platform and filed a complaint. The officer said that I may possibly get my briefcase back, as the thieves, not finding any valuables inside, may throw the bag away in the garbage. With some respite I left for the platform.

On my return journey, I touched Frankfurt twice. There was, however, no trace of the bag.

THE DANISH HONESTY

One year later, in June 1996, I went to Denmark for a couple of days. Being a Delta frequent flier, I booked my tickets to Copenhagen by Air France, Delta's partner in the frequent flier programme. I flew from Indore to Mumbai in the evening, took a midnight flight to Paris and reached Copenhagen around 1 PM local time. I bought my tickets and took a train to Copenhagen Central. It was around 2 PM, more than twenty-four hours after I had left my residence.

Feeling famished, I went to McDonalds. I was standing in front of the McDonald outlet (I refuse to call it a restaurant), looking up at the menu displayed on the wall, trying to figure out an edible item. One of my legs was touching my suitcase, next to which I had kept my briefcase. By the time I decided on the menu and decided to join the queue for ordering, my briefcase had been lifted. It had cost me over 5k rupees and was quite identical to the one I had lost at Frankfurt. I asked many people in the vicinity if they had seen anyone lifting my bag, but in vain. I got so upset that I just walked to the platform and boarded the train to Odense.

I reached Odense and lugged my suitcase to the hotel. It was around six in the evening when I reached the hotel. I ordered a salad and managed to swallow it down before I slept.

Next day when I narrated this story to Elvstrom of AXA Power, he insisted that I report the matter to the police on my way back. I was quite sceptical. However, I decided to honour his advice. On my return trip, two days later, I went to the police station at Copenhagen Central and reported my complaint.

Two days later, I reached home and when I logged on to my computer, there was an email from the Indian Embassy at Copenhagen stating "Dear Mr. Joshi, your briefcase has been handed over to us by the police. Kindly arrange to get it collected within 15 days, else the same will be destroyed" I mailed the embassy that AXA Power's representative would collect the same and requested Elvstrom to get it picked up.

I received my briefcase on the fourth day by DHL. The only items missing from it were a carton of cigarettes, and a folding umbrella. I am sure it must be the doing of a staffer at the Indian Embassy.

SOME MORE TIT- BITS

In June 1997, I once again visited Denmark. I was accompanying the Air India officials who were visiting AXA Power to inspect the equipment ordered by them. On the way, the General Manager enquired many times about the time it would take to reach Odense from Copenhagen. Every time I informed him that it would take around four hours as we had to take a bus to the Copenhagen Central and from there, we would be taking a train to Odense, which at some station would be loaded onto a ferry boat, to cross the sea, and then again, the train would move onwards to Odense. From my earlier visits, I was aware that this leg of the journey was the most thrilling and memorable. During one of my visits, I had witnessed from the upper deck of the multi-storied boat, huge blocks of ice floating around in the clean blue sea water. Very few people would leave the comfort of a cozy restaurant and come out onto the deck to face and feel the chilling breeze. For me it was not an experience I could skip.

When I had mailed Ackerman confirming my schedule, he had informed me that if we came directly, it would cost me 200 kroner and if we came via Copenhagen Central it would cost me 150 kroner. I had not bothered to understand him as many times Ackerman used to confuse me by his odd use of English language.

We landed at Copenhagen airport where the Air India local agent greeted us and handed over our tickets for Odense. He directed us to the train terminus at the airport. That was a big surprise. What progress! At the underground terminus we boarded the shuttle to Copenhagen Central and from there we took a train to Odense.

Probably AI's GM was a patient of amnesia. As soon as the train started and the first ticket collector came over, he asked her, "How long will it take to reach Odense?" I was more than surprised when she replied "ninety minutes".

That was really an amazing progress. They had built a bridge over the sea and a tunnel under the seawater, twenty-five kilometers long, in just around three years. The journey from Copenhagen to Odense was thus cut short to ninety minutes. Back home in Kolkata we have to face traffic jams when we cross the backwaters to reach GRSE. There are two bridges (depending on the route one takes). One is a rotating bridge, which rotates sideways to let the ships pass by, and the other splits in the middle and the two sides lift up for clearing the passage for vessels. Both were built before independence, by the British.

Incidentally, a few years ago, Reader's Digest had carried out a survey in a number of cities by dropping purses with money at different public locations and keeping a watch on them. They then worked out statistics of what percentage of persons deposited the purses with the police or other authorities. Odense had 100% returns. For the benefit of Indians, Madurai ranked second.

--xxx---

THE COW AND THE TIGER

THIS CHAPTER IS DEDICATED TO

ARUN DUTTA

A BUILDER FROM CALCUTTA

WHO WAS MY MOTIVATION

TO VENTURE INTO CONSTRUCTION BUSINESS

The Cow and the Tiger

It so happened that I was on the lookout for business opportunities after I left Migma where I was the Managing Director. I was operating from Indore quite independently and hence, when I left Migma, I did not want to take up a job and report to a stupid boss. I had enjoyed or rather suffered the autonomy of being the MD; such as whenever the driver bunked his duty, I would step into his shoes and become a Matador Driver to ferry the staff to Pithampur.

So, I set up a small consultancy outfit. This did not occupy me full time and hence I decided that I should in parallel get into some other business. Construction business was booming in Indore during those days and I wondered if I could venture into it. I had a reasonable idea of construction costs from my experience of building Magma's factory building. At Migma I had been responsible for its Pithampur project from the stage of the green grass field to the completion of the factory shed and building. Similarly, I had the Gallium's factory constructed at Pithampur.

I, as far as finance was concerned, had my eldest brother-in-law's backing. My eldest sister is a gynecologist and was the Head of the Department at the KEM Hospital at Bombay before she retired. Her husband is one of India's most renowned Heart Surgeons, Dr. S. Bhattacharyya. He has done so many open-heart surgeries that he easily qualifies for the Guinness Book of Records. He lent me some funds for my construction venture.

I did some research and estimated that with these funds, I could construct good, modern houses in an upcoming colony and sell the same for over fifteen lacs within a year. Even after accounting for interest on the capital, I would make a reasonable profit.

With confidence, I went ahead with the plan. I bought a plot of land for around two lacs with the help of a broker. During the next one year the construction went on in full swing. Right from the basic designing, getting drawings prepared from an architect, getting various permits, getting a tube well dug up, and all other construction activities were completed in one year. Two twin bungalows were ready for possession. They had four bedrooms each with attached baths; and had full marble flooring.

I had spent about eight lacs, which for that kind of construction could be considered quite economical. I had managed costs well and saved money. I had gone to Nathdwara in Rajasthan to buy a truck load of marble slabs directly from the mines and thus had managed to save nearly half the money that I would have otherwise spent.

When the bungalows were ready, I advertised in the local newspapers and contacted brokers for finding buyers. The selling price at that time was around 500 rupees per square foot and thus the twin bungalows could fetch us as high as rupees twenty lacs. I was, however, prepared for fourteen lacs. It would give me two lacs of net profit after considering interest on investment.

Many likely buyers visited; brokers brought in a client every time I went to the bungalows four kilometers from my office - eight from my residence. Most of the buyers would be impressed by the construction. All would be Hindus as it was a predominantly Hindu colony. Some would bring their priests; though the *Vastu Shastra* bogie was not very popular then.

In all the cases however, the deal would fizzle out at the last minute. It used to be a typical case of KLPD (I am sure all IITians and North Indian male college students would know the meaning). For those who do not know the vulgar long form; I would say that it is "last minute deception".

The reason for the last-minute withdrawal was always the same. It was the 'tiger' trouble. The plot on which the bungalows were constructed was not rectangular. The front was wider than the rear. The Hindu conservatives call it *'Vaghra Mukhi'* meaning- like a tiger whose mouth is wider than the torso, as compared to *'Go Mukhi'*, meaning – like a cow's mouth which is narrow in the front.

However, progressive the buyer was, he would shy away. Why take a chance and go against the *'Shastras'*, which consider a Vaghra Mukhi house as one with some kind of curse. People staying there would not prosper, they believed.

Later, I met Milind Mahajan, Mrs. Sumitra Mahajan's son. She was Indore's MP, elected to the Lok Sabha six times consecutively and who was also a Minister at the Centre during BJP's five-year stint. During our chit chat, I happened to narrate this story to him. He revealed that their house was Vaghra Mukhi. For the information of all the conservatives and believers, all the members of Mahajan family have made such good progress in life and they could be considered a blessed family.

Coming back to the Cow story, when Dr. Bhattacharya enquired about the progress of the project, I informed him that I was unable to repay as the property was not attracting real buyers and that if he wanted to secure the investment, I could transfer the building to his name. He agreed and said that he would buy the property.

I could have agreed to transfer it at 10 lacs and squared up the loan, but he insisted on payment of the interest which had swelled to around two lacs. He bought the twin bungalows which for me was a rescue operation. He however insisted on paying for my efforts and charging interest on his capital. As a result, he bought the buildings at a higher price. All this took place in 1991. For the next twelve years, the bungalows remained vacant except for a chowkidar's family who got paid Rs. 500 per month.

All these transactions reminded me of an article I had once read in Economic Times.

It was about IDBI (Industrial Development Bank of India). The bank, publicly well known, was in big trouble due to its high volume of NPA[5*] (non-performing assets; though they preferred to term these as 'Strained Assets'.) As per RBI norms there is a limit (of NPA), beyond which a bank is considered sick. Since IDBI was owned by the Government of India, it was being bailed out by a very clever maneuver. GOI funded it by increasing its shareholding by Rs. 7000 crores and IDBI invested it back in GOI's bonds. Thus, no money was transacted except for two book entries. This, on paper, made IDBI a healthy bank and there would

---

[5*] Loans given by the bank, which do not get returned in stipulated period and do not fetch interest.

be no hue and cry about IDBI being a sick bank. What a novel solution for fooling the public!

TIGER'S TAIL

After a year or so, one day, we got an electricity bill for 17000 for that building. Prior to that the bill used to be only for minimum charges of 250 per month. My interest in the matter had reduced considerably because Dr. Bhattacharya was not prepared to rent out the building to anyone except to a bank. I therefore did not pay the bill and the electricity company disconnected the supply and took away the meter. After around 10 years, we started getting notices from the Tehsildar who had the powers to issue an arrest warrant in Smita's name (The power connection was in her name) for recovery of this amount.

Whenever someone came to my house, I argued with him that the meter was taken away without our knowledge and so we could not confirm the consumption reading was correct. And secondly, how could a chowkidar with one or two bulbs in the house consume so much power? I maintained the status quo.

Finally, in 2003, someone approached me wanting to buy the twin bungalows. In these twelve years, the condition of the bungalows had become pathetic; window panes were broken, gates rusted, doors deformed due to rainwater, taps stolen and so on.

This broker had two buyers and after discussing with my sister I brokered a deal for sixteen lacs each. It took more than six months to execute the deal as my sister had misplaced the original documents and the buyer's bankers were not ready for the house loan without those papers. Dr. Bhattacharya had to spend about one and a half lacs in payment of pending statutory dues, property tax and so on. Financially Dr. Bhattacharya was at a loss but this amount was peanuts for him. **And thus, finally the Tiger won over the Cow.**

Incidentally later I learnt that the original owner of the plot of land was a Bohara and hence did not bother if the plot was Go -Mukhi or Vyaghra – Mukhi, And the Broker had concealed the fact,

--xxx---

TALHUNT

THIS CHAPTER IS DEDICATED TO

THE MEMORY OF

LATE KIRTI PATNI

MY CLOSE FRIEND AND A WELL WISHER

Talhunt

During the same period that the 'Cow and the Tiger' episode took place, I also had opened a division and called it "TALHUNT". I was looking for business openings at that time. One day, I was discussing the possible opportunities / business avenues with a very good friend of mine, Kirti Patni, and he made a suggestion. Kirti was my batchmate at NITIE and was from a family of business owners. He had a factory in Indore manufacturing cement pipes. He was a well-informed person and was also extremely good at dramatics and photography. Unfortunately, he passed away a few years later, after he suffered from Hepatitis.

He suggested that I start an employment agency, as it would require very little investment. That started me thinking in that direction. At that time Indore had only one or two operators in that line of business. One day, I was going for a stroll and crossed Deepak Khare's house. Deepak is my sister's (Dr. Pushpa Khare's) brother-in-law who runs coaching classes together with his younger brother. The Khare's classes for Pre-Medical & Pre-Engineering Tests are very well known and thousands of students enrol with them paying a fee of hundreds of rupees per month. Out of thousands, hardly a few make it to the medical and engineering colleges.

So, when I crossed the hurdle of hundreds of bicycles parked in front of Khare Classes, my mind did some quick arithmetic. If I started an employment agency; and if I got at least a thousand applications a year and if I kept a registration fee of forty rupees, which anyone wanting a job or wanting a change in job would not mind sparing, it would fetch me Rs 40,000 a year and that would provide me with some income. I could always look to augment this with other technical consultancy assignments.

I therefore rented a 500-sqft-office space in a commercial building. I got it furnished and equipped with a telephone (depositing 30000 in tatkal scheme), computer, electronic typewriter etc. and formed a private limited company with Smita as a partner. Except for a delay due to communal riots and subsequent curfew, all the operational parts of starting the show were completed quickly. My advertisement attracted around 300 applicants in the first quarter. Smita used to join me in the office after lunch and I had employed a typist and a part time MBA student to visit various industries for their requirement of personnel.

One day, a polished youngster visited me. He introduced himself as Shyam from Bangalore. He had left his house and had spent time with sadhus at Omkareshwar (50 kms from Indore) where he read my ad in some newspaper. He was living a nomadic life and offered to work for me for free. He said some sadhu had told him that he would soon go abroad and he thought I could help him with this ambition. After some hesitation I agreed. He knew how to drive a car, had a Diner's Card and a good personality. After a few months, my initial reservations about him evaporated.

In the first six months we did quite well. Some twenty plus people got employment through us. We billed and collected around one lac rupees or so from the employers who paid us an amount equal to one-month's salary of the person employed.

Suddenly after six months things changed. In spite of several advertisements in the dailies no more applications were coming in. No recruitments were taking place as the good ones registered with us had already been employed. There was a requirement of engineers, managers, even good steno typists in the industry, but suitable applicants were not available. My finances were drying up and I was eating into my savings.

IRRITANTS

During that period one applicant approached me for a job. He was an engineer with considerable experience. His background was such that he could be absorbed in a suitable position in the steel forming industry. One such company belonged to Dewas Tools group, which was owned by Manohar Baheti, younger brother of Dr. Ramesh Baheti, MD of Steel Tubes of India. When I was in Steel Tubes, Dewas Tools had its factory at Dewas within Steel Tube's compound; and I knew Manohar Baheti very well. I also knew his colleague Vishnu Bhagwan who held the Director's post in Dewas Tools.

I went over to him and asked if he was interested in my services. He mentioned that he was. Then I asked him if they would be interested in employing a person of such & such experience. He indicated his keenness. I then gave him the bio-data and arranged for an interview.

Somehow, I did not follow up the matter and after about three months it was by chance that I came across this applicant while on an evening walk. He informed me that he had joined the Dewas Tools group two months back as Works Manager of Dewas Metal Section at a salary of Rs. 13000/- per month.

The next day I went to Dewas Tools and presented our bill to Vishnu who, after consulting Manohar, said that since they had advertised and this chap had also applied against the same, Dewas Tools would not pay my fees. That was an absurd argument. I went up to Manohar but got no result. **I believe the figure of 13 was unlucky for me.**

IRRITANT – TAKE 2

One day, one Mr. Bhargawa visited our office. He was setting up a press shop as an ancillary for Eicher Motors and wanted an experienced technical hand. I had the right person for that job in my databank. He was a mechanical engineer with around ten years' experience of press shop work at Kinetic Honda's Pithampur Plant. I sent him for an interview. Bhargawa did not let me know of the result.

After three months or so I learnt from Shirish, a friend of mine, that this Kinetic engineer had joined Bhargawa immediately after his interview. When I approached Bhargawa with my bill he refused to pay. The reasoning put forward by him was more ridiculous than that of Manohar Baheti. He said "He has not been recruited as Development Engineer, but as Works Manager ".

There were a few other similar incidences where the income remained unrealised. Some employers gave the reason that the employee left within three months of joining and some gave other ludicrous excuses.

SHYAM OR SHAM

One day, a person who was running some business in the Middle East visited us. He wanted to recruit a salesman for one of his shops there. He would not be paying us for our services as the trend then was that the fees were paid by the successful candidate who got the opportunity to go abroad. Shyam immediately offered his own candidature. He was a good salesman and succeeded in selling himself. There was no possibility to get any fees from him, on the contrary he pleaded with me to loan him ten grand to cover the shortfall he was having in buying the air ticket. He promised to return the money soon upon getting his first salary. He, of course, never did so. I initially wrote a few times reminding him of his promise but I received no reply. **Shyam was a Sham.**

THE DRY SPELL

After the first six months or so, a dry spell started and prolonged for a year. The MBA student helping me on a part time basis graduated and left. The steno-typist also left. He went back to Hyderabad to help his father's business. Not a single good applicant was coming in, and we thought it best to close the shop.

Luckily a young lad with business aspirations offered to buy Talhunt. I was quite happy to transfer the Goodwill and a set of 300 odd useless resumes for a consideration of Rs 30,000/-. I never heard of him again and am certain he never earned a paisa from it.

Talhunt had stopped yielding human talent but it did help me gain some real talent.

--xxx---

FRUITS OF 'PROGRESS' (2000)

THIS CHAPTER IS DEDICATED TO

ALL THOSE WHO

WORK FOR

IRCTC

WHICH HAS MADE THE TASK OF

RAILWAY RESERVATION

SO SIMPLE

Fruits of 'Progress'

Twenty-four years ago, at Indore, water supply was available twenty-four hours a day. As of now we get it precisely for twenty-four minutes and that too on alternate days. Earlier the pressure was such that water used to gush out of the tap on the third floor, twenty-four feet above the ground level. Today it hardly trickles from the tap twenty-four inches below the ground level.

Twenty-four years ago, any one could drive from Indore to Mumbai, any time of the day without fear. Today vehicles are stopped in the Ghats until a convoy of at least twenty-four vehicles is formed and then the caravan moves with a police jeep as escort to avoid incidences of looting.

When the Gitanjali Express was introduced, it used to take twenty-four hours to reach Mumbai from Kolkata with one stop in each state. Now it takes much more time and stops at more than twenty-four stations on the way.

Barring such examples, the Indian Railways has certainly made some genuine progress. However, for people from Indore the connectivity continues to be a challenge. For us, therefore, travelling by train is extremely inconvenient and tedious. Getting reservation is another Herculean task. Add to that my luck factor, and then one gets the complete picture.

Recently, I went to Pune via Nasik. I had a meeting scheduled at Pune for which I had to pick up someone at Nasik. So, I left Indore by an overnight bus, which reached Nasik a couple of hours late - nothing unusual. I checked into a hotel and after getting ready in an hour arrived at the house from which I had to escort the concerned person by taxi to Pune, only to be informed that the meeting had been cancelled.

Since I had no other work at Nasik, and many other tasks planned at Pune, I decided to proceed alone by bus. I reached the bus stand by 10.30AM where I learnt that the buses were not plying until noon, due to 'PALKI', a religious procession of lacs of devotees of Lord Vitthal, who walk all the way from Nasik to Pandharpur via Pune. This affects the highway traffic very badly.

I returned to the hotel and reached the bus stand again post lunch. I boarded the so-called Luxury Bus at 2 PM. It covered the distance to Pune by 10 PM taking exactly twice the normal time. The ordeal did not end there. I had to walk a kilometer with my bags to finally manage to get an Auto to reach the hotel.

Shrikant Chendke, a close friend of mine, during one of our chit-chat sessions opined that (He had just gone through the chapter 'American Systems v/s Danish Human Touch' of my book) I take too much risk and do not provide for margins in my travel plans. This reminded me of Dr. Baheti's (MD of Steel Tubes of India) planning.

Once an important industrialist from Japan was to visit Steel Tubes. His three-day visit was planned out to the minutest detail. Steel Tubes is just adjacent to a railway track and to reach the factory's main gate, one has to cross over the tracks. The level crossing used to be open most of the time as there were very few trains plying on that route during those days. Baheti did not, however, take any chances. He had one car parked as a standby on the factory side of the crossing so that in the event of the level crossing's gate being closed, he would walk across with the guest and get into the standby car. Similar arrangement was made for the return journey. However, on both the occasions the standby vehicles only stood by.

The best part of the story was that, on the same evening a Banquette was planned at Indore, in honour of the Japanese visitor, Ching Chang Hu. The return journey consisted of a caravan of fifteen odd cars, Matadors and other vehicles. It started raining, rather pouring, and by the time the motorcade reached Lasudia which is five kilometers from Indore, the road was flooded with knee deep (and for Ching Chang Hu, hip-deep) water. This caused a traffic jam with hundreds of vehicles, mostly trucks, on either side of the road. After we exhausted our patience, we got out of the vehicle and waded through the muddy water while the downpour continued to worsen the situation. We managed to reach an Auto Stand on the other side after a kilometer-long walk. Even Ching Chang Hu and Baheti, who were ten cars ahead, did the same.

The moral of the story is again Murphy's Law. Secondly, if one plans every activity considering the remotest eventualities and provides redundancies, the costs would increase so much that the operation would become uneconomical.

Coming back to my travels, one could say that I am only narrating my bad experiences and not the good ones. I would counter argue that if I kept a log, it could prove that the percentage of such torturous experiences far outweigh the good ones. To support this hypothesis, here I go.

KHARAGPUR VISIT

Once I was traveling with my family to Calcutta. It was in December 1998 when Siddharth had to go to Kharagpur for his second semester. We had decided to take a weeklong excursion to Calcutta. ('Excursion' to Calcutta is a contradiction, considering Calcutta's crowd and pollution level) and had planned to spend a couple of days at Kharagpur.

We had booked Second AC tickets, months in advance. The schedule was simple with enough margins. We would take a taxi to Bhopal in the evening, have dinner in the Waiting Room at the Railway Station, and take the train at one midnight, which would reach Nagpur at 8 the next morning. We would spend the day with Smita's cousin and board Gitanjali Express at 8 PM to reach Calcutta sometime the following afternoon.

We started on time and things went fine till we entered Bhopal Railway Station. The platform was more than overcrowded. Possibly as crowded as Churchgate Suburban Station during peak hours. Except that the crowd was quite static. In the Waiting Room we could manage one relaxing chair with great difficulty. A visit to an overcrowded enquiry counter revealed that all trains coming from Delhi were delayed considerably. (Cause: The devilish fog in Delhi) The wait went on till next morning, interrupted only by the ritual of visiting the enquiry counter every half an hour.

Finally, at 7 in the morning we decided to examine the possibility of taking a taxi to Nagpur. We went out and located one travel agency office which was open. The staffers started discussions with each other. "How far is Nagpur?"; "Is it on the route to Jabalpur?" Siddharth and I went back to the railway station without further enquiry. It was better to choose a known devil.

And finally, the Orange City Express arrived at 11.30 AM. Relieved, all of us slept on our respective berths. The Express reached Orange City just in time for us to have our supper and catch the Gitanjali Express. Smita's cousin had come to the Station and had thoughtfully brought for us adequate food and snacks.

The episode does not end here. We checked the chart for our reservation status. When we had booked our tickets a couple of months earlier, Smita and I had a confirmed booking while Siddharth and Shantanu's status was waitlist number one and two. We were certain that within two months there would be enough cancellations and that they would also get confirmed berths. (The booking was not online at that time.)

We got a rude shock when we learnt that the status remained unchanged. The conductor however gave one berth in the Third AC, which they shared. We only wasted the higher-class tickets, as there was no possibility of getting a refund. It was only later that I learnt that the reservation system was not dynamic and that there was a quota of two berths for Nagpur in Second AC on Gitanjali. Siddharth and Shantanu (wait-list one and two) would have been allotted berths only if Smita and I had cancelled our tickets.

That day Smita vowed that she would never travel with me any time in the future, but she did and later had two more bitter experiences.

THE REAL FRUIT

I was invited to present a paper by The Association of Industries, Chandigarh Chapter. For attending this I was to take the Shatabdi Express from Bhopal, reach Delhi and continue the next morning to Ambala, again by Shatabdi.

I reached Bhopal and had my lunch in the waiting room. During those days (and even now since I go home for lunch every day) having a leisurely, one-hour siesta had become a habit. I therefore dozed off on the comfortable relaxing chair in the waiting room. Shatabdi arrived from Delhi and departed as scheduled after a gap of twenty minutes. For the first time in my life, I missed a train for such a stupid reason as dozing off. Otherwise, generally if I have to leave my hotel to catch a train, say at six in the morning, I invariably wake up without the help of any alarm at least two hours in advance.

Anyway, I contacted Nilesh who checked the timetable and advised me to take Southern Express, which would reach Delhi in time for the next morning's Delhi Chandigarh Shatabdi. I rebooked the ticket and managed to reach Delhi in time. I boarded Shatabdi at 6.40 AM from platform No. 1 at New Delhi station and reached Chandigarh, next to Ambala Cant.

THE REAL FRUIT- II

After about twenty days I was to visit Delhi and Ambala again and for this journey, Praveen had booked my tickets. He used to take care of all administrative work at Static. I finished my work at Delhi and was ready to go to Ambala by Shatabdi[6*]. I checked the departure time from the ticket. It was 6.20 AM. As I said earlier, I got up well in advance, at 3.30 AM, and reached the station at 6.00AM. Just before entering the platform, I asked a coolie, "Ambala ki Shatabdi kahan Ayegi?" (Where will I have to board the Ambala Shatabdi?) He replied, pointing to the platform, number one *"Yahin Ayegi"* (It will be arriving at this Platform.) The Platform remained empty until 6.15 AM and then I saw a rake moving in.

I boarded the Chair Car and took the seat indicated on the ticket. The one precaution I missed out was confirming my seat from the chart since I had gone to Chandigarh just a few days earlier by Shatabdi from the same Platform No. 1, and secondly, since I was in a hurry to occupy the

---

[6*] Shatabdi are fast train connecting Delhi to different destinations.

seat, as Shatabdis normally start right in time, I had skipped the routine of confirmation of seat from the Chart.

The train, however, did not start for the next twenty minutes, and that was when another passenger came in, claiming to be having a reservation for the seat which I was currently occupying. Being more than confident that it was he who had made a mistake, I showed my ticket to him. He took a minute to study it and while returning my ticket said, "*Bhai Sahib, Aap Galat Shatabdi Me Beithe Hai. Aapka ticket Amritsar Shatabdi Ka Hai. Wah To Aath Number Se Jati He*" (Sir, you have boarded the wrong Shatabdi; your ticket is for Amritsar Shatabdi which leaves from Platform Number eight.)

Still uncertain of his statement or rather not wanting to believe him, I went over to the Conductor who was just boarding the chair-car. He said "*Aapki Shatabdi to Bees Minute Pahle Gaiee, Aap Es Ticket Ko Cancel Karaiye Our Dusri Gadi Se Aaieeye, Esise Me Chalna He To Fresh Ticket Lena Hoga*" (Your Shatabdi left twenty minutes ago. Go out, cancel your ticket and take another train. If you want to travel by this train, you will have to buy a fresh ticket.) I had to take a decision within a split second as the train had already started rolling out of the station. I stayed on to avoid hassles of ticket cancellation, buying another ticket, and on top of it, getting delayed. I bought a fresh ticket, paid extra for on-the-spot booking, and reached Ambala in one piece. Later, I learnt that there are eight Shatabdies leaving New Delhi within a span of sixty minutes and at least three of these go through Ambala to different destinations. **And that is why I say, "We have made progress, and I have tasted the fruits of the same!"**

THE SIXTH SENSE

Do I have the sixth sense, or not? I am sure I do not. If you ask my IIT friends, they would say, "No, but he sure has a SICK sense (of humor)" because of my cracking of PJs frequently. Notwithstanding the above, I would like to narrate an episode, which took place during the monsoon season of 1986.

I was to go to Bhopal (I was the MD of Migma then) for a ten-minute job at MPAKVN Office (Madhya Pradesh Audyogik Vikas Nigam) in Bhopal. I took a shared taxi, which used to take five hours (due to ambassador cars and bad road conditions). While taking the taxi ride to Bhopal I decided that I would fly back taking the 3.30PM flight.

At that time, we had only Indian Airlines operating in the country and they had only two flights passing through Indore every day. The first was the Mumbai - Indore – Bhopal- Jabalpur- Raipur – Delhi in the morning and the second was the return flight from Delhi to Mumbai on the same route.

I reached Bhopal at noon and went straight to the AKVN office. However, the concerned officer was missing. He was on an errand and was expected back soon. He however returned only at 3.30PM. During my wait, I went to the Indian Airlines city office just across the road and confirmed that the flight was in time.

At 4PM, after finishing my work at AKVN, I again went to the IA office to check for the possibility of the flight getting delayed as during those days it was nothing unusual. The flights, particularly the hopping ones, used to be notoriously late frequently.

The IA officer informed me that the Indore flight had taken off half an hour ago. I got out of the office, got into an Auto and asked the auto driver to take me to the airport, the most illogical action of my life. People would consider it a foolhardy step, rather simply a stupid act as the airport was ten kilometers away from the city and it would be deserted at that time. I could get stuck there for want of conveyance.

I entered the Airport, which was expectedly deserted. I walked up to the office of the Duty Officer as no other counters were open and asked him if there were any flights to Indore. He looked at me with amazement for half a minute as if I had landed from Mars, and then brushed me aside with a firm **"NO"**

I then climbed up to the mezzanine floor, entered the canteen and ordered an Omelet, as I had skipped my lunch and was hungry. The canteen keeper was packing up for the day but obliged me. While I was having my snack, through the glass window I saw a Focker landing.

By the time I paid for the snack and went down to the ground floor, I saw the Pilot of this incoming flight entering the Duty Officer's Office. I asked him about the destination of this flight and learnt that it was the Raipur Delhi flight. Instead of leaving the Airport, I loitered around in the lounge, never once pondering over my stupidity. I had no thoughts of my own, acting as though I were a robot, only following someone's instructions mechanically.

Just before walking out, I crossed the Duty Officer's Room, which had its door ajar. The Duty Officer spotted me and called out saying, "Hi! You wanted to go to Indore. Is it not? Just wait, one more flight is landing." Beyond that he did not say a word, nor did I ask.

Within ten minutes another Focker landed and again only the Pilot and the Copilot came out of the craft. They were greeted by the Duty Officer in the lounge. From their discussions I learnt that it was an unscheduled flight going to Mumbai. This aircraft had a breakdown a couple of days back and was stranded at Jabalpur, and after getting repaired was returning to Mumbai.

The Pilot was asking the Duty Officer to make arrangements for his overnight stay at Bhopal, as he was not permitted to fly in the Monsoon, which had already arrived in Mumbai. They moved to the Office, continuing their discussion. I had no anxiety, no emotions, and no thoughts in my mind; I just stood by.

After some time, the trio of Pilots and Duty Officer emerged from the room. The Duty Officer said, "Come, buy your ticket." He gave me the ticket (in the column of Flight Number he had written "**NIL**"). While writing out the ticket (it was done manually then), he told me that the Pilot of the Delhi Flight was from Mumbai and that of Mumbai Flight was from Delhi. Both wanting to go home had swapped their duties. The Pilot from Mumbai was senior enough to fly in the rains.

It was already dark by the time I climbed into the nearly empty Aircraft. Only two* passengers were sitting in the forty-seater aircraft. When the plane was landing at Indore, I saw that the airstrip was lit using live "Mashals" (Torches with burning kerosene swabs at the end of wooden sticks) Indore airport had no airstrip lighting at that time. I was the sole person who got down from the aircraft. I reached home by 8.30 PM, safe and sound.

Later, since I am a firm believer of science, whenever I narrated this incident to anyone, more than the listener I myself could not digest the matter. I therefore came up with the only explanation for my illogical, though fruitful act of that day. It was possible that when I was at the IA office, the staffers there must have been discussing the possibility of this flight and I must have registered the matter subconsciously, but then **"WHO IS JOHN GALT?"**

--xxx---

* Two years later, I happened to meet one of them. I was narrating this episode to a visitor when halfway through, he jumped saying, "Damn it, I was also there. We two had stayed back for two days at Jabalpur......." I do not recollect his name, but remember that he was a Marketing Manager at Gallium Equipment Pvt. Ltd. What a coincidence!

--xxx---

WILD GOOSE CHASE (2005)

THIS CHAPTER IS DEDICATED TO

EMPLOYEES WORKING WITH CDA

WHO TAKE ALL EFFORTS

TO

DELAY PAYMENTS TO SSI UNITS

Wild Goose Chase (2005)

So far, I have refrained from writing about my financial state of affairs for the fear of getting branded as one who tells sob stories. However, after finishing over a hundred odd pages, I have dared to touch upon this subject.

Since time immemorial, I have waited to receive any payment within the stipulated time. If I review the bankbooks of the past thirteen years of Static (or even earlier bank books of Migma), every payment (received) will have a story to tell. Therefore, keeping this chapter short and sweet (or bitter?) is going to be a very tough task for me.

WILD GOOSE CHASE- I

We had supplied five lac rupees worth of transformers to DMDE (Defence Machinery Design Establishment) of Indian Navy at Hyderabad. The Expected Date of Receipt or EDR was well past, and so every day we were anxiously waiting for the postman who brought the registered mail. As per the payment procedure of the Indian Navy, 90 % of the bill amount is released immediately (?) on receipt of the inspected goods. The bills get processed and sent to a Black Box called CDA (Controller of Defence Accounts). In rare cases the payment (i.e., unless there are mistakes in the papers sent which happens most of the times) is cleared in about two weeks' time. However, in case the bills get returned, the payment processing has to start all over again.

Payment is received in the form of a Government of India cheque payable at State Bank of India's main branch in the city. Since at that time we had a current account in SBI's main branch, we could utilise the money on the same day we received the cheque. We had the expenses planned, up to the last rupee of the amount. This included overdue salary, overdue wages, bonus which we distributed on every Diwali. We had no alternate funds available; and hence were heavily banking on this cheque.

We had already crossed the EDR and could not get any clue about the payment. We therefore dispatched Praveen, our troubleshooter, to Hyderabad who returned without much information. However, he had managed to get the telephone numbers of the concerned CDA Officers.

After about ten days, since we had not made any progress in finding out the fate of the payment, we sent Praveen again to Hyderabad and he returned with an assurance of speedy payment.

Diwali was just about a week to ten days away when at last the postman delivered the envelope sent by CDA, Secunderabad. Uday opened the same with a sigh of relief, which turned out to be momentary. He handed over the cheque to me, as it did not have the familiar symbol of Ashoka's Lions. The cheque was from Reserve Bank of India payable, at Fort, Mumbai.

The chase took a new turn, but at least the goose was now in sight. We immediately rushed to the bank and tried to get the cheque purchased (in such a case, the bank pays the amount immediately, deducting some interest & charges). However, the bank declined to oblige us.

Then, as an alternative, we asked the Bank official to hand over the cheque clearing documents to us so that we could send our person to Mumbai who would personally deliver the same to their Service Branch at Mumbai and collect the remittance advice once the cheque got cleared. The bank officer agreed and called us at 4 PM.

Uday, our peon Desai, (who came with his travel bag) and I reached the Bank five minutes before time. This time a different Bank Officer called us to his table. He advised us that we should really not spend money in sending our peon to Mumbai unnecessarily. He assured us that he would send the documents by "Speed Line" (some courier company). The documents would reach their Service Branch the next day. He would also advise the branch to telegraphically confirm the fate of the cheque. And thus, we would get the payment even before Desai would probably return if he were to proceed as planned. Further, he cautioned us that even if we arranged to hand deliver the docket, the service branch may not oblige us by handing over the payment advice personally to Desai and in that event, he would have to return empty handed.

After repeated assurances from him that he would take all precautions to ensure the receipt of payment in the shortest possible time, we agreed and all three of us returned to the factory with a new EDR.

As usual the EDR passed without any news of payment. Time was ticking like a time bomb tied to the heroine's waist in a Hindi movie's climax scene. We made a number of calls to Bombay to find out the status of the payment. But the service branch did not provide any service.

Ultimately, when Diwali was just three days away, we sent Desai to Mumbai to trace the payment. With great difficulty he found out that the Cheque had been cleared by RBI's Fort Branch and that the payment advice had been posted to Indore a couple of days earlier.

On the last working day before Diwali, Uday and I reached the main Branch and met the concerned officer. The Bank had not received the payment advice from Mumbai till then. We literally forced the officer to talk to their Bombay Branch by getting him connected through STD/PCO. (Mobile phones had not made an entry then.)

He got verbal confirmation of payment and advised the service branch to provide him the telegraphic transfer code. An hour later he called them up again and got the encrypted code. He fed the code to a machine to verify the authenticity. The machine rejected the code. After another call to Mumbai, he was finally able to get the correct code.

In those days the cash counters of the bank used to close at 2.30 pm. At our request the bank had kept one counter open; the cashier was instructed not to close his books for the day. That day finally we collected the cash at 3.30PM from the back door of the counter. This was our Indian version of **'JUST IN TIME'**.

WILD GOOSE CHASE- II

It was only afterwards that we realised that since DMDE dealt with the ATV project, its funding was from MOD directly and not from Navy's own budget. We, therefore, considered getting RBI Mumbai's cheque as a ONE-OFF case and erased the matter from our active memory, not knowing that we would face a similar situation a few years later.

We were expecting a large payment from Visakhapatnam for supplies made to the Indian Navy. The officer had processed the papers and sent the bills to CDA, Vizag for payment. The Material Organisation at Vizag (MOV) had by then computerised all the bill processing and payment procedures. Therefore, the officer, one Lt. Rao, a nice person, was able to give us payment status on a day-to-day basis telephonically, on the basis of which we had arrived at an EDR.

One day he informed us that the bills had been returned to him by CDA for want of some clarification. We simply had to revise and shift the EDR by a fortnight. We were monitoring the progress on the phone practically every day. The bills got resubmitted to CDA; they got processed at their Bills section and were finally sent to the Cheques section. Accordingly, the EDR was just about ten days away.

Then after about three days, (it was early February) we got another jolt. Rao informed us that there was a serious problem. Navy had exhausted its budget under a particular account-head and hence no cheques were being prepared. Weeks passed without change of status. In desperation, we contacted various senior officers of Navy at Vizag, only to get verbal assurances that the matter would soon get sorted out. There was nothing we could do except to twiddle our thumbs.

Finally, around mid- March, we got the desired envelope by speed post. This time the Cheque was payable at RBI's Delhi branch. History had repeated itself. But thanks to the courier service, we managed to get the realization just before the financial year end, March the 31st. Another case of '**JUST IN TIME.**'

WILD GOOSE CHASE- III

If payment gets delayed for some silly reason, it will get delayed further for a sillier reason.

Way back in 1994, we had quoted for three power supplies to Air India on behalf of our collaborator from Denmark. The equipment was worth some 35 lacs. The order for the same materialised after five years. From my experience of IAF who fly supersonic planes, Air India who fly subsonic planes, and Indian Navy which has its ships moving at a few miles per hour; I have come to the conclusion that the speed of procurement / order processing/ payment is inversely proportional to the speed of their crafts, the missile manufacturer DRDO being the exception.

We had been visiting the concerned officers of AI during all these five years but could not know the reason behind the delay. It was only later that we learnt that the power supplies were meant for installation at a new hanger under construction, which had collapsed once and was being rebuilt.

In international trade, normally any foreign manufacturer supplies items against Letter of Credit from a Bank. This ensures that he gets his payment and that too in time. However, in this case AI wanted to pay only after the power supplies were commissioned. I was able to convince Ackerman, the owner of AXA Power of Denmark that Air India was a Government of India company and could be trusted for payment. He had with some reluctance agreed to AI's terms.

Anyway, as said earlier, the order was received after five years and the equipment supplied in five weeks. We faced a small setback as one of the units refused to work. The problem was sorted out by getting spares from Denmark for parts which had got damaged during transportation. Work finished; it was time to fix up the EDR. Air India was to pay AXA after commissioning, and we were to get Rs.3.5 lacs from AXA when they got the money.

However, as days passed, we saw no signs of movement of funds from AI to AXA in spite of all the follow up from our side from Indore. The problem, we learnt, was severe funds shortage faced by AI. After about forty-five days I finally called up the finance director of AI and blasted off, stopping just short of calling him names. He then agreed that he would advise his Frankfurt office to release the payment.

After a week and a number of ISD calls later, AI's Frankfurt office finally sent a Cheque to AXA Power which they received in a couple of days. In the meantime, the EDR was getting postponed like a mirage. However, on the day Ackerman got the Cheque, we thought that the EDR was just a week away.

After a few days, Ackerman replied to our query by a fax which read, "I do not know what kind of cheque AI has sent. Normally the bank gives us money immediately when we deposit a cheque. In this case, they have sent it to Frankfurt and we do not know how long it will take for us to get the payment. We will transfer your commission as soon as we get paid."

At last, after a period of **THIRTY DAYS AXA** got paid, and as promised, transferred our due payment immediately and we received it in **THIRTY HOURS BY SWIFT TRANSFER.**

WILD GOOSE CHASE 'n'

There have been "n" reasons for delay of payment. Every reason has had some novelty. Recently, we supplied items costing over Rs. four lacs to Vizag. After the EDR was over, we enquired with the officer for the payment status. After a month's follow up, he informed that the payment could not be processed for want of Performance Bank Guarantee.

We have to submit Performance Bank Guarantee (PBG) for 10% of the value of the Order. However, normally we get paid 90% and 10% amount is withheld until the submission of PBG. For the past eighteen years this has been the procedure. This time, however, this chap was adamant and so I called up his boss. He came up with a new concept, He said, "Mr. Joshi, yours is a small-scale unit and hence exempted from providing PBG". I told him that we were covered under 'Micro', even smaller than the small-scale units and that his Financial Adviser would not accept our certificate.

Anyway, we sent him the Certificate of being a Micro Scale Unit and also PBG for 10% value. After a month, we got a communication that the PBG was not accepted as it was for 10% of the basic value of the item supplied and not for 10% of the total value, i.e., amount including sales tax. This again was the first case of its kind in my 18 years' experience. Finally, we got our payment after a two-month delay. How can one plan for something which happens once in eighteen years?

COMEDY OF ERRORS

We were having some differences with one of our clients, Astrix Power of Gurgaon. They had paid us four lacs as advance for a project and, after six months, cancelled the order for the equipment costing fourteen lacs. We had already purchased material worth more than four lacs and hence were not prepared to refund the amount. Over a period, however, we did supply two lacs worth of items and partially adjusted the balance. We had very clearly informed them that we would not be adjusting the remaining amount but instead had sent them a debit note towards loss incurred by us due to cancellation of order.

Then one day, out of the blue, they placed an order on the phone for some transformers for a lack of rupees and wanted the items the next day. We agreed to supply the items provided they agreed to "documents through bank" payment terms. They promptly agreed (Documents-through-bank ensures that the buyer gets the material only after he pays the required amount to his bank which then sends the funds to the supplier's bank). We manufactured and supplied the items to Gurgaon. We submitted our invoice and lorry receipt to our bank. They promptly gave us sixty thousand and supposedly sent the bill for collection to Bank of Maharashtra, Gurgaon.

For two months there was complete silence. Once in a while we called up Astrix only to learn that they were facing funds shortage and would soon be retiring the documents (i.e., paying their bank).

After a lapse of fifteen days or so, I got a call from Wg Cdr Lal, who had taken VRS from the Indian Air Force and was working as G.M. at Astrix, requesting me to help them get the items by making part payment. Since I had already got the bills purchased, the bank was in control. However, as Lal was also an IIT Kanpur alumnus, I agreed to his request and suggested a via media. I explained the intricacies involved in the matter and asked him to deposit sixty thousand in our account and send me a post-dated cheque for the balance amount as per their convenience. I told him that I would clear the bank loan taken against the bill and then our bank could write to Bank of Maharashtra to release the documents.

He promptly followed my suggestion and we squared up the bank loan. Our bank asked us to write a request letter which we did. They made us correct the request letter thrice. The bank manager's knowledge of English was so poor that he could not understand our letter. The fourth and final version of the letter, which satisfied him, was identical to our first draft! All this took the whole week. Finally, our banker wrote to Bank of Maharashtra, Gurgaon, advising them to release the documents.

So far so good; we had sent our bank's letter to Bank of Maharashtra, Gurgaon by our regular courier. After about a week and considerable investigative efforts later, Lal informed me that the courier company had sent the envelope to Goregaon instead of Gurgaon and it was not possible for the courier company to trace and retrieve it.

We were used to such mishaps as they occurred at regular frequency at Static.

Lately there is a new procedure in practice which is called COD i.e., Cheque on Delivery. We had supplied a few items to Kirloskar Cummins at Pune on COD basis. Firstly, our transporter had misplaced the transporter's copy of our Invoice, which is very important, and is valued as if it were currency notes issued by RBI worth the excise duty paid by us. Result: The C of the COD was delayed. Finally, after our transporter submitted some affidavit/ undertaking etc., he got the cheque.

However, we did not receive it for quite some time. Desai's (Our peon) investigations revealed that the transporter had sent it to Palghat instead of Indore. Goregaon instead of Gurgaon is understandable, but Palghat instead of Indore is beyond my comprehension. Luckily however, the cheque was not lost and we finally got it.

In the case of Astrix, however, we had to resend a copy of the bank's letter, which we managed to get from the bank within a week. Reason: mass transfers of bank officers. Finally, we faxed the letter and sent the original over to Astrix by courier. We thought that it was the end of the episode, not aware that there were more surprises in store for us.

On the fourth day, Lal called me up and said *"Joshi yar! Hamari bank main to Kabhi document ayehi hi nahi the"* (Joshi dear, our bank has never received the documents). Our accountant again went ahead with his RAW (Research and Analysis Work). This time he went to the depths of the matter. He went through the bank's files, registers, courier receipt copies and what not.

Conclusion: Our bank had sent all the papers directly to Astrix three months back. Lal's purchase officer located the same in his files the next day. He had simply filed them without checking what the papers contained. But thanks to this act of the purchasing officer of Astrix, an ISO9000 Company, we got our delayed payment due to his stupidity. I am sure Uday, our accountant, and Desai, our peon, can excel at CID or the Missing Persons Squad; they have developed great investigative skills.

POSTSCRIPT

I finished writing Wild Goose Chase on 2nd April 2005. On that day we were pleasantly surprised to receive a cheque worth a lack of rupees from CDA, Delhi. We were not quite sure of this payment, as it was the balance 5 % payment for supply of equipment to the Indian Air Force against an order for three units. Since the order was not fully executed, the payment could have been held up. But Wow, someone was for once kind to us.

The cheque was immediately deposited in the drop box of our HDFC Bank. This modern bank had made life quite easy for our accountant. Log on to the net and you know the status of your account.

Normally on Monday Uday would have checked if the cheque was sent for clearing. He however was unwell and did not come to the office. I was quite busy that week and hence had not bothered to log in. Based on last one year's experience of the bank's efficient working, I had considered the matter of cheque clearing a routine.

On Tuesday our telephone lines developed some snags and we couldn't log in. On Wednesday we had the cheque ready for withdrawing cash for some critical expenses.

Nilesh checked our account. There was no trace of the cheque. He then went to the Bank where the search was made at all possible places. But the cheque could not be traced. And then one wise officer opened his drawer and said, "It is here. We did not send it for clearing as it is a non-MICR Cheque. As per RBI's instructions, clearing of non-MICR cheques has been stopped from 1st April 2005".

I did not know if it was RBI's April Fool Gimmick or a typical case of the GOI where the left hand doesn't know what the right is doing.

Anyway, on Nilesh's insistence the cheque was sent that day and we got the credit after two days. The fact remains: It may be Standard Chartered, ICICI, HDFC or any other bank which claim of providing WORLD CLASS Service; in spite of all that boasting, at heart, basically we are Indians who care two hoots as far as our customers are concerned. I am saying this, as I happened to check the pay-in slip of the bank. It had space for our phone number and the bank should have called up on Monday and informed us of RBI's stupid rule.

--xxx---

GOLDEN DAYS AGAIN

THIS CHAPTER IS DEDICATED TO

PROFESSOR RAJAGOPALAN

OF IIT KANPUR

FOR

INTRODUCING ME TO

OPERATIONS RESEARCH

Golden Days Again (2003)

If anyone asks an IITian as to which period of his life he considers to be the best, the stereotype answer is likely to be 'My IIT days.' Similarly, the NITIE alumni would talk about their NITIE days. Well, my answer would be no different. I consider the two years that I spent at NITIE pursuing Post Graduation in Industrial Engineering as the Golden Period of my life.

NITIE is situated on a hillock between Vihar and Powai lakes and in spite of being in Mumbai, it has a lot of open spaces. In the students' hostel, we had single rooms with attached bath, a luxury compared to IIT hostels. The only disadvantage was that we were just about fifty students in the batch and hence every professor knew each one of us on a first name basis, making it difficult for anyone to bunk classes.

During my first summer I undertook a project with Simon Carves India Limited at their construction site in Baroda, and during the second year I carried out a six-month Project at Pune with Wanson (a sister concern of Thermax Ltd.). I would rate both these cities as amongst India's top ten towns where I would love to settle. Being from a small town myself, I always preferred such places to metros like Mumbai. I dislike crowds and extreme crowds extremely. The stay in Pune and Baroda did have an impact on my future professional career.

While at NITIE we used to get a Stipend of Rs.1000 per month, which was sufficient to cover our monthly expenses. The studies were not very difficult. In short, life was cool and memorable events were aplenty. The courses were quite educative. During my last twenty-five years of Industrial experience, I have been able to fruitfully apply the knowledge gained at NITIE. Often, I hear engineers working in the industry say that they hardly find any use of the engineering knowledge gained during their graduation in carrying out their jobs; I, however, disagree.

THE COMPUTER PHOBIA

While I was in the second year of engineering at IIT, I had to take up a computer language course and I was not a novice. I had studied FORTRAN IV and my fundamentals were quite sound. However, at NITIE we had to learn COBOL. During those days, the programmes had to be punched on cards. We had to then go to IIT, Pawai, and submit our Programme (pack of cards) for processing. Even for one silly syntax error, the machine would reject the pack. That day would be lost since we had only a one-hour slot of the computer time available each day.

Since COBOL is a very structured language, it just does not tolerate any silly mistakes. With my background, I could not (and even today cannot) write a single sentence without making at least one spelling mistake. As a matter of fact, if I were to rewrite the same sentence the next day I would most likely spell at least one word differently. As a result, the COBOL assignments were something I desperately wanted to avoid. And so, I swapped my COBOL assignments with Tandon, a classmate of mine, for some Statistics assignment. In the process I developed a bit of a dislike for digital machines though I was not a duffer as far as designing algorithms were concerned. At NITIE a 1000 machine step programmable computer was purchased for students' use. Just as a hobby I programmed it to play Tik-Tak-To and surely it was always the machine that won.

Now when I sit back and analyse my past, I realise that all this had an impact on the future career.

THE JOB HUNT

Once, at a Health Food shop in the US, I read the slogan **"YOU ARE WHAT YOU EAT"**. I, however, believe in **"YOU ARE WHAT YOU GO THROUGH"**.

So, when the placement period started and I was to take up employment, I was not keen to join a large organisation. My experience at Gajra, though a medium scale industry then, had made me believe that if I joined a large organisation, I would have to work in a small compartment and would get stuck with the routine.

Basically, I am born an impatient person; I get bored doing the same job again and again. Just recently, I met a school friend of mine after a gap of twenty-five years. His first reaction after he learnt about what all I had been doing during this period was, 'How come you are running Static Transformers for more than ten years?' 'I thought,' he added, 'you could never be at one place for more than three years.'

Unfortunately, only large organisations visited NITIE for campus interviews. The best-paid job at that time was offered by Premier Automobiles Ltd. (PAL); one of the two passenger car manufacturers of the country in those days. They paid Rs.3000 per month as the starting salary to persons recruited from NITIE. That was the best package available to NITIE grads then.

Though I did not want to join a large organisation and also did not want to take up a job in Bombay, I appeared for the PAL interview. This was just to prove myself. (I am a big egoist and many wrong things which have happened to me are a result of that[7*]). The result of the interview was better than my expectation.

I landed with a job offer; one member of the PAL selection team was PAL's EDP (Electronics Data Processing) Manager. He was quite impressed with me and declared, then and there, that I would be working in his department. Since I was not keen to join PAL, I tried to negotiate a higher starting salary. I argued that as I had one year's industrial experience prior to NITIE, I should be given one increment above the others. The PAL team did not accept this argument.

[7*] Smita, my wife happened to read this chapter and was delighted to go through the sentence in the bracket. She came out saying, "Ah! For Once You Have Admitted"

During our routine squabbles she frequently quipped, "It is always at the back of your mind that you are more intelligent than the others."

She has stopped repeating this remark after my reply, which was "Why Back? It Is Right in The Front of my mind. Because it is a fact"

I have put this footnote to indicate the magnitude of my EGO.

The EDP manager gave a lot of pep talk and promised me the sky. During the next few days, he continued to lure me to join PAL. My COBOL phobia, however, made me decline the offer. If I recollect correctly, four of my batch mates joined PAL. Three of them later moved on to other jobs. Arun Birla, a BITS Pilani Graduate, progressed from there and as on date is the Marketing Director of Eicher Motors. Ashwin Bondal, an IIT Mumbai product, is the CEO of Selzer Pumps, subsidiary of a US Company. Rajeev Shrivastava later went on to academics and is a professor at IIM Lucknow; while Bhayya, the fourth batch mate continues with PAL.

In retrospect, one would claim that I did not have the foresight and did not visualise the potential of the computers and the benefits of working with big organisations. This of course is true. Had I known or foreseen the explosive growth of computers, I would not have missed this Golden Opportunity. But then now it is only the subject of a "What If" analysis. I am also sure that none of my classmates who joined PAL had these precise reasons in their minds at that time. I think it was the starting salary which made them choose PAL.

As I am writing this, my ego makes me recollect my discussion with a NITIE mate. During the second year, one evening, I was having a chat with Anil Biswas, who was a music freak. We were discussing about different types of tape recorders. I predicted that one day we would have digitalised tapes for playing music. Everyone ridiculed me. I do not know if Anil Biswas ever remembered my prediction of November 1977.

NAAM BADE AUR DARSHAN KHOTE [8*] [*All those 'Big Names'!*]

In the final year of my studies at IIT Kanpur, I had opted for an elective course titled 'Operations Research'. The basic reason was not my liking for the subject, but the fact that this was offered under the PSI scheme. PSI stands for "Personalised System of Instruction". As per this system the course was divided into fifteen sections. The students had to study the subject on their own and appear for tests twice a week. Professor Rajagopalan, a very sober and a friendly person, conducted the course. (I wish him a long life and hope he gets to read this). Every week he took two tutorials, attending the same was again optional. The tutorials were meant to clear any doubts the students had. If my memory does not fail me, I must have attended only a couple of tutorial sessions and that too not to get any difficulties cleared, but to pay respect to a teacher who did not believe in delivering lectures.

Twice a week, tests were conducted. One had to get full marks for each section. After clearing the first section, one could appear for the second. Thus, in a maximum thirty attempts one could earn an "A" grade by clearing all fifteen tests. Clearing fourteen would earn one a "B" grade and so on. A threshold of twelve tests was set for passing the course.

I disliked attending lectures and so I loved this system. I cleared fifteen tests in eighteen attempts to earn an "A", and in the process fell in love with the subject. Operations Research is sort of Applied Mathematics, which deals with optimisation. At NITIE, Operations Research was taught as a compulsory subject. Even today I remember most of the stuff.

And so, when I was looking for a job, I thought I should work for 'Operation Research Group', a consultancy organization of Mafatlal Group. To work with a consultancy organization would be fun, I thought, as there would be a lot of variety in the job. From client to client, the assignments would change. I therefore simply went over to Baroda by an overnight train and walked into ORG's head office. I told the manager my desire to work with them. I was immediately interviewed and offered a job at a salary of Rs. 1200 plus change per month, which was good enough for a single person living in Baroda during that period. During the interview I asked them about the job content, company's activities and so on. I was initially quite impressed by the fact that they mostly undertook Industrial Engineering assignments.

I made my decision to join them and reported for work within a week of passing out of NITIE. I got my first shock when I met my immediate boss who was simply a duffer. In a day I realised that they had mostly market survey assignments, which was not my cup of tea. The only IE assignment they had was from Gujarat Electricity Board, that too in the field of O&M, a subject I dreaded. I had to visit GSEB's office the next day and was tortured when I tried to converse with the concerned people who spoke very fluently but only in Gujarati. By the end of the first week itself I realized that Operation Research Group had no relation with Operations Research and I decided to quit the job.

SECOND ATTEMPT WITH CONSULTANTS

Just before passing out from NITIE, I had started applying to Newspaper Advertisements. I had applied to Kirloskar Consultants, Pune, who had advertised for a vacant post of an Industrial Engineer. On the day I decided to quit ORG I left all my baggage with a friend of mine at Baroda and went to Pune. Just like ORG, KICONS (Kirloskar Consultants) arranged my interview immediately and by the same evening handed me an appointment letter offering me the position of Project Engineer.

Life at KICONS was far better than at ORG. My boss was quite intelligent and all the colleagues were qualified and knowledgeable. My first assignment was to work out production norms for a flask manufacturing company around twenty kilometers from Pune. I visited that factory. It was an easy assignment for me and I believe I did justice to the job.

If I recollect correctly, the average temperature in the factory shed was over 45 °C. The ventilation was extremely poor. The owner of the factory had set the references. He just wanted to know the production norms under the then existing conditions. Working in such a condition was really inhuman. There were two teams of six workmen each. The first person would gather a mass of semi solid glass on the end of a long steel pipe. He would blow it to make a small glass bubble and hand it over to the next person of the team; the second worker would blow it further; and the final blowing would be done in a wooden mould where he had to rotate the tube while blowing it by mouth, to obtain uniform glass wall thickness. As per ILO standards (International Labour Organisation) I had to provide for two hundred percent fatigue allowance to the actual working time element.

The production norms worked out by me indicated that the workers were achieving the output expected from well-motivated workmen. To increase the output further would require change of methods, or improvement of environmental conditions, but that was beyond the scope of our assignment. My boss was satisfied with my report. However, it was only later that I learnt from a colleague the real objective of the factory owner. He wanted the report as a supporting document so that he could pressurise his contract labour later to produce more.

Immediately after I finished my first assignment, I was given another one. I was to assist a senior engineer in preparation of a feasibility report for setting up a project for manufacturing a tabletop offset printing machine for All India Reporter Company of Nagpur, a well-known concern which compiled and published judgments of judicial cases of various courts. Even today, if you go to any lawyer's office in India, you will find a large number of AIR Company's hardbound volumes in the bookshelves.

The owners had contacted a German Company and acquired a maintenance manual and a parts list for a tabletop offset printing machine. They were planning for a tie up with the German Company for the technical know-how for manufacturing the machines in India. On the basis of the parts list and exploded drawings of assembly and subassemblies, we worked out the feasibility report. (I would have liked to call it a pre-feasibility report as a lot of the content was based on 'guesstimation' rather than estimation.)

Typically, the financial part of the report was worked out by KICON's finance department. Since I had a reasonable exposure to Finance from my PG days, I could appreciate the report in its totality. I am not aware of the end result i.e., whether AIR finally went into that project or not, as at KICONS we got no further communication from them.

Both these assignments were completed in a couple of months of my joining KICONS. Then for the next five to six months I was assigned no work. KICONS had a number of divisions. I was working in the Project Engineering Division, which had no business on hand. Since I was the junior most employee, I was not involved in business generation and had to follow Company's rules and regulation. That meant attending the office from 9 AM to 5.30 PM; killing time doing nothing, a gruelling task. I remember those days I used to tell my friends "WHO SAYS NOTHING IS IMPOSSIBLE, I HAVE BEEN DOING IT FOR DAYS."

THE NEXT TURN

During that period my parents were keen (and so was I) to get me married and they had started a search for a suitable match. At Indore they had selected a girl, whom I met for the first time in February 1999 and got engaged to her on 5th March 1979. The marriage was scheduled for 5th May. This posed a million-dollar question. (A bit of an exaggeration) Pune was a much more costly place than Indore or Baroda. The monthly rent for a one room apartment was more than Rs. 1200 which was my gross salary. And so how could we manage? There was no chance of getting a raise for doing nothing and 1200 a month was not going to be sufficient even for our bare survival. This all prompted me to start applying for a better paying job.

I applied in response to an advertisement published by a consultant for the post of Industrial Engineer in a medium scale industry at Dewas, a town around thirty-five kilometers from Indore. I still recollect the advertisement. It stated '… at Dewas near the salubrious city of Indore…' If anyone visits Indore today, he will have to revise the meaning of salubrious in the dictionary.

I was called to Mumbai for a preliminary interview and then was asked to visit Dewas for the final one. The result of the interview was identical to my previous interviews. By the evening of the same day, I was appointed as Industrial Engineer at Steel Tubes of India Ltd, with a salary of Rs. 1800/- plus perks.

--xxx---

MY GOOD DAYS WITH STEEL TUBES

THIS CHAPTER IS DEDICATED TO

ANIL DUTTA,

WHO HAD A GREAT INFLUENCE ON

MY PATTERN OF WORKING

My Good Days with Steel Tubes (1979-1982)

I vividly recollect my first day at Steel Tubes of India Ltd. As I got down from the Company matador (which had ferried us from Indore to Dewas) at the factory gate, the security guard took me to the Security Officer's cabin. The Officer went through my appointment letter and told me that I would have to sign in, in the Senior Executive's Attendance Register, which was kept outside the Company's Managing Director's office. The other staff members who had come in the same matador signed in the register kept at the Factory Gate.

There was no space available in the Company's office to accommodate me, and so I was given a room in the Company's guesthouse. The room had a huge, maybe ten feet in diameter, rotating bed and that was all the furniture in the room. The only advantage was that for lunch I just had to climb down to the ground floor to the Company's canteen.

During the interview for the post of Industrial Engineer, I was told that my job was to establish the Industrial Engineering department and I was to report to Anil Dutta, the Works Director of the Company. Anil Dutta had considerable experience in the steel tube manufacturing line. He was contracted for three years by the Company at Rs. 50000/- per month plus a house, car and other perks. He had earlier worked with Tata's Indian Tube Company for many years; had been trained in some Australian Company and was extremely knowledgeable as far as the steel tube manufacturing technology was concerned. He was extremely smart, dashing and had an impressive personality. During my two and a half years of working with him I learnt a great deal. The main promoter of the company was one Dr. Ramesh Baheti, a highly ambitious person who could manipulate and maneuver any situation in his favour.

On the supervisory and management front, the Company had three different categories of personnel. The first, comprising the Old Guard who were recruited from the local engineering colleges or those who had switched to Steel Tubes of India from other local organisations and had been working with the company since the inception. The salary level for this category was quite low. The second group consisted of persons imported from larger, well-established competitors like Tube Investments, Madras; and Tata's Indian Tube Company. Having better exposure, they were far better than the locals and were paid far more than them. The third category comprised of only three persons- one planning manager, one officer in the marketing department, both from IIM Ahmedabad; I was the third member of this class.

MY FIRST ASSIGNMENT

At Steel Tubes my first assignment was to prepare and implement an incentive scheme. Prior to my appointment, this job was assigned to a team of teachers from the local engineering college as a Consultancy assignment. The team had produced a report jointly with Nandi, one senior engineer belonging to the old guards.

After going through the report consisting of some twenty odd pages, I realised that even the toilet papers had better utilisation. I feel that even a common man would understand that incentive is provided to motivate a person to improve his performance. In industrial parlance, it has to result in better quality, more production, timely completion of jobs and lower costs. The scheme suggested by my friends was very complex in nature and had a basic theme that a workman at the tube plant would get a certain amount which would increase with the quantity of output and after some level the amount payable to him would reduce if the output of tubes increased further. There were many other stupidities in the report. I highlighted these aspects to my boss who immediately appreciated my views and asked me to go ahead and take a fresh look.

RIDICULES AND INSULTS

I was the youngest amongst the technical staff and was paid much more than the Old Guards. Secondly, as per the company norms, I was drawing more than Rs 1600 as basic pay and hence was a senior executive. Within no time I became the blue-eyed boy of Anil Dutta, the Works Director. All this made the Old Guard go green with envy, and as a result they were extremely non-cooperative with me and at times even went ahead to rag me.

I recollect one day, within a week of my joining, in a meeting Nandi asked me, "Do you know the power of Tube Mill One's Welder?" He laughed at my immediate answer, "Yes, it is 120 Kilowatt". Trying to ridicule me he said, "You Know All, it is only 80 Kilowatt, the Nameplate was changed to 120 Kilowatt, as import of high frequency welders with an output power less than 100 Kilowatt is not permitted"

Notwithstanding such stupid insults & humiliation at times, and non-cooperation most of the times from the Old Guard, I would say that barring the last three months, my three years tenure with Steel Tubes gave me sufficient job satisfaction, and I earned considerable recognition. Within a year I was promoted as Assistant Manager, Industrial Engineering; and then to the post of Assistant Manager Planning & Industrial engineering by the end of the second year. Within another six months I was given another raise and I became Manager, Planning & Industrial Engineering. However, until my last day at Steel Tubes I faced umpteen occasions of ridicule and insults from the Old Guard. On the other hand, my performance was always well appreciated by the Managing Director. Only once during my three years' service I had to face his wrath by way of angry words.

It so happened that in the third year, during a Senior Executive Committee meeting, Baheti posed a general question to everyone. He wanted to know if there were any ways and means to reduce the Manpower Cost. Jaiswal, a senior member of the old guards, who was the Accounts & Administration Manager immediately responded by suggesting that the Company should get rid of a battery of twelve peons, one per department who, he said, only served water and carried Dak (mail) to other departments. They were idle most of the time, he added, and went on to say that there should be self-service for drinking water and may be one person who moved from department to department to carry the internal Dak.

Immediately, a mocking smile appeared on my face and I just could not hide my reaction. Baheti noticed it and considered it as me insulting

Jaiswal who was twice my age and fired me left, right and center for it. As a matter of fact, a year earlier, during the weekly Senior Executive Committee meeting, I had put up an identical suggestion. I had seen such "No Peon" systems in operation at Wanson and many other larger organisations and it was quite effective. I had therefore put up a proposal accordingly. However, when the proposal was discussed, it was the same Mr. Jaiswal who shot it down giving a number of reasons to justify having a peon for his department. **The "No Peon" scheme was implemented soon after I left the Steel Tubes.**

The three years I was with Steel Tubes, I had a fixed routine. Get up at 6 AM. Be ready in forty-five minutes. Walk to the Company's bus stop. The matador picked us up sharp at 7 AM. It ferried us to the factory at Dewas and back. It used to reach the factory sharp at 8 AM and used to drop us back at our stop at Indore at 6 PM. Not much traveling was involved in the job. During those three years my salary had gone up reasonably. It had more than doubled by the time I left the company. Just after one year at Steel Tubes I went out on an excursion to Goa; and after another year to Kashmir utilising my leave travel allowance. I would say that professionally and from the point of view of compensation, it was a good job.

WORK DONE AT STEEL TUBES

As I said earlier, my first assignment was to prepare an incentive scheme and to do it effectively, I had to carry out a job evaluation study. There were no grades or pay scales, either for workmen or for supervisory and managerial positions. I completed both the tasks within months, for 300 and odd workmen as well as for the supervisory and managerial posts. As a result of implementation of my proposals, most of the Old Guard got a considerable pay rise, which did soften them a bit.

I was also involved in recruitment and was a member of the selection committee for recruitment of engineers, managers and other staffers. I, along with the personnel manager, went out to IIT Kanpur, and engineering colleges at Bhopal, Jabalpur and Indore for recruitment. I went over to NITIE and picked up Pankaj Patel to assist me.

I was also involved in investment analysis, and Corporate Planning. With my exposure at Kirloskar Consultant, I could handle the job well. As a matter of fact, the company's expansion, (after I had left) took place on the basis of the blue prints prepared by the trio, which comprised the two IIM grads and me.

On the productivity improvement front, which was the basic purpose of my appointment, I believe I did justice to a reasonable extent. I was also sent to Gurgaon to a factory owned by Dr. Baheti's relative for a week to suggest ways and means to improve productivity. It was a small factory manufacturing steel boxes for the Army. It showed very good scope for increasing the throughput. The production lines were not balanced and my report brought out that the production line concept should be changed to batch processing so that the bottleneck machines could complete the job in more shifts / days, while machines with faster throughput could be run only for a few shifts / days a week. The report was very well appreciated by the owner. On receipt of this feedback, Baheti circulated my report to his other friends who owned smaller industrial units.

While with Steel Tubes I also had the opportunity to visit Ludhiana's cycle manufacturing industries and their ancillaries. In spite of being an Industrial Engineer, I was amazed to see the Labour Productivity. The key reason behind it was the payment to workmen, which was made on a PIECE RATE BASIS.

END OF HONEYMOON

In June 1981 Anil Dutta had some differences with Baheti and therefore he quit the Company. He shifted to Ludhiana. Another manager who had come from The Indian Tube Company also left soon after Anil Dutta's departure. The Company Management started suspecting everyone who was close to Dutta. Since I had no plans to leave Steel Tubes, I went to Dr. Baheti and assured him that I would be staying. I told him that I was living in my own house at Indore, was quite satisfied with my salary and job profile and hence had no reason to look for a change. Though he verbally assured me that he had no doubts about such an eventuality (my quitting), his subsequent actions however did make it obvious that he was suspecting my departure. I was no more a member of any selection committees and was to report to a newly recruited Works Manager, one Mr. Agarwal.

Within months, Shrivastava, another senior person, was recruited as General Manager, R&D. I believed that Baheti had realised that Agarwal was No Good for the job and had planned to ease him out. I was a big zero at apple-polishing and no good at political manipulation. As a result, I started getting used as a pawn in the Shrivastava – Agarwal power tussle.

It so happened that the throughput of the seven-tank Tube Phosphating section was quite below its rated capacity. I was to study the same and assess the situation. The process was quite simple. A bundle of tubes was lifted & shifted from tank to tank having acid, water, phosphating solutions and so on. At each tank the tubes were to remain submerged in the liquid for a predetermined number of minutes. The reason for the low throughput was very simple. The workman was using his judgment rather than a timer or a watch and at every tank the bundle of tubes was left for more than the specified time. For example, instead of the specified seven minutes, he would leave the tubes in for 10 to 12 minutes. This was more common during the night shifts due to reduced presence of seniors, and general dull atmosphere because of inadequate lighting. And so, I suggested that we provide timers at each tank and the operator be asked to switch it on as soon as he dipped the tube. An audio alarm would alert the operator as soon as the time was over.

During a meeting when this proposal was discussed, Shrivastava shot down this idea saying that a timer will cost seven hundred bucks and suggested the amount be deducted from my salary. I was speechless at such a ridiculous & senseless argument and had to give up. The turnover of the company at that time was in crores and it was generating handsome profits. Seven hundred rupees would have got rounded off in the company's daily expenditure.

I had the opportunity to visit Steel Tubes after a year of my departure from the Company, by which time Shrivastava had replaced Agarwal. **To my amusement, I found timers installed at each tank in the Tube Phosphating Section.**

SUGGESTION II

Similar was the case of packing of tubes in gunny bags. Some tubes were to be packed in bundles of ten and then covered in gunny bags. Two workmen would pick up these long tubes; tie them up at two places. Then one workman would lift the bundle from the middle while the other would insert the gunny bag over the end lifted free from the stand. He would then slide it down till the middle of the bundle. The lifted end would be lowered. The tubes were then lifted from the middle so that this time the bundle's other end went up and the gunny bag could be pulled over the bare bundle (like socks). And finally, the bag was stitched at the center.

The bundle of tubes weighed around 50 Kgs and lifting it up from the middle, that too at the chest level, required considerable effort. It was bad ergonomics. I had therefore suggested installing a hydraulic lifting arrangement, which could, if implemented, easily double the output. However, this suggestion required an expenditure of a few thousand rupees and therefore was shot down by Shrivastava. **Later, I found this method too had been implemented after my departure.**

I started getting frustrated by such episodes and there was no thrill left in the job. My juniors were handling the planning and other routine industrial engineering tasks, and as a result I was left with nothing much to do.

NEW ASSIGNMENT

During that period, mini computers had entered the market. One day I went to Dr. Baheti and got myself assigned the job of computerisation. I took keen interest in this assignment. I identified areas which could be shifted over to the machine, decided the priorities, negotiated with various suppliers and prepared a blueprint for the Data Processing section.

It was in mid-October 1981 that my father was to be operated for cancer in Bombay's Tata Memorial. All my family members went over to Mumbai, I left for Bombay a day later so as to reach just one day prior to the surgery. I had postponed my departure from Indore to attend a meeting with the Director of Datamatics, who was to guide Steel Tubes in computerisation. My father's operation was a failure and we lost him two days after the operation.

By Dec 1981, the salary increments were to be finalised and I was to prepare a draft proposal for all the staff based on evaluation by their bosses. I had put up the proposal to Dr. Baheti who was finalising the increments while I was sitting across the table. When he came to my name (I had of course left the space blank), he filled up a figure which meant a considerable raise, and the same would have made my basic pay exceed Dr. Baheti's Executive Assistant's pay by Rs. 100/-. Around 4.15 PM, he finished the list and asked me to hand over the same to his Executive Assistant who was a good steno-typist and nothing more. In a happy mood, I reached The Company Matador which would leave for Indore at 4.30 PM.

Just as the driver released the clutch, Baheti's personal peon came running and stopped the matador. Kirti, Baheti's Executive Assistant came, soon afterwards and asked me to step down from the matador. He took me aside and told me that Baheti had slipped up and he was sorry to inform me that my basic pay would be Rs. 200 less. Effectively it meant he would be Rs. 100 above me, on the scale. I nodded knowing what had happened and boarded the matador.

The frequency of such irritating episodes was on the rise and so was my frustration. By January 1982, a new Personnel Manual was introduced. According to the new Manual I was eligible to draw a conveyance allowance of Rs.600 per month provided I had a car registered in my name. This manual was a revision of the original one, prepared by me. This revision was carried out by the company's Personnel Manager. Initially I had my own apprehensions and hence I went over to the Personnel Manager to double check if there was a misprint. On his confirmation I decided to buy a car.

I had accumulated sufficient money to buy a second-hand car. However, I put in a loan application to the Company's Executive Director who sanctioned me a loan of Rs. 10000/- to help me buy a car. Soon I bought an Ambassador for Rs. 30000/-, gave a copy of the car registration to the Accounts Department and started drawing the car allowance.

The car turned out to be a bad buy, and within a month it needed repairs worth six to seven thousand. In the meantime, my friend Kirti (EA to MD} also bought a car, got it registered in his name and parked it in front of his house. He never drove it, as it was not road worthy.

The finance manager, one Mr. Dhoot, also applied for a car loan and for reasons not known to me, his application was turned down. He strongly took up the matter with Garg, the Executive Director. The top management again took a somersault and amended the Personnel Manual by adding a precondition for being eligible to draw the car allowance. "A Prior Approval" was needed from the Executive Director in all such cases. I was called by the Executive Director to be told that I would no longer be eligible for the car allowance.

I was in a fix. However, I instantly reacted stating that in such a situation I would not be able to afford to maintain the car and would have to sell it, and in that case the company should bear the loss, if any, incurred by me, as well as reimburse the actual expenses during the two-month period. Garg promptly agreed to this face-saver.

I sold off the car for 30000/- and prepared a statement of all garage bills; Inflated the expenses by a thousand bucks or so, so as to square up the loan and the allowance drawn by me. Garg had to accept the expense statement and the episode ended with a bad taste. In my life I had never cheated any employer, but these 1000 bucks I made extra in the transaction gave me some satisfaction. I justified it as a compensation for my insult.

THE LAST BLOW

The last blow which made me quit Steel Tubes hit me by February 1982. We had finalised on ORG's minicomputer, had placed the order, and were to start other preparations. One day, I was busy with some work in the office when I got a call from Baheti's PA asking me for the specifications of the System ordered, which I gave him on the phone. A few minutes later another call came for some more information. I went across to Baheti's PA who informed me that an outsider was there in

Baheti's cabin. It did not take much time for me to put two and two together.

From my immediate boss, I later learnt that Baheti had appointed an EDP manager at a salary three times more than mine. This new appointee was working in Tata Exports as EDP manager. He was not even a graduate, but had firsthand experience of working on the unit-recording machine (1st generation machines which worked on programmes coded / written by means of hard wiring).

I was quite upset and took up the matter strongly with Agarwal, arguing that firstly I was quite capable of handling the additional responsibilities of Data Processing and in case it was decided to have a separate department, I should have been consulted. It was a shortsighted decision to appoint a Mechanic rather than an Engineer.

He took up the matter with Baheti who would not change his decision. The argument put up by him was that I was too young to take up so many responsibilities. I laughed when Agarwal conveyed Baheti's reply. I only said "Sir, with that logic you should be the MD and Baheti the Works Manager"

I returned to my cabin, picked up all the computer related files, went to Agarwal and left them on his table. He started pleading that I should continue to be in charge until the new person joined. I however did not budge. I said, "As a Manager Planning & Industrial Engineering, this doesn't fall under my scope of work, I have done all the spade work voluntarily and I am no more interested in this work." And I decided to leave Steel Tubes before the new EDP manager joined.

I contacted Anil Dutta on the phone and informed him of my desire or rather decision to leave. He was at that time providing consultancy to a company called Atma Tubes, twenty kilometers from Chandigarh. He arranged for my interview there. I negotiated my salary for the post of Works Manager and returned to Indore with an appointment letter.

As soon as I handed over my resignation, I went over to Dr. Baheti's room for an Exit interview. I told him on his face that I had lost faith in him and his style of management; narrated the major irritating episodes and walked out. **He remained speechless**.

MY DAYS WITH ATMA TUBES

The only thing good about Atma Tubes was my salary, which had crossed five thousand plus a two-bedroom house, car etc. I used to drive every day to the factory from Chandigarh, which was near a village in Patiala around twenty kilometers from Chandigarh.

The challenging job turned out to be a nightmare. I earlier said that nothing other than my salary was good at Atma Tubes, but that was a gross understatement. The Company was cash strapped; the plant & machinery were antiquated; they would have served a better purpose in a museum. And the worst of all factors was that the owner was whimsical.

As a matter of fact, it was common knowledge that most of the steel tube manufacturers had made money by getting steel from steel plants on the basis of the "Quotas" allocated to them and selling the steel in the black market. (Today's Indian reader would probably find it difficult to appreciate the situation then. During the eighties, practically every commodity was in short supply and attracted a premium in the black market.) Even the early success of Steel Tubes, I suspect, was based on the same formula. One day I was walking along with Anil Dutta and a very senior Steel Tubes official near the scrap yard. I happened to hear the senior official boasting to Anil Dutta, "You see this scrap! We imported steel and claimed transit damage against this junk from the Insurance Company."

At Atma, on many days we had to operate at night as there was no power available during the day. Half the time the raw material was not available, and during the other half the machinery broke down requiring maintenance. I wonder as to how my team could produce tubes at all.

Within six months I realised that I was wasting my time. Sardar Singh, a cut-surd, the owner would call me over to New Delhi and ask me as to why we were not producing enough and before I could reply he in a half-drunken state would add *"Danda Karo Salonko! Tum Bahut Sidhe[9]* Ho. Sabko Danda Karo"*. *"Danda Karo*"* could yield results provided the *Danda* was a magic wand.

The whole situation was beyond my comprehension. The promised investment for new plant and machinery was not forthcoming and the situation was getting worse day by day. The local director at Chandigarh to whom I was reporting had quit the job. The new director, one Mr. Grewal, did not understand T, U, and B of tubes. Anil Dutta was no more a consultant to the company, as his fees were not paid.

Within six months I turned desperate and wanted to leave Atma under any circumstances. I discussed the matter with Anil Dutta who also agreed to absorb me in his own company "Caldyne Consultants Pvt. Ltd."

The only episode worth narrating at Atma Tubes was concerning a complaint against me by the workers to the company's Director that I had come drunk to the factory at night and that the booze bottle half empty was lying in the car. On investigation by the Director, it was revealed that the bottle was a whisky bottle but contained distilled water for the car battery.

The only regret I have is of not making money on the side. I had all the power to sell scrap, purchase material for repair, give petty contracts, and if desired I could have made at least 10000/- per month in addition to my salary. But again, it is my upbringing which never permitted me to indulge in such activities.

Within six months of joining i.e., in June 1982, I moved to Delhi to join Anil Dutta.

--xxx---

---

[9]* Shove the stick up, you are too straightforward…They are bastards. You are a simpleton. *'Danda'* in Hindi is a Stick.

THE EAST INDIA COMPANY

THIS CHAPTER IS DEDICATED TO

SHANTANU, MY YOUNGER SON

WHO

WHEN IN FIFTH

AUGMENTED HIS POCKET MONEY

BY

SELLING FEATHERS

TO HIS CLASSMATES

The East India Company

Solving, or rather trying to solve cryptic crossword puzzles is one of my favourite pastimes. Recently I came across a clue; 'East India' was the obvious answer. This prompted me into writing about my trading experiences.

THE HOLLOW TUBES

I had set up a small consultancy outfit after I left Migma in July1989. Sometime in 1990, during my visit to Mumbai, I called upon Rajendra Kalyanpur, an IIT classmate of mine. He was working with Mahindra Exports then. During our *'Gup-shup'* he abruptly came up with, "*Arrre Ghati Yar* (He enjoyed calling me *Ghati* and, to reciprocate, I always called him *Mota (big/huge)*, which of course described his most distinguishing feature), *tuze to tube ke bareme sab pata hai* (You know everything about tubes), weren't you with the Steel Tubes?"

"I need to buy some tubes for exports. Can you locate a source for me?" he added.

Though Steel Tubes did not manufacture the tubes he wanted, I was well aware of other manufacturers who could supply the water pipes he was looking for, for export to Uganda or Sudan or someplace like that.

I asked him for his target procurement price, which turned out to be Rs. 9 lacs. I realised that there was a margin of at least Rs. 1.5 lacs available for a middleman and so I confirmed that it was very much feasible to procure the pipes he wanted for around Rs. 8 lacs. I asked him if he would mind if I took a commission from the seller.

He did not have any objection as long as I met his target cost and added that he too would like to share the booty. He justified his demand by saying that he spent much more in entertaining his client than what he was entitled to at Mahindra. Anyway, that was his lookout. I would be happy as long as I made money.

I returned to Indore and immediately contacted Rajeev Soni, the Executive Director of Metalman, a company in Indore manufacturing steel pipes. We knew each other well. He gave me a price of R. 7.3 Lacs. At that price the deal was going to be overkill. I discussed the matter with Soni and worked out the modalities of the deal. I took a quotation for Rs. 8.9 lacs in the name of Mahindra Exports while Soni agreed to pay me Rs. 1.6 lacs towards commission once he got the payment.

I rushed Shyam, one of my polished assistants, to Mumbai with the offer. Mota promptly placed the order with Metalman and opened a Letter of Credit. Soon the pipes would be manufactured, inspected, packed and shipped to Mumbai port. The bills and other documents would get submitted to the Bank. Metalman would get paid Rs. 8.9 lacs and in turn, I would get Rs. 1.6 lacs, of which I was to pay Rs. 60000/- to Mota and keep the balance of one lac. It was just a matter of one month's wait.

SET BACK I

The deal turned out to be too good to be true. Within a couple of days, I got a call from Rajeev Soni. He very apologetically informed me that he had given a wrong quotation and that the correct price was Rs. 8.1 lacs (not Rs. 7.3 lacs). This would cut my commission to half. From my general market information, I knew that Metalman would have been quite comfortable with the originally quoted price. But then probably Soni had a bellyache as I was to consume a cool Rs. 1.6 lacs and that probably caused him indigestion.

I argued with him and told him that he was being quite unfair to me. He, however, did not budge. I had no other option but to accept whatever he said. To ensure that my commission did not erode further, I asked him to give me a postdated cheque for Rs. 80000/-, which I would deposit, once he got paid. He promptly obliged.

Some wise men might suggest that to ensure my commission, I should have bought & sold the pipes, without letting Soni know about the ultimate buyer or may be opened a back-to-back LC and so on, rather than a loose commission arrangement. I must therefore mention that I had examined all such possibilities, consulted some commercial experts. But since I was not registered with Sales Tax, Excise & RBI (as exporter) nor had any funds, I was left with a Hobson's choice.

SET BACK II

Within a month, the pipes were manufactured. Mota came over to Indore for pre-dispatch inspection. He went to Metalman's Factory. Everything was in order.

By afternoon, however, Mota came to my office, he was a bit upset. He told me that the deal stood cancelled. He had asked Soni to provide a lifetime guarantee certificate, as it was a necessary condition of Mahindra's Export Contract. For reasons not known to me, Soni refused. This had created a deadlock situation.

I suggested to Mota that we search for some other supplier. I knew another company, which had a plant at Sarangpur about 150 kms from Indore. This company, Siddharth Tubes, had its head office at Indore. A friend of mine, Arun Jain, an electrical engineer, was associated with Siddharth Tubes. With Arun's help we fixed an appointment with Siddharth's Marketing Manager and reached their office without any loss of time.

We explained the situation to the Marketing Manager of Siddharth Tubes and within a span of half an hour, a deal was worked out which was identical to the one with Metalman. The Marketing Manager agreed to pay me Rs. 80000/- on the conclusion of the deal.

SET BACK III

Accordingly, all the actions of Placement of Order, Opening of Letter of Credit etc. were taken care of by Mahindra. The pipes got manufactured and supplied; LC encashed.

I approached Mishra, the Marketing Manager, for my commission. He flatly refused. He said that he had never agreed to make any payment to me. I contacted the directors of the Company through Arun Jain. But the result was negative. For them it was Mishra's word against mine. And they conveniently believed Mishra. The director however obliged (?) me by paying me ten thousand to cover the incidental costs.

Later when I met Mota, he was very cool about the whole episode. He on his own told me that he knew that I was not paid by Siddharth Tubes. I suspect he was taken care of by Mishra directly. Anyway, as far as I was concerned the **TUBES TURNED OUT TO BE HOLLOW.**

DOWN WITH UPS

Many well-wishers of mine, when told about the pathetic financial state of affairs of Static, advised me to go in for trading. But it is easier said than done as the following episode illustrates.

Soon after I bought over Static Transformers in Jan 92, I had made an attempt to market items of similar nature (as that of Static's products) by procuring them from other manufacturers.

Ravindra Abhyankar was my co-director at Static. His brother, Avinash Abhyankar, had a small setup in Pune where he used to assemble a variety of electrical equipment. He used to market 250 watt and 500 watt inverters. Today most urban dwellers are familiar with inverters. However, in 1992, in Indore, most commoners except those using PCs were quite unaware of the existence of inverters. Avinash used to call his inverters "Off Line UPS (Uninterrupted Power Supply)" (inherent contradiction may be excused) and marketed them under the brand name of "Powermate".

Ravi suggested that we could market the same in Indore. I immediately jumped at the idea. I could foresee the virgin market for the product. With the worsening power situation, the product was bound to sell well.

There were two issues which we had to resolve. First was the price and the second one was the quality. Such inverters, which did not produce a pure sine wave, were being sold in Delhi for around three thousand; while Avinash had priced Powermate at Rs 5000 each. He insisted on the price, justifying it by saying that he used proper, genuine components while Delhiwalas used spurious ones and therefore his product, though expensive, was extremely reliable.

As far as quality was concerned, Ravi had more than assured me of Avinash's capabilities as an electrical engineer. Ravi had extremely high regard for Avinash's technical competence. Further, the fact that he was already selling the product in the Pune market made us feel comfortable as far as quality and reliability were concerned.

The utility of the product was beyond doubt. I thought that Powermates could easily be sold to medical practitioners, jewellers' shops and even for household use. We therefore decided to take a plunge and imported five units. Ravi did a good job of fabricating small trolleys with a battery compartment at the bottom.

Our marketing team started moving about to book orders. In order to introduce the product, we also organised a dinner party where we demonstrated this product, in the lobby of a hotel. We invited our friends and acquaintances from nearby industries. However, very few were ready to pay Rs. 10000 / 12000 which was our price for the quarter and half kilowatt models. We were to get only Rs. 2000 as our margin after accounting for the cost of inputs i.e., inverter, battery and cart.

Over the next six months we sold around fifteen units, many of them to my personal friends and acquaintances. In all we had bought twenty units from Abhyankar. Out of the fifteen units sold, only five worked as expected while others conked off soon and had to be replaced.

This meant extra costs of sending the faulty units to Pune and re-transporting them after rectification back to Indore. We considered all this as teething troubles and hoped that this would mature into a profitable line.

However, there was more trouble in store for us. One day, a client called up to complain that his ceiling fan was burnt while being used with Powermate. Investigation revealed that the Powermate had gone berserk and was developing extremely high voltage. We promptly replaced not only the unit but also the ceiling fan.

This episode was repeated with another client. This was a serious warning to us. Our clients used the unit to run costly equipment worth thousands and lacs. If the same thing happened to such equipment, we would be in big trouble.

There was another problem. Some Powermates would overcharge the battery resulting in the same getting dried up and soon it would become unserviceable. Sometimes it was also the client's lack of timely maintenance. Anyway, the end result was that the product had earned a bad name. I recollect one issue in this connection. We had supplied one unit to the Indore bank for use at their cash section in the basement. Six months after the supply their Audit department found that the Powermate was not working. The Battery had gone dry. The concerned Purchase officer pleaded with us. He would lose his job if we did not replace the battery.

We took a firm stance that we would not replace the battery free of cost as we were not at all at fault. For days the matter did not get resolved. Practically every day for about a fortnight the Bank Officers would visit our factory in a Jeep accompanied by a guard with a twelve bore double barrel gun. This would create a scene. Every other visitor had to be explained that we were not involved in any robbery. Ultimately, we did replace the battery and even got paid for the same.

All the same, Powermate had earned us a very bad name. We had to close this business. Somehow or the other we managed to serve the clients for a year or so until we thought our unwritten guarantee and obligations were over.

In the whole process we must have lost at least thirty to forty thousand rupees. We recovered part of it by selling the faulty Powermates in our stock for thirty to forty Rupees, and **FINALLY WE WERE DOWN WITH UP-S.**

--xxx---

TRAGEDY, COMEDY, OR HORROR SHOW
(2005)

THIS CHAPTER IS DEDICATED TO

MR. B RAM

A KNOWLEDGEABLE QUALITY INSPECTOR

WHO WAS ALWAYS READY TO LEARN

Tragedy, Comedy, or Horror Show (2005)

Most of the equipment manufactured by us at Static Transformers are meant for supply to Government agencies and therefore would get inspected by the inspectors prior to dispatch. I intend to narrate some incidents related to these funny creatures. If someone made a TV serial based on this chapter, I am not sure if it would be a tragedy, comedy, or a horror show. I leave it to the wise readers to judge for themselves.

UNCOMMON SENSE

We had received an order for supply of a rectifier for fitment on board a naval ship under construction. Typically, we would have to submit drawings to the Naval HeadQuarters for approval. Since warships are usually cramped with equipment, it is essential to check that the new equipment could be fitted in the available space.

One day we got a call from DND (Directorate of Naval Design). The officer asked us if it was possible to reduce the width of the equipment from one meter to eight hundred millimeters to meet the space constraint. He permitted us to increase the height instead. We agreed to his suggestion.

The duly vetted and approved drawings were received by us soon. The officer had corrected the dimensions in red ink. Other than the overall height and width, he had not changed any other figures. He had reduced the width from 1 meter to 800 m.m. and increased the height accordingly. The equipment was manufactured according to the revised dimensions.

After carrying out the inspection for one full day, the inspector from Baroda rejected the rectifier. He pointed out that as per the approved drawings the transformer fitted at the bottom in the cabinet should have been 850 mm wide while in reality it was only 700 mm.

We could not convince him that it was not feasible to fit an 850 m.m. wide transformer in an 800 m.m. wide cabinet. But for suppliers like us, the inspector is always right. We had to send one engineer to Baroda to convince the inspector's boss and get the item cleared. A common doubt the readers may have is whether the inspector wanted some money from us which was why he was adamant. However, that was not the case; he genuinely wanted the 850 m.m. wide transformer fitted in an 800 m.m. wide cabinet!

NOT A PENNY MORE (NOR A PENNY LESS??)

The bureaucrats in Delhi are masters of framing rules and regulations to ensure that the Government of India does not pay a penny more than what is due (though the contrary is not at all true) and that is why when we got a cheque by Speed Post, irrespective of whether it was for Rs.100 or for Rs.10 lacs or above, fifty rupees were deducted towards postage charges.

Once we received an order for thirty odd fuse links as spares for our equipment in use. The value of the order was about three hundred rupees. The inspecting authority from Mumbai was planning to send one inspector to Indore for inspection, which would not take more than ten minutes. However, we would end up spending much more than three hundred towards hospitality.

Luckily, one of our engineers was scheduled to go to Mumbai for some other work and we avoided the inspector's visit by sending the fuses and the required testing instrument with our engineer to the Inspecting Agency's Mumbai Office for clearing the items for supply.

THE ULTIMATE

The following story was narrated to me by one of the inspectors of the Indian Navy and hence I cannot vouch for its authenticity. However, it is too amusing to be left out of this chapter.

Once his colleague had gone to a factory to inspect some hydraulic tubes. The test schedule included "Pressure testing 3 Bar". For the benefit of non-technical readers, "Bar" is a unit of pressure. Our inspector made the supplier carry out the pressure testing three times saying, *"YANHA*

TO TEEN BAR LIKKHA HAI". (Here, it is written "3 times", 'Bar' means times / frequency in Hindi!).

HOW TO PROVE THAT TWO PLUS TWO MAKE FOUR

Once we supplied a fifteen lacs worth item to the Indian Air Force. Two wise men came from Delhi to carry out the inspection of the Ground Power Unit, used for supplying power to start Mirage & Jaguar Aircrafts, which require power at 400 Hz frequency. (For reference, the power we use at home is of 50 Hz).

Unfortunately, the specifications, which were based on the technology from the Second World War period, stated that the power supply would trip if and when the frequency dropped below 370, or exceeded 430 Hz. Ours was a digitally controlled unit, which produced exactly 400 Hz. It was not possible to change the frequency at all. The inspection and testing took around four days. The wise men left without clearing the equipment (which as on date has logged more than 5000 hours without failure). I was called to Delhi for a grand meeting to discuss various quality matters related to our equipment. One by one all the issues were sorted out except for the frequency variation. I tried my best to convince the wise men that my equipment could only produce 400 HZ or nothing at all. One of them stated that without this test he would not permit me to supply the Ground Power Unit. The aircraft costs hundred and fifty crores and he would not permit it to be vulnerable to damage without under and over frequency protections, he insisted.

What the wise man did not know was the aircraft rejects the power supply if the quality of power is bad, and thus there could be no damage to the aircraft. However, there was no point in teaching someone who knows not that he knows not.

The discussions went on and on and I lost my patience. I told the group, "Kindly feed a computer two hundred plus two hundred and when you get the answer prove that if the answer is more than 430 or less than 370, the computer gets switched off automatically." This annoyed the person even more. Luckily, Squadron Leader Babu from the Air Force came to my rescue and forced them to clear the equipment for trials.

IGNORANCE IS BLISS

Once we manufactured a batch comprising of twenty-five transformers for fitment onboard a nuclear submarine under construction. At the time of inspection, the inspector pointed out that there was a remark on the approved drawings stating "Maintenance Envelope to be provided". Frankly, none of us knew what it meant and so we were stuck. Anyway, the inspection was to continue the next day.

I instructed my workmen to make small steel pouches on the backside of the open-able front doors. By the time the inspector arrived the next morning, we had kept an envelope containing the maintenance manual / drawings of the transformer in the pouch of every transformer. The inspector was more than happy and cleared the lot worth many lacs of rupees.

It was much later that I learnt the meaning of Maintenance Envelope, which in Naval parlance meant the space required around the equipment for maintenance and the same was to be indicated (provided?) in the drawing.

YET ANOTHER BUFFOON

After going through all my (sic/sob) stories a reader once commented, "It is surprising that in spite of the kind of trouble you have been through, you have retained your sense of humour." The fact is that we, at Static, had already adopted a policy that 'if rape is inevitable, you might as well relax and enjoy it.' We had a steady stream of clowns visiting us quite frequently.

One such gentleman visited us from HAL Bangalore. He stayed at his own expense at the cheapest possible hotel, completed the inspection in a professional way, and was to leave the next morning.

In the evening, he approached me, "Sir, I want a favor from you."

I obviously thought that he was going to ask for his birthright. I was wondering if he would keep the amount in four figures. He, however, surprised me by saying, "Your equipment has passed all tests. But kindly dispatch it after three days. I am officially going to carry out the inspection over four days by relaxing at home. You must arrange to give me a hotel bill for these four days with a room tariff of 750 a day. I will claim it from my company."

Praveen, our troubleshooter, went around to various hotels, but no one was prepared to give a blank bill. Finally, we started a hotel business. We got our printing press chap to print two bills of 'Indore Paradise', with an imaginary address. To make the colourful bill (colour printers had not invaded the market then.) look authentic, we perforated a strip on the left side using a sewing machine without thread in the needle and tore off the narrow strip.

THE FIRST COUSINS

Though this is not a Joke book and my friend Ashok criticizes me for my long prelude in my narrations; I am tempted to exclude the following.

Recently I read an anecdote in the Reader's Digest, which I am reproducing below.

Quote:

I was scribbling my name on the receipt for my credit-card purchase when the clerk noticed that I had not signed the back of my card. Before she could complete the transaction, she said I would have to sign it.

"Why?" I asked.

"So that I can compare the signature on the card with the one on the receipt."

Fair enough. I signed it. She picked up the card and the receipt, studied both signatures. As luck would have it, they matched.

Unquote

Jovial Break

This was contributed by someone in the West. It is in that great country where people follow Systems blindly. (Refer the chapter: AMERICAN SYSTEMS V/S DANISH HUMAN TOUCH") India too has its share of such population. This distinguished class comprises the first cousins of the Inspectors fraternity. To highlight their calibre, I am narrating a few episodes.

Once the almighty was distributing intelligence to people before sending them to earth. He exhausted his stock while a few soles were left out. They started grumbling. "How will we manage on the earth without any brains?"

"Go to India and join any Security Department of some Government Organisation; you will have no problems there" - was God's advice.

....

Once, a smart young security guard of TELCO[10*] took his officer to a haystack and proudly said, "Sir, this trucker was taking this stack of hay out without a proper gate pass; I made him unload, before I let him go out."

Whether the guard got a promotion is not known, but that month end TELCO's Materials department found that a truck was missing from their assembly line.

....

MAIN EPISODES

Too often, I have been a victim of dealing with this class of people. Once we had to get our items tested at the Naval Dockyard at Visakhapatnam. The security system was very simple. An escort would come to the gate with an authorization letter for our team. One officer would make some entries in a register and issue us another pass. Then we would move to another window for getting the entry pass for the day. If we cleared that hurdle, we would move to another office at the gate. Some additional entries would be made for the tools & instruments carried by us. The list would get verified by a *jawan* (soldier) who did not know the difference between a screwdriver and a two-ton hammer. Then at yet another office our auto driver would go through a similar drill.

[10*] TELCO is India's largest manufacturer of commercial vehicles.

There was nothing wrong with the procedure except that it took three hours on the first day of our visit. Since our job was to continue for a week to ten days, on the first day we left the tools at the workplace. On the next, we decided not to take the auto inside and managed to cut short the time, though only marginally as the walking (from the Gate to the Ship) time got added. The time consumed in waiting in the sultry & hot weather of Vizag was unbearable; walking a few kilometers instead was tolerable.

When we returned, we invariably had to spend a long time searching for the officer who would sign the pass. A few days later we cut short this procedure by signing the pass ourselves. As long as there was a sign on the pass, the security guards would let you go out. He would not be literate enough to know the difference between Libra and Scorpio. Even today, you can spot a number of long bearded oldies inside the dockyard who could not get out and are spending the rest of their life inside because either they had lost their pass or the officer who was to sign their pass had retired and they were not bold enough to swim across the ocean.

The best remedy to avoid the hassles was suggested by our escort. He said, "When you come in, just turn around and pretend that you are going out without a pass. The security guard would push you into the dockyard. On the way home, do the opposite; you would be thrown out without any delay. This was a sure cure solution, but I was not young enough to try it.

THE INDIAN AIR FORCE

We had supplied a piece of equipment to the Air Force Station at Gwalior. I had gone there and found the IAF officers extremely friendly and amicable. One of our engineers stayed back for a month to carry out the trials of our equipment. He stayed at the IAF Guest House by making a nominal payment. Every day he would phone from the main gate to the concerned officer, who would instruct the security guard to issue a pass and within minutes he would cross the border and move into the restricted area.

Once the trials were over on Mirage aircrafts, the equipment was to be shipped to Air Force Station, Ambala for trials on Jaguars. This was going to cost us a lot and was adding many hassles. The day before the trials were to end, I visited the Gwalior base. Here I spotted a few Jaguars and two transport aircrafts on the tarmac. I casually requested Group captain Kumar if IAF could air lift our GPU and ship it to Ambala with Jaguar detachment. The next day after the trials were over, our equipment weighing 1200 kgs got a free air ride in AN32 to Ambala.

At Ambala the officers were equally nice, but the IAF's security system was injurious to us. We received a communication asking us to fill out forms giving many of our anatomical details, place of birth, right down to the hospital's location (Alas! They stopped at that.) All this information would go to their Security Dept at Headquarters. It would take months before they declared us harmless creatures who could be permitted to enter the restricted area. As a result of this delay due to the security issues the trials of our equipment as well as the payment of Rs. 15 lacs would get postponed by the same period.

AHQ, however, intervened and as at Gwalior we managed entry on a 'Casual Visitor Pass'. The trials of 100 hours were completed in a month sometime in December 2004.

KHANAPURTI

In April 2005, one day we got a call from Mumbai, "Is it Static Transformers?"

"Yes"

"We are from IAF Police; we are sending Sergeant Suresh and Airman Vishnu to Indore for verification."

Two days later, two hefty chaps came and verified our existence. It is yet another story that our engineer, who had done a good job at Gwalior and Ambala, had resigned and left us a month earlier.

RED ALERT (*Nothing to do with FTV's hot mid-night show*)

It was soon after the Bombay bomb blasts (Jan 1995) that I had to visit a ship in Mumbai. We had a representative, one Mr. C. V. Joshi, working for us then. He and I would go in his car to the dockyard, park the car inside and then walk to the visitor's room, praying for the early arrival of our escort from the ship. Similar to the experience in Vizag, after three hours or so we could manage a pass and enter the dockyard. The security guard would check out the car and then we would drive down to the parking place nearest to the ship.

Being the person that I am, I could not resist complaining to the Commanding Officer of the ship. He justified the security system saying, "You know the amount of ammunition we hold here? If a blast were to occur, the whole of Bombay would vanish."

I simply asked, "What if we came in with time bombs in the car, parked it inside as we did today and instead of waiting for the pass, just walked out?"

I hope the D company does not get any ideas.

IN A LIGHTER VEIN

And then there was this fifty-year-old captain. He remained a bachelor right until retirement. His first posting was with the quality assurance establishment of the Indian Navy. For the past twenty-five years he has been assuring quality. In the meanwhile, his parents approached (or were approached by) the parents of eligible girls many hundred times.

During the early years, Naval Officers were in great demand as IT coolies and the MBA Executives were rare species. But our captain, who was a handsome young lad then, always ended up being rejected.

Everything went fine when he went & met a prospective young girl and her parents. By the end of the meeting, the girl would start daydreaming about her life with this naval officer. The parents would also start thinking about consulting their family pundit for the earliest auspicious date.

Our lieutenant (who would get time-based promotions until he reached the post of Captain) would also approve of the girl, but then just before leaving the would-be bride's house, he would approach her father and say "All the qualities of your daughter are as per my specification, I approve of her as my would-be wife. However, if any time after our marriage, I find any of her qualities not as per the specs, or any manufacturing defect is detected, please provide an undertaking that you will replace her free of cost" And that ended the story.

So, is it tragedy, comedy, or horror or simply a stupid show? But as the saying goes, "The Show must go on" and it still does.

--xxx---

THE LAST STRAW ON THE CAMEL'S BACK
OR HOW I STARTED WRITING

THIS CHAPTER IS DEDICATED TO

WORKERS AND STAFF OF

'STATIC TRANSFORMERS PVT. LTD.'

WHO BORE THE BRUNT OF WHATEVER

WENT WRONG

The Last Straw on the Camel's Back
or
Why I Started Writing

To begin with, I would like to elaborate on how I started writing and why the 'diary' is not chronological. One day, to be precise on 27th Dec 2002, I was staying in a hotel in Bangalore when I learnt about the theft that had taken place in our factory. I thought it was the last straw. How to continue? How to repay the debts? These were the prime questions I had to find answers to.

I had just read an Asterix Comics (Very famous French character who keeps bashing Romans; the period is 500 AD). That chapter was titled "Asterix and The Golden Cauldron" wherein Astrix and his foolish fat friend Obelix are banished from the village by the villagers. Reason? A Cauldron full of gold coins which Asterix was to guard gets stolen. And he is then ordered to return to the village only if he could bring the gold back.

These two friends try various means to earn money but end up losing even whatever they have. So, they have a brainstorming session where Obelix says, "Why not tell people our stories and call them 'The Adventures of Obelix'. Maybe people will pay us for that." And that inspired me to start writing.

THE LAST STRAW ON THE CAMEL'S BACK

December 29th, 2002: I reached Bangalore at 2 PM after 40 hours of gruellingly/ boring journey from Delhi. The visit was for chasing a payment of about three lacs due from Hindustan Aeronautics Ltd (HAL). I spent the rest of the day with Yatin, my batchmate from IIT, K.

The next evening, I returned to the hotel after visiting HAL. To know about the progress of work back home I called my office at Indore. It was then that I got the last (till then) bad news. Our PCs and printers were gone and so was some 500 Kgs of copper from the factory.

We work from 9 am to 5:30 pm, six days a week and have a guard who stays in the factory from 5:30 pm till the next morning. It is only on Sundays or holidays that the factory remains unmanned from 9 am to 5:30 pm. Even on these days if I am in town, I normally go to the factory for about four to five hours to sit in peace, review various matters and plan for the coming week.

As a matter of fact, before I bought Static Transformers Pvt. Ltd. (STPL) in January 1992, there used to be no night watchman. Considering it to be quite a risk to leave the factory unguarded, I had immediately appointed a chowkidar who would report at 5:30 pm and stay there during the night locking the factory from inside.

On my return to Indore, I learnt that some people had come in a white Maruti-800 (as we learnt from workers of the neighbouring factory) on Sunday morning. They had simply opened the lock, gone in, unscrewed all the connections, removed the PCs and the printers from the office on the first floor and reels of copper wire from the assembly hall, relocked the doors and vanished. They left the computer monitors, etc. intact.

Our chaps reported the matter to the police at the local police station. My sister, who knew the IG, got him to instruct the police to put in all the efforts to search for the culprits. Till date, after about three weeks of the theft, we are clueless in the matter.

Around six months back we had bought a CD writer and had taken back-ups. So, what we lost in addition to the hardware was the information we had stored during the past six months. Since in our factory we have a lot of dust, we had taken a wise decision of keeping the 3rd PC with a CD writer at home. And just a few days earlier my friend had borrowed the scanner and not returned the same. As a result, the damage was limited. However, in spite of having a manual and an electronic typewriter, we had to manage with handwritten letters or go to a PC station for work till we bought a new PC / printer (PCs in those days were expensive equipment).

The above episode acted as a trigger to my attempt to write this (kind of) autobiographical compilation.

EMPTY ASSURANCES FROM INSURANCE COMPANIES

Just after taking over Static Transformers Pvt. Ltd., I had the Company's assets insured. At that time, we were banking with The United Western Bank. Since our raw materials, work in progress as well as all the fixed assets were hypothecated to the bank, they also insured these goods. It so happened that at one time we landed up with double insurance policies - one bought by us directly and the other by the Bank. It was a big exercise to get one policy cancelled and the money refunded. From that time onwards we had stopped getting our assets insured.

Around two and a half years back we had changed our bankers. We borrowed funds from Maharashtra Brahman Sahakari Bank. This bank also had been debiting our account with insurance charges.

And so, after the theft, my colleague went to the Bank to find out if we could get a claim from the insurance company, only to learn that the bank had insured only the building but not the fixed assets or the stocks. Though the claim would not have been much, it would have been better than nothing.

At that time, in India we only had Government owned Insurance Companies and so my experience has been limited to dealing with them. And though the amounts involved have been very small, I have never been able to get money from them for any claims but have only been left wiser.

Way back in 1987, I was the MD of Migma Equipment Pvt. Ltd., a company held by a group from Delhi. The same group also owned Gallium Equipment Pvt. Ltd. For Migma, I had set up a unit at Pithampur, an Industrial township 35 Kms from Indore, for manufacturing automobile components. My colleagues wanted me to set up facilities for manufacturing rolls used in tube manufacturing units at Pithampur. So, we bought a plot of land and before the factory construction started, got an open policy for about Rs 80 lacs.

A small shed was constructed and building material was procured. One day there was a storm. It was so intense that the roof of the godown was severely damaged. The asbestos sheets were broken. To our estimate the loss was worth Rs 20 to 25 thousand.

The next day we called the insurance agent who went through our policy papers and pointed out the matter in small print which said that no claim below 1% of insured sum would be entertained. As I said earlier, I was only left wiser. I learnt "**Think Big but Also Read the Small Print**".

A similar episode occurred in 1990. I had already parted company with Migma Group and had set up a consultancy office. I had an Ambassador car at that time. One day I found that the boot of the car had been broken into and the spare tire stolen the previous night. I immediately rushed to the police station and reported the theft. The policeman came to my house and took my statement. He was writing in Hindi. Finally, he read out the statement and took my signature. His handwriting was so bad that even the chemist who knew Hindi could not have deciphered the same.

That day I called my insurance agent for submitting my claim. The cost of the extra-tire (stepney) etc. was around Rs 2500/-. The agent informed me that before the insurance company paid me, it would need a '*Khatma*' report from the police. This report indicates that the police are unable to locate the stolen goods.

I had employed a few assistants to help me in my office work and I assigned the task of getting this report from the police to one of my smart assistants. After ten odd visits to SP's office, made every alternate day, he finally could manage to get the *Khatma* report by paying the police official Rs 300.

The insurance agent took all the papers including the *Khatma* report, which also had a copy of my statement in Hindi. He visited me the next day and showed me the copy of my own statement (written by policeman and signed by me) where the last line read, "The cost of the stepney was around Rs.1000." My agent informed me that the insurance company was ready to pay me Rs.1000 but then I would not be getting the advantage of No-Claim Bonus in the next premium I would be paying to them, and that meant I would have been a net loser. Not only that, but it would have taken three years before I would have been eligible for full No-Claim Bonus.

During those days it was quite common to get the car done up and get the insurance company to pay for it by way of false claims. **But to do that one had to be a wheeler-dealer.**

My third category of experience in insurance claims pertains to health insurance. During the last fifteen years I had been abroad many times. During most of my visits, I got myself insured for medical expenses, as I am well aware of the high cost of treatment abroad.

Planning a visit however, is a tricky job. It involves ticketing, getting the visas stamped, getting an insurance policy and so on. I always ended up in an 'egg first or chicken first' kind of a situation. Especially at a place like Indore, I have yet to find a Travel Agent who knows all the procedures precisely. Especially if you are visiting a number of countries and you have to reschedule your itinerary, it becomes quite an exercise. I have ended up paying for the medical insurance more than once for a visit, and had to write off the premium paid when the trip got cancelled.

It was during my visit in December 2001 to the USA and Denmark that I somehow missed getting myself insured. It was because my ten-year US visa had just expired and secondly because of the 11th Sep episode, getting European and US visas had become a tough task. I had to personally visit the Danish Consulate at Delhi, and the US Consulate at Mumbai, for visas. I returned home just in time for my departure.

I always start my journeys on a Saturday or a Sunday from Indore so as to utilize all five working days for work. Unfortunately, the Insurance Companies are closed on these days. This was another minor reason for my not getting the medical Insurance done up.

And as luck would have it; it was during this trip that I had a trip. It was while I had gone out shopping with my sister and brother-in-law in Chicago that I slipped on the pavement and hurt my shoulder badly. By the evening I experienced severe pain, and my shoulder had swollen like a football. We all thought that it was a bone fracture and were left with no option but that of praying to GOD.

By the next morning however, the pain was bearable. The swelling came down to the size of a tennis ball and to the size of a ping-pong ball by that evening. However, the large black patch of blood clot took more than a month to subside. Readers would recall the last sentence of chapter," American Systems………..", wherein I have cited Murphy's Law which says "If anything can go wrong, it does." I just wish to add **"however, God saves you from disaster"**.

--xxx---

DRAMA IN REAL LIFE (2012)

THIS CHAPTER IS DEDICATED TO

SMITA, MY BETTER HALF,

FOR

ENDURING LIFE WITH ME

FOR 33 YEARS (AND CONTINUING)

Drama in Real Life (2012)

There are many skills at which my better half is far better than I am. Stage acting is one of them. I did participate in dramatics up to two years after getting married. Not that my interest in theatre suddenly abated, but that my performance as an actor was not good enough for me to pursue the activity.

The first play I took part in was during my sixth standard in school. The play was about a stupid king who gets conned into wearing clothes supposedly weaved out of very thin gold threads and visible to only those who have never committed any sins. My role was that of a kid standing on the roadside with balloons in hand and shouting "Raja Nanga! Raja Nanga" (The king is nude! The king is nude!), as the king walked on the road. I believe I did perform remarkably well.

Then, during my high school days, I used to take part in Marathi Dramas staged during the annual Ganesh Festival. When I was at IIT, I took part in a satire, which was staged to expose the mismanagement at the campus hospital where a student's life could not be saved because the oxygen bottle could not be opened in time. I got noticed by an artist at IIT and was given a role that year in a one-act play, '*Bakri*' *(the goat)*, which was staged during the competition at the annual gathering of Miranda House of Delhi. For the benefit of the less informed, Miranda House is a Girls' college, famous for its Bold and the Beautiful. Needless to say, we got the best play award. Even today I can sing the theme song in tune.

My male ego prevents me from not mentioning a small episode which took place during the debate competition of the festival. The topic was 'Violence v/s Non-Violence' One after another, each speaker was arguing away vigorously. Then a Good Figure came on the stage and spoke in favour of Non-Violence. During the slot for Audience Questions, I stood up and asked her, "If you go to a jungle and face a tiger and if you shoot the tiger, it is violence or else the tiger will eat you up. So where is your non-violence?" There was a thunderous applause from over five hundred young females, which engulfed whatever the speaker mumbled in reply.

My logic may have impressed the pretty faces, but such short-cut logic was of great disadvantage to me in academics, especially when it came to Humanities and Social Sciences. One of the electives I had chosen during the second year (first semester) at IIT was 'Introduction to Economics'. It was child's play for me. But in spite of performing well in the exams, I got a 'B' grade and so I approached the professor in-charge. He showed me my end-sem (semester) answer book, wherein he had given zero marks for one particular answer of mine. Had I scored full marks for that question; I would have received an 'A' grade.

The question was "Prove that the costs are minimum when the average cost equals marginal cost".

I had answered the question in precisely five lines using calculus (A branch of mathematics developed by a very well-known physicist, Sir Isaac Newton) The professor however expected a two-page answer stating, "You manufacture the first item you spend so much, then you manufacture two items, and the cost for the second is slightly less, so in total you spend so much; and so forth". I simply walked out of the Prof's office without further argument. There was no sense in debating with a person who did not appreciate Calculus. I am sure that day Isaac Newton must have tossed and turned in his grave.

Coming back to dramatics, I did participate in full-fledged three act plays during the annual festival at NITIE. I got to play the lead roles in these Hindi dramas but then it was the case of 'Andhon Me Kana Raja' (One eyed amongst the blind is like a king). After my marriage, Smita and I acted in two dramas, one staged during the Ganesh Festival and the other during the 'Annual Festival of Maharashtra Commerce' (An association of commerce students). Then the curtain was drawn on my acting career. However, as I said in the beginning, Smita is certainly good on stage. She got offers from various Local Theatre Groups. Over the years, she acted in a number of dramas and won various awards including 'The Best Actress award' in the All-India Drama Competition held at Delhi, Nagpur, and Mumbai.

Indore has a large Maharashtrian population. A lot of cultural activities take place in the Marathi circle. A number of amateur theatre groups are active. Smita became a member of one such group. Unfortunately, all these groups had only limited vision of participating in the same competitions held at Delhi, Nagpur etc. Year after year their teams would go there, win prizes and come back. None however graduated to become professionals.

Once, Anil Chafekar and Avinash Gokhale, both branch managers in banks, and also senior members of one such Amateur Theatre Group, visited us and appraised us of a week-long drama festival planned that summer. The organiser was very well known to them, they said. For seven consecutive evenings seven very popular dramas were to be staged by professionals from Mumbai and Pune, in an open-air theatre. The cost of the project was three to four lacs. The yield expected was double that amount.

This organiser was collecting capital. Avinash and Anil both said that they were contributing Rs. 10000/- each and requested Smita to chip in the same amount. They assured that the investment was safe and in the worst possible case if there was no profit, the capital would be intact and would be returned within a month. Further, the investors would be getting good front seats for watching the plays.

Since the amount was small and we had a verbal guarantee from two Bank Managers, Smita and I consented. The week-long drama festival was a great success, if assessed on the basis of the attendance; audience count was in thousands each evening. However, the investment never came back. Anil and Avinash coolly evaded the responsibility. Later, I learnt from Anil that he himself had not invested any money. It was an honest admission of dishonesty. Avinash claimed that he had written off his ten thousand worth of investment. I suspect he must have recovered the amount from some of the Bank's rich clients, as the pain of losing hard-earned money never showed up on his face.

ANOTHER 10,000/-

I had faced a financial loss of a similar amount earlier when I shifted to Indore from Delhi to set up a project for Migma. Our first essential requirement was of a telephone connection. Back in 1985, there was a waiting period of over two years for getting a connection, though it was possible to get one in the BLACK market or by way of some government quotas. While I was making general enquiries, Vijay Shitoot, an ex-classmate from Indore, offered me a connection for Rs. 10,000/-. Since he was staying in the same colony as ours and was not a known cheat or a con man, I had no reason not to believe him. Furthermore, he was distantly related to Smita. So, I paid him the amount but soon realised that I had been had.

Since Vijay was related to Smita, she got extremely upset and hence kept visiting him, asking him to repay. He was, I learnt later, extremely short on cash and had lost considerable sums in his farming and dairy business. He however agreed to repay by way of supplying wheat from his farm. He did honor that commitment and for the next six or seven years we did not buy any wheat from the market. The loan (if one can call it that) got squared up over this period, without interest though.

BACK TO ACT II

In the present case however, the organiser of the Drama Festival had no farming business. As a matter of fact, we had not seen him ever and would not recognise him even if he walked across to us. In business, you lose money many times and for no fault of yours. You have to treat the loss as sunk cost. I, therefore, never brought up the matter for discussion. Smita however, was just not ready to forget the matter. She wanted to recover the amount at any cost.

An year before Smita had acted in a three-act play called "Doctor Tumhi Suddha?" (Doctor, You Too?). The drama had won some prizes at the Delhi competition. Anil had directed the play and Avinash was the male lead.

It was easily possible to collect twenty thousand rupees, over and above the expenses such as the theatre rent and other costs, if a show was organised at Indore. So, we put forward this idea to the team and everyone agreed. The returns would be split between Avinash and Smita as long as the same were not over Rs.10000/- each. This was to compensate us for the earlier financial loss.

The preparations started. It was agreed that each participating actor / actress would sell tickets worth three to five thousand. The collection was expected to be around Rs. 35000/- as there were seven / eight active members in the group. Selling tickets was the only major job. Staging the drama was child's play for the team.

Until the day of the drama, we had sold Rs. 4500/- worth tickets, and collected most of the amount. Avinash had collected an equal amount, which was utilised to meet the expenses of staging the Drama. Other team members kept saying that they were on the job and would be adding to the kitty. However, we were quite puzzled by the answers of Anil and a few other members of the team as they had started becoming evasive as we moved towards the scheduled day.

ACT III

The drama was staged successfully. Avinash's collection and minor contributions from a couple of others covered all the costs. Anil and another senior colleague did not contribute a penny to the collection.

This behavior, after having agreed on the basic objective, was just inexplicable. This time Smita was so annoyed with the group that she stopped participating in their further activities. Later we heard that Anil and Deshpande disapproved of Avinash who used to come to the practice sessions in High Spirits, and hence they had decided not to put in their bit. Avinash probably smelt ....a rat and out of embarrassment never asked for his part of the spoils. We thus retained our collection. How stupid could human behavior become!

--xxx---

MIXED PICKLE

THIS CHAPTER IS DEDICATED TO

DR. MISHRA & ASHWIN BONDAL

FOR

THEIR VALUED COMMENTS

AND

ENCOURAGEMENT

Mixed Pickle

For the past few weeks, I have not been able to write further. The reason: On Ashok's suggestion, I gave my manuscript to a doctor friend of his. The idea was to get feedback from a person who did not know me and also did not have a technical background. Dr. Mishra happened to be a voracious reader. Within days he returned my manuscript with five pages of written comments.

My motivation to continue to write went sky high when he called me a raconteur. There were words of praise. He wrote, "It is surprising that in spite of facing so many vows, you have not lost your sense of humour." He however added that I must break the monotony by inserting some good episodes here & there.

Very honestly, during the last three weeks, my mind has gone blank. I cannot recollect even one good event worth mentioning (on the professional front). Even today I have been sitting idle with a blank sheet in front of me for more than an hour, trying to figure out some good episodes to pen.

My thoughts wandered until I remembered the preamble to a small story written by my favourite science fiction writer Isaac Asimov. He was once given a topic and asked to write a Science Fiction impromptu. He came out with a two-page story called 'Square Peg in the Round Hole'. I decided to apply the same trick to myself and came out of the Catch – 22 situation.

Presently, in my hotel room, a sachet of mixed pickle is lying on the table, left over from last night's dinner. And that triggered my grey matter for use as the title of a new chapter. To give due respect to Dr. Mishra I thought I would cover "Not-So-Bad" episodes.

BRAVADO ACT

It was in April 1986 that I happened to travel abroad for the first time. I was with Migma then, and my senior colleague, Anil Dutta, decided to sponsor me for visiting the Hanover Industrial Fair.

I had to personally go to Mumbai to manage the visas and ticket, which I bought through Sita Travels who also managed to get me my German visa. During those days the UK required no visa for Commonwealth citizens. I managed the Austrian visa in half a day. However, I could not get my French visa due to shortage of time.

My ticket (being the cheapest by choice) was for Bombay – Geneva – Dusseldorf – Paris – Lion (A tourist place in France). The return ticket was: Lion – Paris – Geneva – Bombay. It was not a reroutable ticket, by Swiss Air. No other ticket was available which I could manage in the shoestring budget. And there was no time left for obtaining the French visa. I, however, boarded the flight as scheduled. My thinking was simple. I would fly to Paris on the scheduled day of the return journey from wherever I was, by buying a ticket locally, and board the onward flights to Geneva & Mumbai.

After twenty days of quite an enjoyable (except for food), educational and memorable tour, I took an early morning flight to Paris from London. There I booked my registered baggage to Mumbai and reached Charles De Gaul international airport, well in time for my return flight. I stood in the queue and reached 'Visa Control'. The uniformed officer asked me to go back shouting "No Visa". I tried to explain that I just wanted to go out to get boarding cards from the Swiss Air Counter. However, the officer was adamant. I tried another counter but the efforts were counter-productive.

I was not sure if the airlines had counters inside the arrival area (I believe there are none at Indian Airports). I was scared and panicky. However, my worries vanished when I looked around and spotted a Swiss Air Counter nearby. The counter girl only asked me for my seat and food preference and gave me the boarding cards in a jiffy. Rest of the flight was a smooth sailing though 33000 feet above the sea.

REVERSE SWEEP

Memories of my visit are still extremely vivid in my mind. I can replay them on my mental screen like a movie on a CD player.

The first day when I landed in Dusseldorf Airport, I started searching for one Dr. Dutta who was to receive me. For twenty odd minutes, I moved around with my bags asking people for directions. Most people did not, or pretended not to understand English. I was quite upset and felt a pang of homesickness. But soon Dr. Dutta located me and took me to a hotel or rather a paying guest type of accommodation. I still remember my cab ride as it was for the first time in my life that I was traveling in a Mercedes Benz.

I kept my bags in the room and walked with Dutta to his residence, which was about half a kilometer from there. It was around ten in the morning and extremely cold & cloudy. The idea of going to Dutta's apartment was that I would know the location. I returned soon, got ready, and walked back to his house, from where he was to escort me to an industrial exhibition on 'Steel Tubes'.

I had no problem in returning to his house within an hour or so but then by the time I reached his house, I was freezing, my teeth chattering. I felt that if I touched my earlobes they would break and fall off. Dutta offered me some brandy to help me fight the cold, which I gulped down.

By the time we reached the exhibition, I felt extremely thirsty and my head was spinning like a CD. Dutta took me to a stall and asked me to have coffee. Till then I never had a coffee that strong and, contrary to Dutta's expectation, I felt worse and very thirsty as if I had spent a month in a dessert without water. And to add to it, at the Industrial Exhibition, very few spoke English. All this set in a severe depression in me.

It was only late in the evening that I could trace Roy, a friend of Anil Dutta, who was also in Düsseldorf during the week. We knew each other well and he helped me pep up my spirits.

Then onwards the tour became very educational and worthwhile. At Hanover Industrial Exhibition, I went around and spotted a Slitting

Machine[11*]. The Germans had priced it at Rs. 20 lacs. I studied its specifications and asked the stall keeper if he would be interested in buying rather than selling a machine, with identical specifications from India at a price of Rs. 14 lacs

After my return to India, the German, along with his colleague, visited India; and placed an order for a Slitting Machine with a company in Mumbai owned by Mehta & Joshi who were well known to us. The order got executed and Joshi offered to pay us 3 percent commission amounting to forty-two thousand, an amount exactly equal to what I had spent on my visit.

Anil Dutta, our group head, however, refused to accept it, arguing that it was not morally correct to take commission from friends. When we worked as consultants, this same Anil Dutta was sponsored by many Tube Mill equipment suppliers for visits abroad on some pretext or the other. But then if human beings did not behave like this, the English language would not have the phrase 'Double Standards'.

I, however, was satisfied with my ingenious approach of selling a manufacturer a product, which he himself manufactured. **It was a successful "Reverse Sweep".**

CULINARY EXPERIENCES

I am not a gourmet, but am very used to home-cooked Indian food. Though, after spending five years at IIT and eating hostel meals, I would claim that I could eat anything with pleasure as long as it was not cooked in Hall III or Hall I mess. Over the period I have, however, been spoiled by Smita. She is so good in the kitchen (amongst many other places) that my taste buds are fine tuned to nothing but the best.

During my visit to Dusseldorf, I went to a Greek restaurant and had my first encounter with mustard sauce. My God! It was so pungent and acrid that I feel it should be declared unfit for human consumption. But then it reminds me of my dinner with Ackerman in Taj, Delhi. Ackerman was

---

[11*] A Slitting Machine is used in Steel Tube and other similar industries

the owner of AXA Power, Denmark. He was visiting India with his family. I had taken him along with his wife and son for dinner at the Taj in Delhi and had ordered "Indian Thali". He had a bite of Masala Papad and since he had had a couple of bottles of beer earlier, he dared to finish the entire Papad lavishly sprinkled with red chili powder & finely chopped green chilies. When it hit him, it was a bit too late. He literally was in tears. His already pink face turned red with agony or rather Agni. He said "Joshi, I now understand why you use water and not tissue paper like us. Your ******* chilies are so bloody hot, the paper would catch fire"[12*]

However, other than that mustered devil, every other item was insipid. (I wish there was a much stronger adjective than insipid to describe the tastelessness). At Hanover, I stayed at a paying guest accommodation quite close to the exhibition ground. For four days, every evening I used to walk back to the room. There was a German Restaurant on the way. I would stop there for dinner. The cold weather and lots of walking during the day would make me hungry. But I would lose my appetite as soon as I would have my first bite. For four days I would point my finger to an affordable item on the menu card, which obviously was printed in German. English was Greek and Latin for the waitress who took the order. I would remember the entry number of the item. Next day I would order, ensuring not to repeat the item.

The fifth day on my way out of the exhibition, I met one Mr. Rao from Bangalore. He too was suffering from malnutrition. We therefore decided to locate some Indian Restaurant. We moved to the downtown area. There we saw some policemen standing on the curb. We enquired with them for guidance. One of them immediately spoke to his office on a walky-talky, hailed a cabby and directed him to take us to The Taj Restaurant.

It was a Pakistani restaurant where I had the pleasure of speaking in Hindi after about a week's gap, especially so, because the listener could

---

[12*] First non-real statement, plagiarized from a Joke book to add spice.

understand what I said. As I ordered my food I said, "*Chicken Masala Aur Nan Aur Dekho Tushara Pas Jitney Hari Mirchi Hai Sab Dal Do.*" (And look here; put all the green chilies you have, OK?). The same was my request to Mrs. Phadke whom I visited a couple of days before I left England.

SORRY SONIA

During one of my later visits to Germany, I was to visit Leachmoteren, a company situated at a very small town near Munich. I reached there on a Thursday afternoon and was picked up from the railway station by a Company car. The one-and-a-half-hour drive was quite enjoyable due to the picturesque scenery. However, the driver had rendered me speechless as he and I understood only two words in common: "Leachmoteren" & "Joshi".

The driver dropped me at the hotel on the outskirts of the town from where I telephoned the Company. The concerned officer informed me that they were working only half day and were closed for a long weekend (Practically for half a week and therefore weekend was an incorrect description). He would be glad to pick me up on Monday morning, he added.

And so, for four days I was alone. The hotel room was nice. I used to stuff myself during breakfast as that is when I could identify what I was eating. My frequent walks in the cold weather to the town used to work up my appetite. The lowest risk item amongst eatables was a pizza. Pizza was not common in India in those days. I survived on pizza, which I would bring to the hotel room and eat as and when the hunger was unbearable. That is the story behind my pizza phobia. **Sorry Sonia.**

BRAVADO ACT II

After the third year at IIT, during summer vacation, I, along with two friends, went for a three-week course on Mountaineering at Nehru Institute of Mountaineering at Uttarkashi through NCC. The course was very memorable and full of thrilling experiences in my life.

As a part of the training programme, we, fifty odd participants, were taken to a base camp, around twenty kilometers from the institute where we stayed in dormitories. After lunch consisting of puri bhaji, we were left on our own at another location. We were to cross a mountain range through the jungle by ourselves and reach the base camp i.e., the forest bungalow near a village where we had our lunch. We were told to follow the "*Pagdandi*" (The nearest word I know in English is calf path, a trail).

It was around two thirty when the crowd started drifting into the jungle. We all broke up into smaller groups. Shyamarghya Mukharjee, Amitabh Shrivastava, my IIT mates; one Rao from Bangalore (I have lost count of the number of Rao's from Bangalore I have met) and I were together. Within half an hour somehow, we had lost sight of other groups; we had strayed from the *Pagdandi*. We were in the middle of a dense Himalayan jungle; there was no trace of any human beings or dwellings. We were in a fix. I had one puri leftover from lunch and all of us had already consumed water. Canteens were mostly empty.

We took a very wise decision (?). We thought that if we climbed up to the mountain top, from the summit we would be able to see the road, which ran along the base of the mountain range on the other side. So, we would just climb down on the other side and hit the road, and walk along the same path to the base camp. I was hardly twenty-one and had reasonably good stamina and physical effort was not a problem for me. But then climbing in the dense forest is not a joke.

After about half an hour of treacherous climb we thought that we would soon be at the top, but then there was a surprise in store for us. We found another peak ahead of us and we therefore had to continue our adventurous journey. By six thirty we crossed the mountain range and within minutes, while we must have hardly climbed down two hundred meters, the sun set and it became pitch dark. For the first time, in spite of our training at the institute, we realised that climbing down is far tougher than climbing up.

With nightfall, the mercury also dropped down suddenly. It was also quite windy. We all were wearing wind-cheaters and our climbing exercise of the previous four hours had kept us warm. Notwithstanding all this, we started shivering.

We thought of staying put there until we got traced or found. Luckily Shyag and I had a bad habit of smoking and hence each had a matchbox. We found a small clearing and lit a campfire there. There was no shortage of wood; we were in the dense jungle. The campfire would also save us from wild animals. The jungle was known to have cats.

For the first time (and the only time in life so far, touch wood), I was scared of death. I wished I had some pen and paper. I could write my particulars and keep it in the wind-cheater pocket. The tiger would spare the wind cheater as it was made of synthetic material. That way someday my fate would be known back home.

At around 10 O'clock we heard some movement in the nearby bushes; the rustling sound was certainly caused by a large animal's movement. Shyag and I woke up the other two who were sleeping (it was their turn to rest). We tried to intensify the fire by adding pinecones. Otherwise, we remained frozen.

Then we sensed a strong stench. I immediately realised that the stinking smell was of raw meat. I recollected my childhood visits to the zoo, especially the tiger cages. During my childhood, we would sometimes sneak into forbidden zones to see the tigers in their cages from close quarters. I was therefore more than sure that it was a cat carrying it's prey. Then the source of rustling sound moved away. We were sure the beast had come within a few meters of us.

At around midnight we heard some rustling sound mixed with human voices. It was from a hillock across us. We started shouting in unison "We Are Lost", one word at a time, until the echo of the previous word from all around died down. We got a response in the same fashion. "We", "Are", "Also", "Lost". So, they were our course-mates and were moving away. We had the following exchange of shouts.

"We Are Four Us"

"We Are Twenty-Seven"

"We Are Not Moving"

"We Are Going Ahead"

Shortly they moved away beyond earshot.

It was at around 2A.M that the army major in-charge of our training and two havaldars with rifles and torchlight came to our rescue. From them we learnt that this gang of twenty-seven had reached a small village and with local help had reached the base camp. They had told the major about our whereabouts. Escorted, we climbed down to the base camp. On the way down, for the first time I saw three porcupines cross our way. I found a quill nearby which I brought home as a souvenir. It was not until we reached the base camp that we realised that we were extremely hungry and thirsty. Fear and anxiety command higher priority over sense of hunger or thirst.

At the camp no eatables were available except some lumps of badly cooked rice in a big aluminium pot. I do not relish rice as such, but that night it tasted sweeter than *arugulas*.

REST OF THE NIGHT

Out of the four of us, two slept in the sleeping bags in the open veranda of the forest guesthouse. I, along with the fourth, sneaked unauthorisedly into one room through a window. In the morning we found a trail of bloodstains in the veranda including some on the sleeping bags of our two brave friends. Some animal must have crossed them with blood dripping from its prey.

Though it was the end of the episode for us; two more participants were still missing. In the morning the major and other army men (who were our instructors) were sitting with grim faces when we saw these two walking towards the guesthouse. They were Gadwalis and yet they had strayed in the jungle, and to fight the cold had taken shelter in a cave. **Well! All Is Well That Ends Well.**

MIXED PICKLE PART-II (JUNE 2020)

For the last ten odd years, I had stopped writing. I had completed 31 out of 32 chapters and had left the last chapter titled, "WHAT ALL CAN GO RIGHT AND HOW IT DOES NOT". I in the meantime was looking for a publisher without success.

Recently our e-group of my NITIE classmates had become quite active, especially as most of us were locked in due to COVID-19 pandemic. We started having ZOOM meetings. In the process I got in touch with Ashwin Bondal, my NITIE classmate and IIT Mumbai alumnus. He is an avid reader, an intellectual and in my opinion within the NITIE group, "**More equal amongst the equals**".

I started mailing him my manuscript chapter by chapter and started getting critical comments. After about 20 chapters, he came back with: "Good story, but why is it always one woe or misfortune? There must have been cases of unexpected good fortune too. You need to narrate them too; only if it maintains the balance."

I was on the verge of mailing this chapter (Mixed Pickle) when the above comment was received. I therefore decided to add a small episode as part-II of this chapter.

EXPECTED GOOD FORTUNE

We had indigenised a Russian equipment for the Indian Navy. I am constrained to write the technical details of the equipment but can only state that it plays a critical role in keeping the warship operational. As a matter of practice, Navy procures spares from the Original Equipment Manufacturer. One has to provide a list of spares to Navy with prices and internally Navy fixes up "Bench Mark Prices" by comparing with prices of similar items. In our case, Benchmarking was done on the basis of Russian spares prices which were significantly high.

We had filled in the RFQ (Request for quotation) and were invited to attend NLC. Having attended numerous NLCs, I still am not aware of its full form. In effect it is a price negotiation meeting. Normally it is held once a week and a number of contracts are negotiated and finalised for order placement.

The participants comprise of 10-15 naval officers including MOD's FA (Financial Adviser). The meeting is chaired by Material Superintendent, who is a Commodore in rank. During the meeting you are served tea and snacks in fine cutlery. Though the purpose is only haggling over the price, the decorum of the meeting matches that of UN council discussing some serious world crises. It normally takes 30 minutes to a few hours to conclude a case, depending on the contract amount.

The value of spares we had quoted was around 60 Lacs. There were 25 types of items required in different quantities. The NLC was scheduled at 11 AM on a Friday in February of 2013. During those days we were doing a lot of business with Larsen & Toubro's Marine Division at Rabale in New Bombay. As a matter of fact, they were carrying out marketing activities for our products. I therefore had planned to be at L&T, Rabale on Thursday and attend the NLC on Friday at Ghatkopar, Mumbai. On Thursday L&Ts rep was to attend the NLC for Rs. 1 Crore worth of our equipment to be supplied to MO, Visakhapatnam.

On Thursday at around 5:30 PM, while I was with Mr. Mahajan, GM of L&T's Marine Division, we got a call from L&T's Vizag rep. He informed us that the NLC remained inconclusive as Navy found L&T's offer too high priced. This would in-turn cause delay of order from L&T; that however was not a major setback. In my dealings with Indian Navy, this was the first time of an inconclusive NLC. I got worried about my next day's scheduled meeting. I did not wish that the lucrative spares' order got postponed.

Next day I left the hotel at Rabale and took a taxi for Ghatkoper. I called my office and got various calculations done. While waiting for my turn for NLC, I wrote out a discount letter. I was ushered in at 11:30 AM for the meeting. After pleasantries, I said "Sir, I am offering a 30% discount on 17 items and 5% on 8 items" and handed over the letter to the secretary. Everyone was so pleased with the 30% discount that they just stopped short of clapping.

The chairman said, "Thank you Mr. Joshi I wish all our vendors were like you, our life would have been much easier".

My trick of giving heavy discount on C (low valued) items and low discount on A (high valued) items had worked.

I walked out precisely in 6 minutes. 6 seconds per Lac for NLC. A new record set.

--xxx---

MY CONSULTANCY DAYS

THIS CHAPTER IS DEDICATED TO

MY FRIEND SHIRISH

WHO

DID ALL THE SPADE WORK FOR

THE PROJECT

My Consultancy Days

TWO MONKEYS AND THE CAT

I recall the story from 'The Panchatantra' in which a cat acts as an adjudicator for two monkeys quarreling over equal distribution of butter. To balance the pans the cat keeps taking portions of butter from the heavier side, and at the end both the monkeys are left high and dry.

This is precisely what happened in 1989-90. After I had left Migma in July1989, and before I took over Static Transformers in January 1992, I was operating from a small consultancy setup at Indore. I had formed a Private Limited Company called 'Smit Consultants Pvt. Ltd.' (clever readers would recall my wife's name). One day, a company from Calcutta contacted me. It wanted to set up a facility for manufacturing Valve Tappets. The Calcutta company was a Vendor to TELCO Jamshedpur, and was supplying a variety of machined components. By the time I was out of Migma, it was the largest supplier of Valve Tappets to TELCO, Pune and TELCO, Jamshedpur. I was therefore more than pleased to provide technical help to this Calcutta Company.

For working out the Consultancy deal the Calcutta Company asked me to visit them at their cost. The Company assigned me the job of examining the feasibility of setting up the tappet-manufacturing line. The investment required would only be for the foundry as the Company already had all the requisite machining facility at Hawra (Calcutta's neighbouring district). It was quite a viable project. I prepared a preliminary report and collected my fees. I was to provide further consultancy until the project went full stream. I was really thrilled to get the assignment as it was my first interesting, and at the same time, a paying consultancy assignment.

Just then an influential industrialist from Jamshedpur approached me, and called me over to Jamshedpur. During my visit he asked me if I could help him set up a tappet project at Jamshedpur. I informed him that TELCO had given an LOI (Letter of Intent) to a Calcutta company and that there was no scope for two / too many players. Secondly, I could not be working with two parties on the same project at the same time, to avoid conflict of interest.

He said that he had got the LOI given to the Calcutta party cancelled and got an LOI in his own favour. This Jamshedpur industrialist was also a vendor to TELCO and supplied components manufactured at his press shop. He would have to invest not only for the foundry, but also for the machining facilities, as he currently had none. As a result, it would not have been a viable project. (i.e., the investment would be substantial while the business disproportionately low to yield any profits). But he was adamant and had made up his mind to go for the tappet project. I therefore started working as a Project Consultant to him.

I explained to him that the project could become viable only if we could add some more items/ products to utilise the foundry capacity and thus increase the volume of business without much extra investment. And so, I explored the feasibility of manufacturing cylinder liners for TELCO. But after a lot of groundwork over a period of one year, the project was finally dropped and **I ended up not only without any butter, but I also lost the bread.**

GOOD FROM FAR IS FAR FROM GOOD

While working out the project feasibility for manufacturing valve tappets and cylinder liners at Jamshedpur, I advised my client that it would be worthwhile exploring the export market as, with prices offered by TELCO and with the small quantities required by them, the project was not financially lucrative. My client immediately agreed and asked me to search for potential buyers.

During that period (1990-91), there was a lot of emphasis on pollution control in Europe and I thought that it might be worth contacting manufacturers there rather than the end users as the foundry is quite a big source of pollution and the manufacturers would have to invest a lot to be able to achieve their pollution standards and hence would be looking for a source of supply from developing countries. I was sure that they would be happy to let Indians carry out the dirty work.

At that time the fastest means of written communication was the fax; email / Internet was not available. I started contacting various manufacturers in Europe, the UK and USA. My efforts of about two months yielded some results.

A large multinational company belonging to the GKW group showed keen interest. This MNC had a company in England by the name GKN Sheepbridge Stokes. It supplied cylinder liners to most of the auto manufacturers of England and Europe, and was keen to outsource part of its requirement as it was overbooked.

After a lot of correspondence, at their request, I got two samples manufactured locally - one from a Vijayawada company and another from a Pune based unit. I couriered them the samples. This was done to build confidence about Indian technical capabilities. Within a few days their report was received. The liners met all the required quality parameters. The report included a comment by their Inspection Department, which said at one place, "Microstructure better than ours".

My Jamshedpur client was quite excited when he reviewed the development and sent me over to England to discuss the possible collaboration. I visited the company and we discussed broad parameters for our collaboration. We negotiated the price of the cast cylinder liner and fixed it at 3 pounds each for the initial type of liners which we were to manufacture and supply.

During that period the exchange rate was Rs. 55/- to a pound. I had done my calculations and was quite sure of the viability / profitability of the venture. It was already the beginning of 1992 by the time I visited England. On my return, I was to prepare a detailed feasibility/ project report and then was to visit England with my client to work out the final agreement with the British Company.

But then there was a surprise in store for me. For reasons beyond my comprehension the pound slid down to Rs. 45/-, which meant one liner would fetch us Rs. 135 rather than Rs. 165, a steep drop of around 20%. The pound remained at that rate for quite some time. The British were not ready to increase the price and my Jamshedpur client became scared of the uncertainties involved. **The project was dropped – dreams shattered**.

YET ANOTHER MIRAGE

In 1994, one day after my consultancy phase was over, I was busy in my office at Static when two visitors came to meet me. They introduced themselves as Gawarikar, General Manager; and Laghate, President of Mahindra Sintered Limited, a metallurgical concern manufacturing auto components.

They were planning to set up a plant for manufacturing cylinder liners in India. Apparently GKW had some financial stake in this Company and Peter, the Executive Director of GKN Sheepbridge Stokes, had advised Mahidra to consult me for the proposed project. Accordingly, Laghate and the party had approached me.

With my previous experience, I advised them that the project viability could be enhanced if they could export part of the production. If they planned the project purely on the basis of the domestic market, with their overheads it would be difficult for them to compete with the small-scale manufacturers, from Agra and Rajkot, who dominated the spares market.

I did not hear from them again. Probably, Mahindra Sintered dropped the project. This of course did not cause any loss to me, as I had not planned on getting any business. However, the reason for mentioning this small episode would be clear by the end of this chapter.

After two years, in 1996, I received an envelope at my residential address. It was sent by GKN Sheepbridge Stokes. Their letter mentioned that they were looking forward to importing liners from India. They had enclosed drawings and specifications of a variety of liners and had talked of numbers amounting to millions of pounds per year.

Based on my earlier experience with them I took the decision of not spending any money in sourcing the liners. I, therefore, did not respond to their queries while they kept sending more and more enquiries.

Casually I mentioned about this matter to Shirish, a friend of mine who was working as an Export Manager of Gajra Bevel Gears Ltd., an offshoot of Gajra Gears. He took keen interest in the matter and assured me that he was willing to do all the spadework on behalf of his company and that he would cover my interests in case the exports materialised. He only wanted me to be associated with his exploratory work and to keep advising him on technical matters. Within a day he made me meet his director to discuss our mutual working arrangements.

We worked out a deal, according to which I was to advise them on the technical matters. I had made it very clear to Gajra Bevel that I would not be spending any money from my pocket for carrying out any work necessitated by this business and that they would have to cover my costs of traveling etc. I was to get a small percentage from the export proceeds i.e., the profits which would accrue from the export of liners to GKN Sheepbridge Stokes. This could work out to a few million rupees a year if the liners were successfully exported in the required quantities.

Shirish did work hard to source liners from manufacturers across the country. The prices offered by GKN were not very lucrative, but were good enough to yield a modest profit to an established manufacturer. His search did yield results. India Pistons, a large Company based in Chennai, agreed to supply the liners at the offered price.

Shirish and I flew to Chennai to discuss the modalities, schedule of supply and to work out the finer details. On our return Shirish checked up all the figures. The business was going to be quite profitable to us i.e., to Gajra Bevel and me. Naturally, the next step was to get a formal order from GKN and agree on the supply schedule.

GBGL asked me to visit GKN in the U.K. Jain, GBGL's Senior Manager looking after exports (Shirish's boss) was already in Europe on the way to US. It was therefore planned that he would join me for a day at GKN Sheepbridge Stokes for discussions with the customer. His itinerary was all packed and he could squeeze in just one day for the proposed meeting.

Accordingly, my tickets were booked and I left my home for catching the evening flight to Mumbai from where I had to catch a midnight flight to Frankfurt for an onward journey to Manchester. I checked in for the flight, cleared security, and was waiting for the departure announcement.

After some delay, as we started walking towards the aircraft parked on the tarmac, some Indian Airlines Officials came running and asked us to return to the Departure Lounge. He informed us that the flight stood cancelled as one of the aircraft's tires had been punctured. They would be getting a spare wheel from Mumbai the next day and we could then proceed to Mumbai. They were courteous enough to arrange prepaid taxis for the passengers to return to the city.

That day, Shirish had to work late till midnight, informing concerned people about the event, rescheduling my programme and rebooking my tickets for the next day's flight. Next day I caught the afternoon flight to Mumbai.

GKN's car picked me up at Manchester airport and I reached Chesterfield after a two-hour drive. More than thirty hours had passed since I had left home, most of the time I had spent at the airports waiting for the flights. As a result, I was dog-tired. Peter, GKN's concerned Director, and Jain of GBGL picked me up from the hotel within minutes of my arrival, not even allowing me time to have my bath. This was because Jain had to leave for London within an hour to catch his flight to US. Within an hour we concluded the deal and left the details to be worked out the next day. Two days later when I came out of the Indore airport, I was grinning from ear to ear.

Just within a few days of my return from England, GBGL got a fax from GKN informing that Peter was visiting Ahmadabad and would be in Mumbai for a day on his way back. He was keen to meet the Chairman of GBGL. I S Gajra, chairman of GBGL, was equally keen to meet Peter as he had recognized the bright business prospect. He insisted that I also be for the meeting at Mumbai. On the scheduled day, therefore, I flew to Mumbai in the morning and phoned Gajra's Mumbai office on reaching the hotel booked by GBGL for my stay.

Peter had already reached Oberoi Hotel and we were to meet as soon as I arrived from Delhi by the early morning flight. I learnt from GBGL's office that the Delhi Mumbai flights were delayed due to fog at Delhi airport, which happens to be an annual ritual.

I went over to Oberai and joined Peter at around two in the afternoon. Every half an hour GBGL's Mumbai Office kept providing us a report about further delays in flights arriving from Delhi. By ten pm we gave up all the hope, and I dropped Peter at the International airport for his flight.

I returned home the next day morning. Though all this did not have any impact on the proposed business, I wasted my day and GBGL wasted money on my travel.

SUPPLY STARTS

The work started soon after my return from England. The first sample lot of twenty-four liners reached GBGL from India Pistons within a month and a half. I went over to Dewas to inspect the same and found everything in order including the microstructure. The lot was immediately shipped to GKN by courier.

We also received GKN's inspection report quite fast. Every parameter of the liners was found within limits except for some very minor variation in an insignificant dimension. This could be easily taken care of during supply of the Pilot Lot. We now were to get a formal order from GKN. **It was certainly time to count the chicken.**

But then GKN went **COMPLETELY SILENT**. As days passed, we started getting nervous. India Piston was chasing GBGL every day to know the status. Countless number of faxes and phones by Shirish yielded no response from GKN.

Then one day I called up Peter. On the phone he informed me that GKN's Order Book had hit rock bottom due to recession in the auto market in Europe; GKN had to cut down the volumes of their own manufacturing and that he would contact us as and when things improved, which never did. **NET RESULT: THE EGGS NEVER HATCHED; THEY WERE INFERTILE.**

HIT AND MISS, RATHER MISS AND HIT

As mentioned earlier, during my consultancy days I had sent samples of cylinder liners to GKW, UK. I had one of the samples manufactured at

PEFCO, Pune. PEFCO had a Foundry where they manufactured a variety of specialty cast products for the automobile sector. They were pioneers in manufacturing chilled cast valve tappets, and were competitors to Migma. `

One fine morning, I was contacted by PEFCO for providing them machining know-how for Mahindra Tappets, which required quite a special process. Since I had personally developed this process at Migma from a b initio, I had no difficulty in taking up this small assignment. PEFCO paid me nominal fees. I, however, had no complaints, as it was unexpected extra income for a couple of days' efforts. As a result of this assignment, I got acquainted with most of the senior managers of PEFCO, Pune.

Since PEFCO does not deal with consumer products, it is not well known to the common public. Even less known is the fact that the Company is owned by Korus Group. Korus (India) Ltd., the flagship company of this group, is however widely known for being the leader in supply of stationery items, especially the carbon papers.

So, one day when someone from Korus' local office came to Smit's office, looking for me, I thought it was in connection with PEFCO. Surprisingly, however, he just noted my phone numbers and informed me that he was doing so as per the instructions from his corporate office at Mumbai.

Within an hour, I got a call from Korus, Mumbai. A senior manager talked to me and inquired if I could visit Mumbai and meet their chairman in connection with some consultancy assignment. I immediately consented as I was looking for such opportunities.

During my meeting with 'Babuji' (a common term of respect for a senior person), the sixty plus chairman of the group, it turned out that Korus was looking for additional business / product lines for their Pithampur Plant. This factory at Pithampur Industrial Area, which is around 35 kilometers from Indore, was set up for manufacturing tube well drilling rigs. And it so happened that their order book was drying up resulting in poor financial results. During a top-level meeting at PEFCO, Babuji had posed this problem and sought suggestions from PEFCO's senior managers. Their CEO recommended that the Company should seek my help. And that is how I was contacted.

During my visit to Korus, Mumbai, I agreed to look into the right opportunities. On my return to Indore, I visited their Pithampur Works to assess their strengths / facilities. I realised that they had reasonably good facilities of machining, fabrication and for assembly, for a light engineering factory.

BACKDROP (1990)

As I have written, during that period I was looking for various business opportunities. One project which I had examined was that for setting up a unit for manufacturing Oxygen Generators. While I was at Steel Tubes, I had learnt about a relatively new technology, known as PSA (Pressure Swing Adsorption). The atmospheric air consists mainly of nitrogen and oxygen and, in layman's language, equipment based on this technology filtered out oxygen and separated nitrogen for use. So, it was possible to discard nitrogen and collect oxygen. It was a clean system requiring only electric power. In India, no one, to the best of my knowledge, was using this technique to fulfil the requirement of oxygen then. Most industries where oxygen was needed were using bottles (heavy cylinders filled with oxygen).

In one of the informative TV programmes called 'The World This Week' I had seen that in US they used oxygen tents for asthma patients. These tents were connected to a small machine working on electric power. This machine, the size of a Birla Yamaha Gen-set, was supplying oxygen to the patient. I could easily infer that it was a PSA based oxygen generator. I had therefore researched and located two manufacturers, one in Germany and the other from the US for a possible tie up for manufacturing oxygen generators in India.

The applications for such equipment were many; including hospitals, oxygen-pubs and fisheries. I was certain, the way pollution levels were rising, oxygen- pubs would be common in near future. I had therefore spent Rs. 30000/- in getting a market survey done to assess the demand for such equipment. I had assigned this job to Kirloskar Consultants,

Pune, as I was aware that their market survey division was good at carrying out such jobs. KICON's report was very encouraging.

The German manufacturer did not respond to my faxes while the US Company showed interest in the idea of a tie up. I therefore visited them and worked out a collaboration agreement for USD 25000 (equivalent to Rs. 8 lacs then).

I worked on the project details and found that it was a viable one requiring a total investment of Rs. 30 to 35 lacs. I therefore approached the financial institutions for funding only to learn that they did not finance the "Technical know-how fees". On my own, I had no such funds available for investment and by that time I had already spent about a lac or so on the project for the market survey, visit to the US, etc. I did not want to write off this amount and so I started to look for a financial partner.

All my efforts turned out to be futile. I then tried to sell off the project and advertised in the Times of India. I got a reasonably good response. More than ten parties showed interest. Since most of them were from Bombay, I went to Bombay with my junior colleague and stayed at a reasonably good hotel at Juhu for two days. I held meetings with some of the prospective clients. This too did not yield any result. Most of the likely clients showed keen interest, but later for reasons best known to them developed cold feet. My expenses on the project had gone up by another twenty-five thousand by way of advertisement and traveling costs. The shortage of funds and this dead investment started causing extreme concern to me.

KORUS OFFER

Against this backdrop the call from Korus and my visit to their plant turned out to be a boon to me. Oxygen generators could easily be manufactured at their Pithampur plant and Korus had the strength to market them.

During my next meeting with the Korus chairman, I, therefore, suggested that they take up manufacturing of oxygen generators. Keen for additional business, Korus agreed to buy the project at Rs. 1.5 lacs (I was so desperate for money that for fear of refusal, I did not ask for more). It was agreed that I would get paid once AMOX, the US Company, agreed for the tech know-how transfer to Korus. They then asked me to go to the US, along with their representative to get the formal agreement signed with AMOX.

This was the purpose of my very brief visit to US. We worked out the itinerary and from Indore I booked my ticket on a KLM flight. I reached Louisville, Kentucky; and so, did Korus' executive. The collaboration agreement was worked out and signed in a day. Though AMOX and I had agreed for USD 25000 as the Technical knowhow fees, in the earlier written document (agreement with Smit) it was kept at USD 35000 so that if the project got financed by any Financial Institution, the entire USD 25000 would come from them.

That evening AMOX's President took me out for dinner. At that time, I brought out the fees issue and told him that they were to get USD 10000 more and they should split this amount with me. He agreed and assured me that he would transfer half of this additional amount as soon as Korus paid AMOX. This USD 5000 (Around Rs. 1.60 lacs then) was going to be a bonus for me; so far - so good.

RETURN JOURNEY

All this happened sometime in May 1991. During that period my brother-in-law, Dr. Avinash Khare, was in Paris. Avinash is a nuclear physicist working at the Institute of Physics, Bhubaneswar. He travels abroad so frequently that had there been a scheme for taking up UN Nationality, he would easily have qualified. Avinash is a very decent and compassionate person, very simple, sober and soft-spoken. He never loses his temper, not even in his dreams. It is a great disadvantage to have such a brother-in-law. You often get compared.

Before Avinash had left for Paris, I had informed him that I was likely to go to the US and in that case, I would return via Paris, and break my journey there to spend a couple of days with him. However, that was subject to getting my visa. Pushpa, my sister, was at that time at TIFR, Mumbai, for some summer research project and she could communicate with Avinash by some primitive email type communication. I was able to inform her of my visa status.

I went to Mumbai on Thursday for the said US visit. I was to leave Mumbai on Sunday. I collected my ticket from Korus' travel agent and went to the French Consulate for my visa. I submitted all my papers, after waiting in line for more than two hours. The lady at the counter asked me the routine questions and informed me that I could collect my passport on Monday. I explained to her that I would need my passport on Friday evening at the latest. She however arrogantly denied entertaining my request. I had therefore no option but to collect my passport then and there, of course, without the French visa. I informed my sister at TIFR of the fate and left for the US on Sunday as scheduled.

After my work at Louisville, Kentucky, I flew to Newark to meet my cousin, as my return ticket to Mumbai was for a later date. The next day, I went to New York and was loitering around in the downtown area when I spotted a queue of ten odd persons in front of a building. I was amused to note that it was the French Consulate. Without a second thought, I joined the queue. Within fifteen minutes I was facing the lady at the counter who asked me to pay ten dollars, which I promptly did. Within minutes she handed me back my passport, with the French visa stamped.

Before I left Mumbai, I had informed my sister (for onward transmission to Avinash) that I would try to get the French visa in the US and if I succeed, I would visit Paris and that he should check with KLM on the day of my arrival, if I were on the passenger list.

I started my return journey from New York's JFK airport, where I was told that my reservation was cancelled because I had a double booking (one made by my Indore travel agent and another one by Korus' agent). This set back was, however, momentary as seats were available and I was accommodated on the flight to Paris. All this is only the background. My real ordeal started only during my return journey.

It was around 2 PM when I landed at Charles de Gaulle Airport. I cleared immigration control, collected my baggage and proceeded to the reception area, looking for Avinash. I searched for him everywhere until around 3 PM. It was then that I felt that I should take some other steps.

I got help from a Sri Lankan who gave me some French coins and guided me to use the public phone. I got through to The Institute of Physics Nucleare (French Spelling), only to learn from the lady attending the phone that Dr. Kare's (That is how the French pronounce Khare) room was locked. She had no clue of his whereabouts.

With only a few hundred dollars left with me, I decided to take a cab to the Institute rather than waiting for the uncertainties, and specifically before dark. The cabby told me that it would cost me around 70 to 100 dollars.

It was my first visit to Paris (though I had transited through Charles de Gaulle airport earlier) and I enjoyed my hour-long drive to the Institute of Physics Nucleare.

It was a small building with picturesque surroundings. The office lady took me to Dr. Khare's room, on the door of which hung a large padlock. I simply stuck my visiting card on the door mentioning the time and followed the lady back to the office. I took Dr. Khare's residential address, which simply was "Messo International". I learnt from her that he was in the room till one PM and had not been seen thereafter.

It was 4.30 PM and panic had started setting in. The temperature was in single digits. I had to locate Avinash one way or another. I went to the cab (I had not taken out my bags till then) and asked the driver to take me to Messo International, which was half an hour's drive back towards the town.

I paid off the cabby. The drive had cost me USD 115. My balance had dwindled to nearly 200 dollars with two days to go before my scheduled flight to Mumbai. I lugged my bags (one without wheels), climbed 50 odd steps, which led to a large cemented area the size of a football field, with the main building on the other side. The entire layout of the building reminded me of Roman architecture where one walks, walks and walks and climbs steps, before reaching the main building.

But finally, I was at Messo (Mess / Hostel) International. On the ground floor there was a large cafeteria and a small office room in the corner. The lady at the office looked into the register and said "No, no Dr. Kare" It was a jolt to me and I requested her to check again and again until the decibel level of her identical replies started going up.

I lugged my bags to the cafeteria, swallowed some snacks without noticing / tasting the food. I made general enquiries and learnt that at that campus they had Messo China, Messo Mexico, Messo India and so on. I met some Indians there who advised me to look for Avinash at Messo India. With no better option, I dragged my bags to Messo India, which was about half a kilometer away. Due to the tension and the physical fatigue, I did not realise until I stopped to cool myself outside the Messo India building, that the time was around 6 PM and the temperature was nearing zero degrees.

Dr. Khare was not staying at Messo India. I had to look for some other alternative for spending two nights with less than 200 USD in my pocket. I kept my bags in the reception area and talked to as many people as possible, explaining to them of my predicament. It was not possible for the residents to accommodate me in their rooms as the rules barred non-residents from getting in beyond the reception area.

On someone's advice, I went out searching for a hotel nearby. I scouted around, took a bus ride. No one spoke English (or at least pretended that they did not understand English). I believe I paid much more for the bus ticket, but was in no position to argue with the conductor. The nearest hotel had vacant rooms. The tariff was over 400 USD per night. I was back to square one and back at Messo India.

It was around 7 PM when it started snowing. Enough was enough. I made an emergency plan of taking a taxi to the airport and staying there until the day of my flight. But since it was not yet dark, I decided to wait for some more time before I pressed the eject button.

During the next few hours, I must have narrated my ordeal to at least ten or more Indians staying at the Messo India. It was only at 9 PM that (the sunlight had started fading) I met Rao, a young South Indian again from Bangalore. He was an engineer working with some MNC. He was in Paris for training. He listened to my story and agreed to help me.

It took him considerable time to make the caretaker of the hostel look the other way, while he took me to his room. Once in his room, I felt the pang of hunger. I had to do with an apple, which I had bought at the cafeteria and a small bottle of wine I had bagged during the flight for Avinash. By 10.30 PM I was sleeping like a log on the wooden log floor.

Before I had gone to sleep, Rao had informed me that Dr. Vaid from Indore was staying there and so also one Mr. Das from Kolkata who was working at the Institute of Physics Nucleare. This was some encouraging bit of information.

I hate people brushing their teeth in public. But I was most pleased to meet Dr. Vaid who entered the room with foam all around his lips. In a small conference, it was decided that I would go with Das to the Institute of Physics Nucleare and look for Avinash. In the event he did not come out of his vanishing act, I would return in the evening with Das and stay with Vaid who would show me around Paris and ensure that I board the train to the airport on the day of my flight.

All set, I went with Das to the Institute. We had to change twice on the suburban trains, using the tickets with magnetic strips (this was a 'first' for me).

Once at the institute, I rushed to Dr. Khare's room, which was still locked, my card still there untouched. I stuck one more card on the door with a fresh date and time. Das left me there to go to his building. Before he left, however, he gave me a lot of coins and taught me to operate the coffee vending machine to get coffee which was mild enough to drink.

I waited in the library till 2 PM. Every 15 minutes, I used to walk to Dr. Khare's room and back to the library, once in a while peeping in the office. The lady would smile and say "No, Dr. Kare".

Finally, at 2.15 PM Avinash rushed in, panting heavily. For a moment both of us were speechless.

His side of the story was quite odd. He had telephoned KLM a day before to learn that my booking on the flight was cancelled. He however rechecked a few hours before my arrival time to be told that I was on the flight and so he had rushed to the airport. The suburban train was considerably late due to a local strike of railway employees. He reached late at the airport and looked for me all over the airport. He reconfirmed my name on the passenger's list. Knowing well that I would not have much money with me and that it was my first visit to Paris, he got tensed up and could not sleep at all through the night. Next day early in the morning, he went straight to the Eiffel Tower and kept waiting at the gate till about 1 PM. His reasoning was that if I were in Paris, I would certainly visit the Eiffel Tower. He gave up his wait and returned to the Institute only at 2.15 PM.

For the rest of my stay in Paris, Avinash took good care of me, showed me around Paris, and offered me his bed and in spite of my protests, slept on the wooden floor. The rest of the journey is, as they say, history.

As far as Korus is concerned, they paid me after a considerable delay. I had to visit Korus Mumbai to force them to pay. And as things always go wrong with me, on the day of my visit to Mumbai, there was a total strike of transporters. No buses, taxis or locals. I had to walk from Parel to Korus' office a few kilometers away. Korus did not reimburse the cost of my Indore-Bombay & Bombay-Indore ticket (forming part of my US visit) on some pretext or the other. Smit Consultants P Ltd had that amount as debit balance for many years in the books of accounts until it was written off.

Korus manufactured and sold a number of Oxygen Generators, but later closed the line for reasons known to them.

The fair American was not fair. He never transferred me any funds. However, life has gone on all the same.

[13]

---

[13] After 20 years, during Carona days, many plants sprung up in India to manufacture Oxygen Generators based on PSA Technology.

AGAIN, AGAIN AND AGAIN

THIS CHAPTER IS DEDICATED TO

MY FRIEND

VISHWANATH KRISHNAN

WHO

ENTERTAINED ME WITH HIS PJS

Again, Again And Again

At IIT as well as at NITIE, I was quite infamous for my PJs[14*]. Some fellow students even dared to exaggerate and termed my jokes SJs[15**]. One such joke, which tested as to whose wits lasted longer, narrator's or listener's, goes as follows:

Narrator: "There were three brothers. 'Again', 'Again and Again', 'Again &, Again' and 'Again'

Two of them, 'Again, Again and Again', 'Again and Again' died. Who was left?"

Listener: "Again" or "Again?" depending on whether he or she got the catch or not.

And then the narrator would go over the question once again. This closed the loop of question and answer often ended with either the narrator getting a black eye or the listener performing Houdini's vanishing act.

****

During my first year at IIT, I made friends with Shyamarghya Mukharjee, my neighbour at Hall III. An aeronautical engineering student, he hailed from Dhanbad and had a public-school background. We two became quite close, but drifted a bit apart when we branched off in the fourth year.

Being aware of my atrocious language skills, he once said, "****, (This time, these asterisks are not for footnote indication) you are going to be a big man one day. I will write your biography then". He used the last four letters of my first name and distorted the pronunciation to make it sound feminine. In retaliation, we also distorted his name using the first four and adding the eighth alphabet of his first name.

[14*] Poor Jokes   ** Sick Jokes
[15]

We lost touch once we passed out of the institute. I was only vaguely aware that he had joined TCS. A couple of years ago, i.e., after twenty-seven years of leaving IIT, I got to know Shyag's whereabouts, thanks to the e-group (Class of – 75). He was at Hyderabad, still working for TCS.

I called him up and met him during my visit to Hyderabad. Our meeting took place at the airport. We hardly spent twenty-seven minutes together. The gap of twenty-seven years had not weakened our bond. The nearby passengers must have been puzzled to see two of us hugging while loudly calling each other by our nicknames.

The period of twenty-seven minutes was too short to update each other with twenty-seven years' worth of information. Anyway, I reminded him of his promise and told him of my misadventure of attempting to write my autobiography. He gladly agreed to edit it.

Accordingly, on my return I promptly sent him a copy of my incomplete manuscript and asked him for his comments. Putting his views mildly, he said, "Don't you think it is a bit too repetitive?"

Shag's comments dampened my enthusiasm to continue to write and indexed my memory. The "Again and again" joke surfaced into my active memory cells.

But then I thought: What the heck! If I have been getting screwed repeatedly, I will write about it again and again, pointing out the subtle differences in each session. I am not at any risk of having a black eye as I will not be facing the readers. And of course, he or she has a choice to shut the book and watch TV.

With this background, I have started scribbling once again; this time, with a statutory warning to the readers, "You are free to skip this chapter, if you find it repetitive. However, no claim of full or partial refund will be entertained."

FROM PLUS TO MINUS

Just after taking over Static, I got a call from Calcutta. We had a local representative there. He informed us that the Indian Navy / GRSE (Garden Reach Shipbuilders and Engineers Limited) was interested to place an order for six ICCP (Impressed Current Cathodic Protection) Control Panels with us. We quoted, and then gladly accepted the order.

For the benefit of non-technical readers, I have to first explain the basics of Cathodic protection. The warships (Or any other ships for that matter) float on salty sea water all the time. Salt water is highly corrosive and eats away the hull of the ship. The eating away or the corrosion is a kind of electrochemical process, vaguely the opposite of gold or silver plating. The corrosion has to be arrested; else the ship would turn into a sieve within a few years.

To stop the electrolysis going on near the surface of the hull of the ship, an electric current has to be passed in the reverse direction so as to nullify the original corrosive process. Hence the name of the protection system.

Simple as it may sound, in reality there are a number of practical difficulties. Firstly, the level of corrosion has to be measured all the time and accordingly the quantum of current is decided. The sensing is done by measuring the potential difference between the hull, and an electrode dipped in seawater near the hull of the ship. The potential is of the order of 0.15 Volts or approximately one tenth of a pencil cell voltage.

Secondly, the order was placed with us specifically for the units based on "Magnetic Amplifier Technology" which is a First World War technology. I am sure none of the electrical engineers below the age of forty would even have heard of it. This outdated/ obsolete technique has gone out of electrical engineering textbooks long ago. It was something similar to asking for a cell phone with Morse code technique.

Anyway, we got on the job, got the drawings approved and built two units. It involved a lot of experimentation to get the design right. We consulted the best of electrical engineering consultants available at Indore. All of them failed to build the unit and gave up halfway through.

However, taking clues from their unfinished work, we completed the job. All this delayed our supplies for which we paid a penalty.

We called the inspectors for inspection who asked for approved QAP, a mandatory requirement. The QAP was prepared and sent to Delhi. It was promptly rejected and returned. After countless amendments, finally the QAP was approved. It contained a lot of funny entries and abbreviations like CHP, IRs, SC (i.e., Customer Hold Point, Internal Records, and Supplier's Certificate). In addition, it had a lot of IS, BS, NES, MIL and other specification references.

The people at Delhi who scrutinized and approved the QAP were unaware of the difference between a diode and a transistor but were masters in their job of preparation of QAP, and so they had added all the checks for hardness, tensile strength of steel parts like angles, channels and sheets. As far as testing of electrical performance parameters was concerned, they only insisted on IR and HV (Insulation resistance and High Voltage test) checks and of course they asked us to add Red Warning Plates of "Danger-415 Volts".

Sometimes I wonder as to how many red '**DANGER- --- VOLTS**' tallies I would find at a Quality Assurance Officer's house. I am sure if he could, he would stick one on his wife's forehead (Voltage would depend on her statistics).

The electrical functional testing part however was left untouched by the person scrutinizing / approving ATP (Acceptance Test Plan) probably because it was Greek or Latin to him.

SMOOTH SAILING

Then onwards, for a brief period of a few months, everything went smoothly. Two units were inspected and shipped to Calcutta. The next two units for the next ship were also cleared and dispatched. We even got ninety percent payment against the supplies.

The units were tested on shore for which we had to send our electrician to Calcutta. The ICCP control panels were taken to the ship and installed.

The ships are built at GRSE at the jetties, which are on the Hubli bank. The water there is not salty and thus ICCPs could not be functionally tested there. (Water cannot conduct electricity easily unless it is sufficiently salty) The actual performance of the equipment therefore could only be tested when the ship went out to the sea.

ROUGH WATERS

A few months later we sent our electrician for the first sea trial. Our units worked fine when the current was set manually; but in automatic mode, electricity refused to flow. Our electrician used his limited knowledge and fiddled with the wiring, which did not improve the situation, but only spoiled the wiring. GRSE as well as NHQ (Naval HeadQuarters) created a big hue and cry and asked us to rectify the equipment immediately. The ship returned to GRSE within three to four days.

At Indore, we went over the circuit and found no reason for our equipment's unexpected behavior. For the next sea trials, we therefore sent a senior engineer along with an electrician, who only further messed up the internal wiring.

After a few months the ship was to be handed over to the Indian Navy and hence the panic mounted. We were pressurized and were threatened with getting black-listed as a supplier. I therefore stepped in and decided to go to Calcutta to sort out the matter.

I landed in Calcutta on the day the ship was to sail out. When I saw the state of the wiring of the equipment, I was sure I could do nothing to amend the situation and hence I asked the GRSE officials to remove the units and replace them by the units supplied for the next ship.

The naval officials and the GRSE staff managed to do it in a couple of hours, whereas in normal conditions it would have taken them a couple of weeks, especially to do the necessary paperwork. We Indians are good crisis managers.

By four in the evening, I checked the units' functioning, which was perfectly fine. I simulated the sea condition by supplying the same voltage signal (potential difference) to the unit which is the measure of the level of corrosion. It was then that a sailor standing nearby said "Sir, but at sea this signal is negative." Wisdom suddenly dawned on me; the mystery stood solved. Shouting Eureka, I rushed to the LO's cabin (Electrical Officer).

I explained that there was a mistake in what was given to us as the functional requirement of the ICCP Panel. The unit in 'as is' condition would not work in sea in automatic mode. The only solution was to change the negative signal coming from the sensing electrode to positive, which was not feasible for me unless I changed or added some electronic circuitry. And as the ship was to sail at 10PM, it was not feasible to complete the job before it left Calcutta.

It was therefore of no use my sailing with the ship. He however, insisted that I go along. I, therefore, went back to my hotel; called up Indore and asked for a small electronic card, which would change the negative signal to positive, to be immediately couriered to Visakhapatnam, which was the destination of ship's first leg of the journey. I boarded the ship with my travel bag at 9 PM.

MY SECOND SEA VOYAGE

Just after a few months of my marriage, Smita and I had gone from Bombay to Goa by sea. It was a short journey of sixteen hours and that too by a passenger liner. The warships are different. There is hardly any space for movement. One cannot even stretch one's arms and yawn in peace without hitting the sidewalls or the roof.

On board the ship, I frequently lost my way. Moving from one location to another was like moving inside an anthill. I felt extremely claustrophobic. Though I did not get seasick during my five-day voyage, I felt sicker watching sailors throwing up in the plastic buckets placed (or firmly tied up[16*]) at various locations.

The ship left early in the morning and reached deep into the sea by noon. Most of this time I spent on the deck. Every few hours the colour of the

---

[16*] The ship's rolling and pitching movement can make things fall and hence every item on board is firmly secured.

water kept changing until it became deep blue. I realized for the first time as to why Navy blue is that dark blue a colour. The landscape on the bank of the Ganges was lush green. One has to see it to believe the beauty of Bengal. By noon, the land was out of sight. One could only see water, water and more water all around.

Since my units were put on manual mode and were set to pump full current, which they were doing without complain, I had absolutely nothing to occupy me. Some civilians from GRSE who shared my cabin played cards sixteen hours a day, while I spent most of my time on helo-deck (where the helicopter lands on the ship).

A BRIEF DETOUR

For the benefit of readers, I would add another experience of mine here. Once Smita had accompanied me to Visakhapatnam. She was keen to see a warship. I therefore took her to the dockyard and got permission to visit a warship as well as a submarine.

As the two of us climbed up the gangway (narrow bridge connecting the shore to the ship), the Commanding Officer of the ship and some sailors stood in attention and saluted Smita. From there, until we finished the ship's tour, she was "Yes Madamed" by everyone. It was a big surprise for me. I then learnt that since the ship is feminine (She), as a tradition every lady is given such an honour and respect. Further a ship is SHE and not HE or IT because it carries everyone in her belly. Amusing, is it not?

From there we went over to a submarine. Life in a submarine is worse than that in hell. There is no space to even walk in pairs. You have to walk behind one another. Hats off to our submariners! In my opinion, of all our defence personnel, their life is the toughest.

DETOUR ENDS

Coming back to my current ship journey, I watched the Russian Guns' trials, which fired thousands of rounds of ammunition in a minute, creating a wall of defence against the incoming missiles; then witnessed the mid-sea fuelling exercise during which a tanker moved side by side our ship and tons of fuel was loaded in ours. Both the ships moved in parallel at full speed. One of our electricians was on INS Deepak (the fuel tanker) to attend to the trials of one of our other equipment. The ships moved so close that we could recognize each other. I realised that watching such feats on Discovery or National Geographic was nothing compared to the real-life experience.

Finally, after five days of trials of various equipment on board, the ship reached Visakhapatnam harbour. As soon as she docked, I was summoned by Deepak's LO as the trial of our equipment there had failed. I went across by a motorboat and advised my electrician to tune the equipment.

The electronic PCBs, which converted the polarity of the signal from negative to positive, had reached my Visakhapatnam hotel. I carried the same to the ship on the same day and fitted them. Both our units immediately started behaving as desired.

The chapter was finally over only when these makeshift PCBs were replaced by our electrician a few months later. On my return to Indore, I wrote to all concerned that all this had caused us a lot of extra cost of traveling. Primarily the fault was of wrong specification of the equipment, which said: pump current if **"THE SIGNAL IS MORE THAN ZERO". And a negative signal can never be more than zero.** The current was to be proportional to the signal on a scale of 1 to 20. However, as always was the case with Defence contracts, we had to give up and write off the expenses for no fault of ours.

The specification still continues to be the same. I wonder if some other supplier may in the future go through similar trouble as we did. Supply of six ICCPs gave us six lacs and I am sure we spent more than that in manufacturing, modifying the units, and for the many visits to Calcutta. Anyway, we are quite used to such happenings.

But the best part of the story is yet to be told. A few months later, during my visit to GRSE, I learnt that the entire paint of the ship hull was worn off and GRSE had to get the hull repainted at the dry dock at Mumbai. It cost Navy / GRSE Rs.80 Lacs. How they had managed to hide the cause of this damage is not known to me. Babus know the tricks of the trade. However, it did not take me a second's thought to realize that it was the case of over protection. **For five days we had, on LO's advice, pumped 100 Amperes each i.e., two hundred amperes continuously which had caused the works.**

--xxx---

THE OXYMORON: TOUGH TENDER

THIS CHAPTER IS DEDICATED TO

THE MEMORY OF

LATE MR. A. D. PATIL

WHOM I CONSIDER MY GURU

IN ELECTRICAL ENGINEERING

The Oxymoron: Tough Tender (2004)

The Indian Navy was in the process of setting up a base at Karwar. This project was called Project Seabird. Two years ago (i.e., in June, 2002), we got an enquiry for a large number of items from Siemens Ltd. The headers of all the documents were marked Project Seabird. The items included transformers, rectifiers, battery chargers and one large inverter. The technical documents, which gave detailed specifications, were voluminous. We needed to feed the entire information into our PC because, in our offer, we had to write almost the same thing. We then used the famous "cut-paste" technique to prepare our quotation. During that period Praveen was on leave. Amongst all of us he could type the fastest. We, therefore, got the tender fed on a CD from a professional typist and had to pay Rs. 5000 for the work. Readers can guess the volume of the paperwork.

Within days we received an identical enquiry from L&T and ten others, all large electrical contractors. It took us quite some time to work out the costing and prepare our quotes. All the technical documents had a list of approved vendors. As per that list, Static Transformers was accredited for supply of Transformers, Battery Chargers, and Power Conversion Equipment.

The total value of our offer was around eighty lacs. Out of these, two large chargers were worth thirty lacs each. In addition, one item was a very large inverter with a lot of paraphernalia. I was sure (and I had checked with experts in the field) that no Indian company had built that big an inverter. I had earlier visited Sicon once. Originally an Italian company, which was later taken over by Socomac of France, Sicon had the technical capability to manufacture the item. In spite of Internet access, none of the parties involved was able to locate a supplier for the inverter and so we stepped in with our offer on behalf of Sicon. Socomac had its presence in India, when Sicon was acquired. The Indian Company had set up a plant to manufacture lower ranges of inverters at

Gurgaon. I had taken the prices from them on the phone and quoted on that basis. The price was over one and a half crore.

Later, I visited Socomac's Delhi office and worked out initial details with their senior executive, A. D. Patil, M.Tech. from IIT Bombay. In the event of an order, they would supply the main equipment while we would take care of the paraphernalia and other naval formalities. This would give Static at least ten to fifteen lacs towards commission alone.

The documentation of our offer consisted of at least a hundred pages. We had a lot of telephonic interaction with most of these large electrical contractors over the next six months, especially with Siemens. MECON, a GOI consulting firm, had done all these tendering on behalf of the Indian Navy.

We kept getting technical queries, which we promptly responded to. Somehow, we were very enthusiastic when we interacted with one Mr. Vishwanath of Siemens who was very amicable. We had sent our offer to L&T Madras office too. Surprisingly BHEL, Bangalore, asked us for quotations of only transformers and battery chargers, though on our own we had sent offers for all other equipment. We had somehow given the lowest priority to L&T.

After about a year, in July 2003, the price bid was to be opened. Only four or five had technically qualified. Siemens, L&T and BHEL were included in the qualified list. I telephoned Vishwanath about the result. He was quite sad. He said "No, Mr. Joshi, we have lost. We were second lowest. L&T is lower than us by half a percent. Anyway, thank you very much." I could only mumble "Ya, you win some; you lose some."

Immediately I contacted L&T to congratulate them. One arrogant female was on the line. She showed off (only telephonically) about how they were smart in costing and blah-blah.

COOKIES CRUMBLE

After about a month's time we checked up with L&T and they informed us that they had yet not got the order.

One day, I was visiting Cmde Chandra who was DQA (Navy) and, while in his office at RK Puram in Delhi, I happened to enquire about Cmde Anil Vyas with whom I had lost contact after the V. Kumar's episode. I had met him only once, casually, in South Block, outside the Defence Minister's office when he mentioned that he had moved to the ATV Project. Later, someone had informed me that Vyas had retired. Chandra however replied, "Oh, he sits next door. Do you want to meet him?" and without waiting for my reply he lifted the intercom and dialled. He said, "Anil, Joshi is with me. He wants to see you." Then he said, "Just walk across to Seabird's Office and ask for Vyas."

At the Seabird office, I had hot tea with biscuits and an hour-long chat. I told him about our offers for the Seabird Project, and mentioned that we would work with L&T without any problems, as they were professionals. We were aiming at the business worth eighty lacs direct supplies of transformers, battery chargers, and some earning from Sicon supplies worth one and a half crores.

It was really good news that an honest and upright officer (Refer chapter: 'The Whistle Blowing Act') who was sympathetic to us was in-charge of the project. But as I said earlier, in my case, every single good news is followed by two bad ones.

He burst two bombshells. "Hold it. The battery chargers requirement has been withdrawn" (sixty lacs worth orders gone with the wind) "and who says L&T is getting the order? It is BHEL who will get the Order. Being a Government Company, they are getting 5% price preference." This was not really the second bombshell, except that working with BHEL was slightly more difficult than with L&T, who would have been more open and less formal and would also provide better payment terms.

He informed me that BHEL itself would be manufacturing the big inverter. Commission from Socomac evaporated into thin air. Anil advised me to visit Bangalore and meet the BHEL people and try to sell/promote Socomac.

FUTILE VISIT

I visited Bangalore along with Socomac's Indian technical expert and gave a presentation. I also gave them our product catalogues and requested them to consider our offer for equipment, other than transformers.

During this visit we had engaged one freelancer engineer, Kameswaran, at Bangalore for liaison work. He subsequently informed me that the entire BHEL team had been transferred and replaced and that they would not be including us for supply of other items unless they were categorically instructed by Mecon who had passed the buck to the Navy. And in spite of letters written by Navy's Seabird Office, for reasons unknown to us, our name was not included.

PRESENT STATUS

We have received the first (Non budgetary) enquiry for transformers, worth a couple of lacs, and our people have quoted for the same. We don't know whether we will get any orders or any more enquiries, or whether BHEL will make or import the large inverter. Whatever it is, now we are not sure whether even the money spent so far on travel, telephones and stationery will be recovered or not. Another piece of bad news was that Cmde Anil Vyas was retiring on 31st August 2004, just twenty days later.

Lastly, in the days of so-called globalization / privatization, BHEL still gets 5% Government preference and for private companies we have MRTP (Monopolies & Restrictive Trade Practices Act). Anyway, we are in India and hence have to live with these illogical rules. So, for us, as far as the Project Seabird is concerned, **"It had a flying start and it has flown away."**

The English language is very peculiar. The word 'Tender' has been used in all its good senses since the 13th century. Some crazy fellow started using it to mean "Offer for a Contract or Supply" in the 16th century. I wish he had used the word 'Tough' or 'Tedious' instead.

PART II

This story does not end here. Around six months later, Nilesh happened to meet some L&T engineers at Bangalore. They were from their Heavy Engineering Division (HED). From Nilesh they learnt that we could supply the large inverter for the Seabird Project.

Our correspondence and subsequent visit to L&T revealed that BHEL which was executing the Seabird contract could not manufacture the 1000 KVA inverter and they were therefore looking for another source. L&T's Heavy Engineering Division made an offer and got the order from BHEL for supply of this 1000 KVA inverter.

We therefore made an offer to HED. Mr. A. D. Patil and I met them in New Bombay and held discussions with their Engineers. If I am not mistaken, we made four to five visits for technical clarifications. It was during these visits that A.D. and I became close friends. His Electrical Engineering fundamentals were very clear. I learnt a great deal from him. Unfortunately, he passed away recently. He was suffering from cancer and had fought the killer disease for around five to six years, had gone through chemotherapy thrice. Even when the treatment was going on, he used to go to his office for work. Whenever I faced a technical difficulty, I simply used to call him on phone and he used to take keen interest in explaining me the subject matter.

Equipped with our technical inputs, the HED Engineers made visits to Bangalore to clear technical issues of the said inverter with the Navy / MECON officials. We were sure to get the order due to the TINA (There is no alternative) factor L&T faced.

On the third visit, L&T came up with a very stringent Technical Requirement. They stipulated that the equipment should have IP56 degree of protection. IP56 Protection means that the equipment should be practically air / water tight; no dust or foreign particles should be able to enter it; no ingress of water should take place when water is splashed on it from all directions. This was a Herculean task, and in my opinion was not at all called for.

A 1000 KVA Equipment of the size of a large truck mounted on wheels was bound to generate at least 50 KW of heat which needed to be thrown out into the atmosphere. Socomac was not ready to deviate from their specifications, and HED did not dilute theirs either. They were bound by the customer's requirement.

I came out with a solution which I believe was most practical, not very expensive and could have satisfied the customer. I suggested that our main equipment could be at IP56. The main equipment would be air conditioned. Only the heat sinks would be protruding out from the back of the equipment (like the cooling tubes at the back of the 1st generation refrigerators.) These too, I said, would be enclosed in a large cabinet with only inlet and outlet fans with filters. L&T representatives understood and agreed to get a clearance for the scheme from the Navy.

During our next round of discussions, we found out that L&T could not convince the concerned officers of the Navy who wanted the moon. I wish they had asked me to accompany them for their meeting with the Navy; maybe then the result could have been different.

Anyway, the customer is always right. To meet this requirement, we needed to build a sealed unit with air conditioners to suck out 60 KW of heat. It was a criminal act of wasting power.

We quoted for the enhanced requirement. The price went up by 30 to 40 lacs. L&T negotiated and asked us for 'no regret price'. During the same visit we had another meeting with their purchase manager who haggled for a few lacs. We returned with the hope that the order would be received soon.

After considerable follow up, we were called for the last round of discussions and were asked if we could supply the inverters at Rs. 1.5 crore without the additional increase of 30 to 40 lacs which we had asked for air conditioning, etc. We flatly refused.

As a result, L&T decided to build the equipment themselves, which over the period they did and incurred a huge loss which was more than what they would have incurred had they bought the equipment from us.

The logic was, if they bought and sold it, it would have been a trading activity and would have been reflected as a glaring mistake of the Heavy Engineering Division. The concerned Director of L&T had therefore ruled that L&T design & build the equipment themselves. The loss incurred would have been hidden in their Total Income & Expenses of the manufacturing activity. Great Management Funda of a professional company! We, as usual, had wasted our time, energy and money in the matter.

LOSE – LOSE SITUATION

We had been supplying transformers to ONGC in Assam. The value was small, up to a couple of lacs in one lot. However, last year they sent us a slightly bigger tender. For this tender, they wanted us to deposit earnest money of Rs. 30 thousand. Our earlier earnest money of 13 thousand, which was due for more than a year, was not returned by them till then.

We asked our agent at Sibsagar, around 400 kilometers ahead of Guwahati, to request ONGC to adjust this money and permit us to send only 17000 more. ONGC however refused on the grounds that the files were different.

And so, we sent our offer with a DD of Rs. 30 thousand. The total value of five different types of transformers was around 11 lacs. The tender forms had the routine terms and conditions attached with them, including the one which I quote: "ONGC reserves the right to split the order". Normally, this is a standard condition of every Government Organisation.

More than five parties had quoted against the above tender of transformers. The tender was opened and a comparative chart got prepared, which our agent faxed us from Assam. In totality we were the lowest. However, individually our price was not the lowest for all the five types of transformers. Five different bidders turned out to be the lowest for the five types of transformers. One was from Calcutta, one from Mumbai, and others from some other cities, besides us at Indore.

We got a call from our agent a few days later. He informed us that ONGC has decided to place five orders with five parties. This way, they were to save a few thousands and all the five would lose on the expected margin because the cost comes down when you produce a lot worth eleven lacs, as compared to a smaller one worth two lacs each. In case of earnest money two files could not be merged, while ordering one file could be split into five!

Anyway, suppliers are not choosers. If we refused to supply, they would not send tenders to us in the future and secondly, we would forfeit our earnest money of 30,000. We therefore executed the order.

Before dispatch, ONGC's Inspector visited us from Baroda, stayed at a hotel for a day and after finishing his work, left the next evening. If we account for his traveling expenses (borne by ONGC) it would amount to at least ten thousand. ONGC may have inspecting offices at Calcutta & Mumbai, but I am sure they did not have offices in the other two cities. And so ONGC's total Inspection cost was at least 50 thousand. Thus, in totality, I am sure, they spent more in procurement as against what they would have spent if they had placed the full order with us.

We had never faced such a situation with other Government Organisations during my dozens of years of experience. But there is always the first time.

In 1997, a Management Guru coined the phrase 'WIN–WIN SITUATION', for a business deal which benefits the buyer as well as the seller. English Lexicographers could add 'LOSE-LOSE SITUATION', for describing the narrated type of cases.

--xxx---

MANAGEMENT GURUS

THIS CHAPTER IS DEDICATED TO

THE MANAGEMENT GURUS

OF

MIT, HARVARD AND THE LIKE

Management Gurus

Once, while I was traveling to the US, with nothing interesting to do, I surfed various music / movie channels sitting in the aircraft. While doing so, invariably one comes across a channel where some corporate guru is preaching Management 'Fundas'. I listened carefully. The speaker was narrating the bold and unparalleled decisions taken by Enron's top echelon. I was familiar with the name, as the giant corporation was about to set up a Power Project in Maharashtra. Since I dealt only in thousands and at most in lacs, that too in rupees, I could not learn much from those who dealt in millions & billions and that too in dollars, I, therefore, switched to some tolerable Hindi movie.

Just a few years later, on a similar journey, except that it was towards Mumbai, another Management guru was talking about a course being conducted at Harvard Business School on the Decline of Enron - lessons to be learnt and bla - bla. This was a typical case of "Nothing Succeeds like Success and Nothing Fails like Failure".

Anyway, before I continue writing this chapter let me put out a disclaimer. I myself have undergone a number of courses in Management and in no way intend to criticise or challenge the great gurus of Management. Nor do I intend to write case studies for Management students. As I said at the beginning, I am only narrating real life episodes. Readers are free to draw their own conclusions.

DELEGATION

Professor Kaul at NITIE had delivered two or three lectures on Delegation as a part of "Industrial Behavior", a course we had to study during the second year of my post-graduation. Fully convinced of the importance of delegation, the matter got engraved in my relatively virgin grey cells.

It was in 1985 that I shifted from Delhi to Indore to set up a project for Migma group. We had bought a plot of land in the industrial area of

Pithampur. The area was totally barren. The heat could have killed us. We needed some greenery to look at. We had dug up a well and had started the factory building construction. I decided to plant trees all around the two-acre plot in the coming monsoon. We brought a large variety of plants from the forest department and instructed a team of workmen to plant these around the boundary. The workers were from nearby villages and were the first-generation industrial workers. They had probably spent a lot of time since their childhood carrying out agricultural work.

I was happy to see some green patches, as the plants were taking roots. However, my happiness was short-lived. After a dry spell of a couple of weeks (I must have been away from Indore, else I would have noticed and salvaged the situation), we found that most of the plants were lifeless, practically none had taken roots.

On the spot inspection revealed that our workers had planted the plants along with the polythene bags!

QUALITY CIRCLES

When I did my PG, the QCs (Quality Circles) were not in existence, or the Japs had not divulged the secret of QCs to the world till then, or maybe I bunked the class when QC Fundas were taught. Only later on I got a general idea of QCs and their objective.

One day, I was sitting in the reception of CG (Crompton Greaves) office at Indore. The magazines lying there were older than what I would get to read at my barber's saloon and so I shifted my attention to the notice board. One notice was titled 'QC AWARD FOR THE MONTH'. Then followed about fifteen sentences, the gist of which is given below.

Rajesh Tawde has been awarded for the best QC suggestion of the month. He faced a problem in giving expense account after his return from tours. Now he notes down all his expenses on a daily basis before going to sleep. This has relieved him greatly.

What I have written in three sentences was explained, elaborated in fifteen sentences on the notice. I am sure, I was not drunk. Probably the guru employed was fifth class pass (or fail).

BELIEVE IT OR NOT – HOW FOOL PROOF CAN ONE PLAN?

Sometime last year, I had gone to Mumbai for ship trials of an equipment we had developed for the Indian Navy. There was a lot of spare time to kill on the ship. And so, while I was getting bored onboard INS – Vidyut, I got into conversation with Lt. Cdr. Biswas, a young Naval Officer, who was pursuing a part-time MBA. I narrated a story to him, which I now plan to pen.

At the end of my narration, contrary to my expectation, he inferred that our planning was bad and that we should have anticipated the likely situation; taken precautionary measures. I was speechless and did not continue the conversation any further. I would like the readers, however, to make their own judgment.

THE STORY

In 1998, we quoted for the supply of some transformers to Larsen & Toubro Ltd. They placed the order worth Rs. 6.5 lacs for epoxy cast transformers, which were to be used in a refinery project at Haldia. The transformers were produced and the inspector was called for inspection. L & T has a practice of appointing free lancers for inspecting the goods at the supplier's Works, probably to avoid permanent overheads.

We were very pleased with this profitable order, especially because L & T was to pay us on proof of dispatch and secondly it would add L & T's name to our Customer List.

The inspector, a Maharashtrian from Pune, arrived at Indore. I was out of town at that time. The inspection went on smoothly on the first day. For us at Static Transformers, manufacturing and testing of such transformers was a routine business and hence no special arrangements were made.

The next day, the last test of the Heat Run was started. Heat Run is a test during which the transformers are loaded to the full capacity for 8 hours and the temperature at various points measured. This test ensures that when used by the customer at his site, they would perform as per the specification and not get overheated.

The test was to end at around five. During these days, in Madhya Pradesh, we were having a power cut from 6 PM to 10 PM and hence completion of this test prior to that was necessary. By 4 PM the workmen and the supervisor who were carrying out the heat run were relaxed. Generally, if anything has to go wrong during the test, it does in the first three to four hours. From the trend of the temperature observations, it was felt that the test would be satisfactorily over.

But suddenly, some smoke was observed. of one of the cables used to supply power to the transformer. The cable would catch fire unless the power was switched off. The heat run was therefore stopped and the cables removed.

The damaged cable was (not a part of the transformer) removed and found to be unserviceable. Another cable was not readily available. Any way the testing would have to be redone, as it has to be continuously done for eight hours. Deshpande, the inspector, was to leave by 8 PM flight and so he did. However, before leaving, he told our chaps that he would be soon visiting Bhopal (which is 200 Km or 4 hours' drive from Indore) and at that time he would come over to Indore for the heat run test.

Our chaps prepared the cable the next day and carried out the test at 125% loading and were ready for Deshpande's visit.

So far, so good. Whatever happened was part of the game. It would cause a delay in dispatch of goods and receipt of money by a week or two, but then if everything happened as planned, life would be boring.

I was back at Indore and learnt about the events. Deshpande got busy with something else and could not visit us as promised. Our frantic follow up started with phone calls and faxes. Nilesh even visited L & T Mumbai to urge them to speed up the visit, but to no avail. More than a month passed and there was no news from Deshpande.

And one fine day, it so happened that I was out of office for some work and so was Nilesh. Pandit, our senior supervisor, was on leave. Deshpande called up from Bhopal at around 10 AM. Uday Mulay picked up the phone. Deshpande asked for Nilesh, Pandit and me in that order. Since no one was available he then asked Uday if the transformers and the test set up were ready.

Since Uday, who is our accountant, was not aware of the details of the matter, he could not confirm the readiness. He however noted down his Bhopal telephone number where Deshpande was available that day. Deshpande advised him that he should be contacted at the earliest.

I reached the factory at 11 AM and so did Nilesh. Immediately after I learnt about the call, I asked Uday to connect me to Volta's Bhopal number where Deshpande was to be contacted.

Uday tried many times, but could not get the call through. Then it was my turn to try but even my attempts were a failure. Just after dialling, the telephone used to go dead. In fact, by 1998, the telecommunication in India had progressed so much that normally one could get his call through even to Antarctica in the first attempt, however we could not get through to Bhopal.

Suspecting that there was something wrong in our telephone instrument we went to the nearby PCO. The result was still the same. Uday & I drove to my residence, just a kilometer away and tried to call from there. The result was no different.

During that period, I used to call Jayanta Apte in Delhi quite frequently, and it would be very difficult to get his number. So, I used to go to the telephone exchange to call him. From the exchange I could always get his number in one shot.

Uday and I therefore drove to the telephone exchange. (Only BSNL was there in the country then). We did not succeed in getting the call through. We tried calling the Navy's Bhopal office, some relatives at Bhopal, but to no avail. All Bhopal lines were dead.

We must have called fifteen different Bhopal numbers, twenty times each from four different locations /instruments. We even booked a trunk call.

The result was still a lemon. By 5 O'clock (it was too late to send someone to Bhopal and to locate Deshpande) the number of calls we made, probably exceeded the total calls made by brokers in a month at BSE.

Finally, at 5.30 PM we could get the call through; only to learn that Deshpande had just left for the Company's Guesthouse. We called up the guesthouse, but he had not reached. We called every five minutes until at 7.30 PM, when we finally could get Deshpande on the line.

He curtly said "Mr. Joshi, I had planned to reach Indore by evening and tomorrow being Sunday we could have finished the testing, and I could have returned to Bhopal. I have some work scheduled here on Monday and am booked to fly from here to Mumbai by the afternoon flight. So now we have to plan the testing during my next visit."

I urged him to take a taxi and reach here either the same day or early the next morning. I got the following response.

"You see! I can't start now. And I can't reach by 9 AM tomorrow by which time the test must start, so that the same can be completed by 5 PM, before your power cut. I am therefore not in a position to plan it this time. You should have phoned me earlier." There was no point urging him further. So, I asked him as to when he intended to visit next.

"I am a Maharashtrian. *Aani Mazzya Ghari Ganpati Bastaat. Me Ata Ganpati Nantar Yein;*" was his reply in Marathi, meaning: Being a Maharashtrian we have the religious function at home during the Ganesh festival, and therefore I will visit after that.

The result was that the inspection got postponed. To cut this long story short, the second Inspection took place three and a half months after the first and so the funds were received three and a half months later than planned in our funds flow. Had the phones worked on that Black Saturday, we would have got the payment at least two and a half months earlier. Our turnover that year was only around fifty-five lacs. Thus, our receipts of one and a half months' production got delayed by two and a half months due to the failure of the telephone network.

As I wrote at the beginning, I narrated this episode to Biswas and asked him as to how one could plan in advance for such (unforeseen) events. He came back saying, "It is your fault Mr. Joshi, you should have instructed the telephone attendant, briefed him and should have told him that he might get such and such call and he should reply in such and such way."

I feel he missed my point completely. It is up to the wise readers to make their own judgment. **Recently Management Gurus have conveniently coined a phrase "Black Swan". However, no one ever imagines a situation where in spite of not being in Australia all swans we faced were always black.**

--xxx---

GOING CHRONOLOGICALLY
OR
THE FIRST MISTAKE OF MY LIFE

THIS CHAPTER IS DEDICATED TO

TAPPU PATNI

FOR HIS VALUABLE

CRITICISM, COMMENTS, AND SUGGESTIONS

Going Chronologically
or
The First Mistake of My Life

BACKGROUND

I lost a good friend, Kirti Patni, in 1998. He suffered from hepatitis B. He was an Electrical Engineer, a topper from Indore's most prestigious engineering college and belonged to a rich family which owned a couple of cement pipe manufacturing factories as well as ACC's cement dealership.

Kirti, though a couple of years senior to me, was my batch mate at NITIE. He was a keen photographer, dramatist and a voracious reader; and as a result, had diverse interests. He married Rekha, an architect by education, while he was at NITIE. Kirti had returned to Indore after post-graduation. I too was back in my hometown by 1985. We, therefore, met often and as a result Smita and Rekha befriended each other.

Tappu Patni was Kirti's son who had to leave his engineering studies midway due to Kirti's untimely demise. In spite of the separation of Kirti's brothers and unprecedented expenditure incurred on Kirti's treatment, this young lad has done well and by now is a financially sound and a successful businessman.

He visited us last Wednesday. During our chat, he talked of various books he had just read. He, a public-school product, had inherited Kirti's reading habits. As a result, he too was aware of things around the world. Our discussions shifted to my diary and Tappu showed keen interest in going through it.

The next day I left for my Mumbai-Pune-Goa-Karwar tour. However, prior to departure, I instructed my office to deliver a hard copy of my diary to Tappu and it was delivered on Thursday evening. On Friday Tappu called me to tell me that he had started to read and liked the book.

Thanks to BSNL's service, our conversation had to be stopped prematurely for lack of clarity of voice.

A day later he again called up to say that he had finished reading it and that it was very good. He however had a few suggestions. I should organize the chapters chronologically so that readers who did not know me are at ease with the incidents described by me, he said. Secondly, he advised that I should introduce the characters appearing in the text to the readers better, so that they could visualise the situations more vividly. He also advised me (politely) that I should ruthlessly discard pre-IIT episodes.

From my side, I assured him that I would consider his advice positively and asked him one simple question. "I appreciate your comments, but answer my one question. If at all my so-called diary gets published, will people read it?" His response took me on an ego-trip. He said "Why not uncle? If Chetan Bhagat's 'Five Point Someone' (inspiration behind Amir Khan's Three Idiots) is appreciated by people, why not your book?"

For a few years prior to this incident, I had not scribbled even one page. Coming to think of it, I really cannot say why. Tappu's statement however tickled my grey matter and here I am writing on a Sunday morning in my hotel room. I have taken Tappu's advice seriously and hence the title of the chapter and a reasonably good introduction of the Patnis.

Many people have a habit of reading a book directly from the first chapter, skipping the introduction / background. Tappu probably did the same. I will therefore elaborate upon the questions raised by him and some others, though there may be a bit of a repetition.

Another friend of mine argued that if you are not writing an autobiography, then "what is the message you want to convey to the readers?" I did not know that every non-fiction had to convey something. But coming to think about it, I believe (though I have not explicitly brought it out in the book) that one's decisions (and the consequences) depend on one's experience. I have mentioned this in the introductory part where I have stated, "One Becomes What One Goes Through". I will try to bring out this aspect at length in the next couple of chapters.

After reading my diary, Rekha asked me if I ever did any introspection. A big word for me! In my view everyone does it, consciously or subconsciously. Further, how honest one is with oneself while one does 'introspection' is a big question. While carrying out this exercise, is one absolutely unbiased, or does one continue with one's prejudices? Anyway, I will try to keep this in my mind while I write further.

GOING CHRONOLOGICALLY

Firstly, I am not writing my autobiography. I am just narrating various events of my (mostly) professional life. I believe that had I written chronologically; this diary would have become a boring book. Secondly, it would have appeared that I am writing about myself; whereas the 'I' in my book stands for ANYONE in my shoes.

Had I written chronologically, "Until Things Did Not Go Wrong" would have been the first chapter of my book wherein I have described about my life at IIT, Kanpur from July 1970 until April 1975, as I have stated nothing went drastically wrong during that period. Then, as explained in "What If", due to my illness I lost my admission to the PG Course as well as two job offers which I had and I was forced to join Gajra Gears for lack of any other alternative. Then after a stint of nine months with the company, I joined NITIE for post-graduation in industrial engineering. "Golden Days Again" covers this period i.e., July-1976 to May 1978. This chapter also covers a further period till April, 1979 during which I worked with Kirloskar Consultants at Pune. "My Good Days with Steel Tubes", covers the next three to four years; to be precise, until December, 1982. I have yet to cover events from then onwards until 1989.

"My Consultancy Days" and "Talhunt" deal with events of the period July1989 till December 1991. The remaining chapters are mostly related to events post January 1992 while I was (and still am) at Static. I therefore now intend to cover the gaps, in the next few chapters.

THE FIRST MISTAKE OF MY LIFE

By the time I completed my post-graduation I had a good job offer from Premier Automobiles to join them as a Management Trainee in their EDP (computers) Department. It was the highest paying job of that period for NITIE grads. Incidentally my batch mates, who joined PAL at that time, today belong to Who's Who of the Indian Corporate World. My aversion to COBOL, a computer language and my experience of Gajra Gears however made me believe that I would perform better in a smaller organisation rather than merely being a cog in a big wheel. A consulting firm would offer me a variety of job content.

As I have mentioned earlier, I believe that "One is what one goes through" My Gajra Experience directed my destiny and hence I joined ORG as a Management Trainee. After a week's stay at Baroda with ORG. I shifted to Kirloskar Consultants, Pune, in July 1978.

If I really were to be another Chetan Bhagat, I would admit that not joining Premier automobiles and opting to join ORG/ Kirsolskar Consultants at one third the salary was the first mistake of my life I had committed.

By 1979, on 5th March to be precise, I was engaged and was to get married on 5th May the same year. At a meagre salary of Rs.1200/- per month for doing nothing at KICONS, I could not continue with them. I therefore searched for a job and joined Steel Tubes of India, Dewas, near Indore, as an Industrial Engineer at a basic salary of Rs.1800/-+ perks per month.

From May 1979 to May 1982, the job satisfaction as well as the compensation was rising rapidly. By the time I left I was drawing a monthly basic pay of Rs.3200/-. However, during the last few months of my job with Steel Tubes, I was getting neglected, discriminated against, and insulted by the top management. This insulting behavior was unbearable to me and as a result I searched for a job and joined Atma Tubes at Dera Bassi near Chandigarh as Works Manager at a good salary of over Rs.5 K per month plus, house, car etc.

I am mentally debating if I could call it (i.e., leaving Steel Tubes) the Second Mistake of my life. My bloated ego made me refuse to compromise with the situation at Steel Tubes and even today it makes me refuse to admit that it was the second mistake of my life. While at Atma Tubes from May 1982 to Dec 1982 every day I went through a nightmarish experience. The frustration was growing exponentially and finally, in Dec 1998, I shifted to join A. K. Dutta at New Delhi in his Consultancy Company, Caldyne Consultants.

MY DAYS WITH CALDYNE

I shifted to Delhi in December 1982 to join A. K. Dutta who had a small consultancy outfit. He provided consultancy to the steel tubes and strips manufacturing industry. Our clients paid us handsomely. For consultations we travelled by air and stayed in five stars hotels at client's cost. Of course, they did benefit greatly from our advice. For two and a half years life in general was cool.

There were many interesting episodes and incidences of this period which I remember vividly. Most of them were on the family front and there is nothing special about these. Maybe just one of them - though on a non-professional front - is worth mentioning here.

DELHIITES

I was staying on the ground floor of a well-constructed two-storied building. The landlord's family occupied the first floor. Mr. Mahan was a rich businessman. His construction companies were operating in the Middle East countries.

On the first day of each month, I used to climb up to his residence and pay the house rent. Once on the first of March or April I went up to pay the rent. I rang the doorbell. Mahan's Nepali servant opened the door and informed me "*Woh to hospital Gaye Hain*" (He has gone to the hospital). I therefore returned with the money.

Next morning the story repeated, and so it did on the third day. I probed to know why Mahan went to the hospital every day so early in the morning. Bahadur clarified, "He got a heart attack four days back, and has been in the hospital since then." During those days in Indore (I cannot vouch for it now), even if anyone had measles, the entire colony would be aware of the news within no time, that too without having mobiles, land lines or email.

Anyway, that evening Smita and I decided to pay a visit to the hospital. Smita was expecting then and it was already showing. We went by scooter in the bitter chilly evening to the hospital, which was ten kilometers from the house. Mohan's room was crowded with his relatives & friends.

After the formal "What happened? And how are you now?" etc., we started for our return ride. Mahan's wife and daughter also climbed down the stairs with us. They summoned their car and drove off. We went to the scooter parking and returned to the house. Mahan's car, and Smita & I reached our house exactly at the same time. I am sure, had it been Indore and for that matter any other place, a pregnant lady would have been given the privilege of a car ride. But then Delhi is Delhi, I suppose.

CALDYNE CONSULTANTS

At Jamshedpur (Tata Nagar) in Bihar, Tata's have a number of manufacturing plants including Indian Tubes where they manufacture Steel Tubes. Anil Kumar Dutta (AKD for short) had worked with Indian Tubes in a managerial position. He along with his few colleagues had left the company and formed CALDYNE (Cal for calories & Dyne for unit of work). They had planned and accordingly set up a factory to manufacture valve tappets and valve seat inserts which are Diesel Engine components. They were financed by Bhagat Duggar, a rich Marwari businessman. But they had miserably failed in their endeavour as they could never manufacture a tappet or an insert in spite of a large investment. Later on, the unit was locked up by the lending Bank.

This group of stalwarts had internal disagreements and so AKD shifted to Delhi and started consulting for Steel Tube & Strip Manufacturing which was his stronghold. He then shifted to Indore and on contract worked with Steel Tubes of India as Works Director for a large compensation package.

As a matter of fact, he had conducted my final selection interview at Steel Tubes. AKD was a metallurgist, and along with his expertise in tube and strip manufacturing he had a very influential personality. He was very bold, and dynamic but extremely egoistic.

His contract with STI was over by January, 1982. Thereafter, he started giving consultancy to other manufacturers from Delhi. Ramesh Baheti, the ambitious CMD of Steel Tubes, considered Dhirubhai as his role model. Steel Tubes had extracted whatever they could from AKD and distanced him after it had become a well-established Company.

My life during my stay at Delhi was cool. We had to provide consultancy and our clients included Bharat Tubes, Avon cycles, Tube Investment (Madras), Steel Tubes & Strips etc.

In the meantime, Caldyne's unit at Jamshedpur started bleeding. AKD sent me to JSR to study the feasibility of the unit. My three-day visit only confirmed what was very evident, that the factory was not at all a viable unit. This unit was being remote controlled by AKD's colleague from Calcutta, and locally managed, rather mismanaged, by AKD's nephew.

AKD therefore dissociated himself from the group and formed Migma Equipment Pvt. Ltd. His brother, Arun Dutta, younger by 12 years, financed Migma. Arun was a geologist (that explains the name Migma), working with Geological Survey of India. He, along with his few colleagues, had obtained a loan for house construction from GSI. He took the lead and constructed a multistoried apartment in Salt Lake. During the process he realised that there was a vast margin between the market selling price & construction cost of a building. He therefore kicked his job, and became a builder/developer. By 1992, he had made enough money to finance Migma.

Readers from Calcutta would recall that during a rainy season a building constructed by him collapsed, killing a few people. Dutta & his wife went on the run and finally, after two months, surrendered to CBI. Incidentally, as of now, he is doing very well.

THE PROJECT

When I was at Delhi, life was cool in spite of the extreme weather conditions. I however was to move out soon. AKD was very keen to set up a manufacturing unit as he thought that consultancy could not continue forever. In retrospect, I believe it was incorrect. We were really very comfortable with consultancy. We should have concentrated and diversified then, but my colleague Bhatia (my batch mate from IIT Kharagpur) & I were quite young for Dutta who was more than twice our age and had a towering personality. We therefore played 'follow the leader'.

AKD's ego then made us plan for setting a factory for Valve Tappets, Valve Seat Inserts & Cylinder Liners, for automobiles and other diesel engine manufacturers. I visited practically all automakers as well as engine manufacturers in the country and carried out a market survey which ascertained that a market did exist for the products.

Based on AKD's technical inputs, I prepared a project report and put in an application for land allotment and loan for the project with Rajasthan State Industrial Development Corporation (RSIDC). It was rejected on the grounds that there was a power shortage in Rajasthan. We then applied to Indian Overseas Bank. Dutta visited IOB's head office at Madras to return with the bad news that our application was turned down.

Then during one of his visits to Indore for consultation with STI, (STI had hired us again to help them in setting up a Cold Rolling Mill) he was advised by Ramesh Baheti to set up the factory at Pithampur, an Industrial location which was 35 Kms from Indore then (Now with a new road 20 Kms). The Govt of Madhya Pradesh was offering 20% subsidy to Industrial projects there.

Incidentally, Dr. Baheti had insisted that I should not be sent on this new consultancy assignment. However, when IDBI (Not IDBI Bank) was sending their team for project evaluation, he agreed to my presence there as I had prepared the project report and financial projections, and no one else in our group could defend it.

One day AKD returned from Indore by flight and announced that we were setting up a plant at Pithampur. The choice of the leader to set up the project was me, primarily because I was more street smart, knew finance and had better leadership qualities than my colleagues. That I was from Indore was the official reason.

Before I shifted to Indore, I recruited a would-be chartered accountant, Pradeep Batra, an intelligent strategist for taking care of Finance Management at Delhi. My happy days at Delhi came to an end and I shifted to Indore.

--xxx---

MY DAYS WITH MIGMA EQUIPMENT
OR
THE SECOND MISTAKE OF MY LIFE

THIS CHAPTER IS DEDICATED TO

PRADEEP BATRA WHO

AS OF NOW OWNS

THREE FOUNDRIES

ACROSS THE COUNTRY

My Days the Second Mistake Of My Life
or
My Days with Migma Equipment

I came to Indore in May 1985 and stayed with my sister for a few months until I got my tenants to vacate our house, built by my father. This was another influencing factor which shaped my future. My father had willed that the house should be my property after my mother's demise. This, unlike many other young Indians, made me not to have the urge to save money and build a house since I already had one. Had I been from a poorer family, I would probably have been richer today.

Time has come to introduce two more characters - Ashok Patankar and Kiran Phadke. Ashok was my classmate from the 4th Standard till BSc-I. After completing BSc, he had joined Cipla as a Sales Representative. He should have had no complaints as the job suited him and he suited the job. But then, he had an itch to do something on his own and so, while I was in Delhi, he contacted me and told me that he wanted to set up a lamination unit. He had picked up Kiran Phadke, a B. Com grad, for this task (or the picking may have been the other way round) Kiran met me in Delhi with the plan.

I invested some funds in the project, helped them with machine selection and "Packtron" was born. They started operating from Ashok's house, making profits from the very first month. Firstly, there was no borrowing and secondly Kiran worked very hard. Kiran treated me like an elder brother and did all sundry jobs for me and my family smilingly, without any expectations. It is unfortunate that he has reportedly taken to the bottle now.

The first set of things to do for setting up the production facilities at Pithampur was to apply for a loan to MPFC, to SBI (State Bank of Indore) for working capital, and for allotment of land to MPAKVN, which I did from my makeshift office at a rented place.

MY FIRST BRIBE

I got into the act and moved on all fronts. I faced the first hurdle. For days and days, I used to visit and meet MPAKVA officials for land allotment. However, there was absolutely no progress and then Kiran advised me to grease the palms of the top boss. Two of us therefore went to the MD's house the next day and after a brief talk I kept an envelope containing Rs.1000/- on the coffee table. He immediately said, "Oh! There is a plot of around two acres in sector one in front of Bajaj Tempo. But a power line goes overhead and there is a pole in the plot. We got the plot of land allotted in a week's time. I had graduated to the law of the land.

One by one I went through various tasks to set up the factory. The project cost was 75 Lacs and I had got a loan sanctioned for Rs.50 lacs with Rs20 lacs subsidy. We were to invest only 5 lacs. But when MPFC went for refinance to IDBI, on IDBI's advice the loan amount was reduced to Rs. 47.5 lacs with Rs7.5 lacs equity. Not bad at all. I will go on record to say that Pradeep Batra (a qualified CA by then), who subsequently became the owner of Migma stated that I had taught him the fundas of project financing.

From 1985 until 1989, I slogged, many times staying overnight in the factory. As the Managing Director of Migma Equipment Pvt. Ltd., I could not have relaxed. Since over twenty years have already gone by, I do not recollect various woes I had to face, but my luck had swung to the worst extreme. Though I had a good team with me, we could not move fast to develop the products. Mr. Dutta had a bad habit of appointing people and promising salaries which drained our budget. He appointed one Mr. Bhatnagar, a retired Labour Commissioner; Pradeep Bhatia, a Metallurgical Engineer. I had recruited Bhonsle, a Metallurgist and Works Manager of PEFCO, a Korus Group Company; and Phandse from PEFCO Pune who was their Machine Shop in-charge. During that period, PEFCO's share was the largest amongst TELCO's tappet and insert suppliers.

One mistake we had made was to set up a project without having sufficient funds and without realising that the promised subsidy would be paid after many years and after a lot of follow up and bribing. God only knows how I managed finances. It was a common practice to over bill the purchases of machinery, take a kickback from the supplier and inject the money back as promoter's funds. The next mistake was our lack of technical knowhow. By the time I realised all this, it was too late. The interest meter of MPFC was already ticking.

Another big problem faced by us was that during that period, for getting a single nut/bolt or a screw we had to go to Indore; and for items of even slightly higher technical content, we had to depend on suppliers from Pune or Mumbai.

The biggest mistake we made (I would say it was a blunder) was that we thought that we had the knowhow to manufacture technically tough castings. For the benefit of non-technical readers, tappets are chilled cast items and VSI & liners are centrifugally cast (as of now VSI are also manufactured using Powder Metallurgy) items. I had never doubted our technical knowledge as AKD, Pradeep and Bhonsle were all metallurgists by profession. As a matter of fact, Bhosle had many years of experience in manufacturing these products.

And yet the choice of machinery was grossly wrong, all selected with the help of these stalwarts and also weighed in by Phandse. I am not a metallurgist and it will not be an exaggeration to say that I did not know the difference between steel and cast iron then. I did not recollect how much time we took to get our tappets approved at Telco Pune, but then we were a bit lucky as PEFCO workers went on strike during those days. Telco had deputed a purchase officer who used to go to Pithampur with me in my car from Indore, and by evening one wooden box full of tappets used to be loaded in the car. I had to drive fast on the return drive of 35 Km with a railway crossing on the way, and load the Box in Vijayant's bus going to Pune by 6PM.Once in a while when we reached late, we would chase and overtake the bus within a few kilometers, and load the box.

Once on our return journey, we stopped at a petrol pump, without observing that it was not petrol, but a diesel pump. Only when the pump attendant filled up the tank, and asked for a much less amount than my expectation that I realised the stupidity. We lost half an hour in emptying and refilling the tank. Thanks to the Birlas, the Ambassador car's engine used/ burnt the residual diesel without any complaint.

ON THE LIGHTER SIDE

For the benefit of the younger generation, I would like to insert a popular joke of those days here. The roads then were full of potholes and travelling by Ambassador was like riding a camel at 40 to 80 Kms per hour. So, the joke goes: Mr. Birla died and was denied entry to heaven. He argued that he had done many good deeds during his stay on earth, such as building so many Birla temples. Chitragupta rejected his plea saying that it was a popularity measure and was done using a lot of black money. Then Mr. Birla thought for a while and said' "I made the Ambassador and anyone who takes a ride in it even for a kilometer, says, 'Hai Ram'". The gates were opened immediately.

GRINDING JOB

Jokes apart, we really had to do a lot of grinding. The tappets had to be ground in a centre-less grinding machine, and also were to be surface ground. The machines selected by us for these operations were not at all capable of grinding to the accuracy required. I told AKD and informed him that I had negotiated for a cylindrical surface grinding machine costing Rs. 60000/- for which I had got a loan sanctioned by the manager of our State Bank of Indore Branch. AKD, however, vetoed my decision, asserting his position. He was the big boss. He was influenced by Avon Cycles' owner Indrajeet Singh Pahwa to go for a second-hand German Machine. We lost considerable time waiting for this machine.

This second-hand German machine was to be sent from Ludhiana to Delhi and then to Indore. In the meantime, we were having lot of inhouse rejection of tappets because of poor accuracy of our machine which was a cup type grinder. I was therefore following up with AKD on a regular basis. Finally, the German machine was dispatched from Ludhiana. Two days later "Replay – Believe It or Not", I got a message from AKD that "The machine bed had broken into two parts during transportation." Probability of a machine bed breaking into two parts during transportation is one in a hundred thousand. But then I am used to such odds.

Here I would like to mention one more fact. In the absence of a proper surface grinding facility in-house, we tried to outsource the operation. We scouted in Pithampur and Indore Industrial areas. The lowest quotation we got was for Rs. 10/- per tappet, while we sold the finished tappet at Rs 8.3 per piece!

Finally, another secondhand machine arrived. One bottleneck got widened.

For centreless grinding we had no choice but to go for HMT make machine costing three times the machine we possessed. With our machine the production rate was very low, and machining required a heart surgeon's skill. The HMT machine was costing Rs 3.5 Lacs while we did not have even that many thousands.

VISIT TO USA

I was young and had not travelled to the USA until then. I therefore applied to the Rotary Club's cultural exchange program. I was interviewed by Rotary Club Officials who included Dr. Athle, a radiologist staying a few houses away from my residence, and Mr. Anantraman, Chief Manager (Credit) SBI (State Bank of Indore). These chaps were so impressed by me during my interview that Dr. Athle came to the house in the evening for informing me that I was selected by their club. This interview later helped me to get a loan from State Bank of Indore for the centreless grinding machine.

Then there was the final interview at Bhopal. Here around fifty candidates had assembled from all over MP. My personality was certainly far above the other candidates, barring a few exceptions. I, therefore, was expecting to get selected for the 40-day cultural exchange program. My interview was over, but I had to stay there till the evening for another round of interview and then would know the final result.

A JOVIAL BREAK

While we waited for the outcome of the interviews, one candidate told all of us a joke which best suited the occasion and which I can't exclude from my diary. Rotarians arranged a cultural exchange programme with the Martians who sent a couple to the Earth. A Sardar family was their host. Over several weeks both the couples exchanged 'cultures'. On the last day of the stay, they decided to exchange partners to experience each other's ways of reproduction.

Next morning, the dejected surd with red ears faced his wife who had a big smile on her face. Mrs. Singh asked him "So, how did things go?" The surd answered "Bull shit. What about you?" "It was fantastic. He undressed and kept twisting his ears until he was at the peak of his excitement. And we enjoyed all the night."

The Surd replied "Oh! Now I get it. That is why that bitch was twisting my ears.

By that evening the result was out. I was amongst the team of four.

LADY LUCK

Just then one consignment of tappets packed in wooden boxes and despatched by a special Matador to TELCO, Jamshedpur, was received there in damaged condition. This forced me to travel to Jamshedpur to sort out the matter. AKD advised me to reject the Rotary Offer and convey my regrets to them. He also offered to sponsor my visit later, which was never to happen. Irrespective of AKD'S advice, I could not have gone to USA in such a situation as at Migma the buck stopped with me.

The HMT machine was priced at Rs 3.5 Lacs while, as I said, we did not have even that many thousands to spare. I had applied to SBI for a loan. Our Bank however was not willing to oblige as our balance sheet was not healthy. This is where I used my contact with Anantraman, chief manager, credit. He practically had to bulldoze the credit manager of the bank's zonal office. Reluctantly the zonal manager stretched the limits, went overboard and provided us the funds.

PACKING & RUST PREVENTION

These are two things I have not been able to master. At Static Transformers we packed the items in various ways, but transit damages to goods have occurred regularly.

At Migma there were a lot of complaints of rusting of tappets and once I decided to coat them with rust preventive solution used for vehicle bumpers. That lot of thousands of tappets was rejected at Pune, and my local representative there had to employ labour to remove the rust preventive coating with kerosene and toothbrush.

THE WAY OUT

In spite of all these obstacles, we had become the largest suppliers of tappets to Telco, we were operating below break even as our turnover was around 2 lacs per month (25000/- tappets per month at Rs 8.30 each). For a project with an investment of 80 lacs, it was just not enough. We had also developed tappets for Mahindra, Eicher etc. However, VSIs were not developed till then. There were no sources of funds to keep the factory alive.

I had already realised that we could not break even with tappets alone and had therefore visited Maruti Udyog for supply of chilled cast camshafts. I had collected the drawings from Maruti's Gurgaon factory, and promised them to deliver the samples within six months. The Maruti officials laughed aloud and said "It is impossible".

But then I did supply samples which promptly got rejected. In spite of a number of attempts we could not make any progress. The reason was simple. They wanted a hardness of more than 50 HRC at the top of the egg-shaped cams and more than 25 HRC on the sides.

Our cams had at all these points a hardness of more than 50 HRC. Technically more than 50 is also more than 25 but then the customer is always right. They theoretically should have specified the requirement as 'More than 25 but less than 50'.

We made more attempts and when we thought we had achieved the results, I went to Maruti with fresh samples. A camshaft was cut and checked. The results were no better and Maruti's quality officials sang the same song. I then asked them to show me a Japanese cam shaft. They agreed immediately. A Japanese cam shaft was brought and promptly cut; hardness checked. It was more than 50 at all three points, identical to our supplies. Maruti officials cut a few more Japanese shafts only to realise that they were unnecessarily rejecting our samples.

We went a step further. Our camshaft was sent for a 1000 hours engine trial.

It was already early 1989 and by that time we were facing severe paucity of funds and had bled so much that on a couple of occasions our matador would stop half way to Pithampur with its empty diesel tank.

OUR DELHI OPERATIONS

At Delhi, AKD had set up another company by the name Gallium Equipment and had made my colleague Yogesh Bhatia its MD. This company was to manufacture equipment required by steel tube and strip manufacturing plants. This in my view was a wise decision. For all of us in the group, steel tube and strip was our core area of competence. We knew these things like the back of our hand. Further, for funding, AKD had roped in Mr. Mehta, a financially sound person who manufactured cold rolling mills, the main equipment required for the strip plant.

Yogesh was sent to the USA for getting trained with an American company manufacturing strip storage equipment. Gallium had started operations from a rented factory shed at Faridabad. This company (Gallium) supplied its first equipment costing around Rs.20 lacs to the cold rolling mill of STI. The equipment never worked satisfactorily and was later bought back at a depreciated value of Rs.13 Lacs.

See the irony - one got paid Rs.20 Lacs for equipment which did not work satisfactorily while we had to struggle hard for a tappet worth Rs.8.30 each.

SEPARATION

Anyway, I will end this chapter by narrating one final episode of my separation from the group. Yogesh was technically a sound mechanical engineer. With shrewd Batra to manage finances and AKD to get orders with advance payments, Gallium was bound to do well. Moreover, they were operating in our known field. They had also recruited Anique Husain, Yogesh's IIT batch mate.

But at Indore we were struggling hard and somehow managing the show. While people at Delhi travelled by air, I had to frequently travel by train /bus to Pune, Igatpuri, Jamshedpur. My only hope was the Maruti camshaft. This, if successful, would have given us good returns as its selling price was Rs.80 while the cost of raw material was Rs 18. Further, Maruti was to buy 20 to 30 thousand cam shafts per month.

In the process I started getting step motherly treatment. Once, when I went to Delhi, at the same time AKD had invited a young lad working at Tata Exports, Dewas for an interview. This diploma holder stayed in a good hotel with his wife while I was asked to stay put in the office, we had just vacated but was still in our possession. It did not even have drinking water and I stayed thirsty throughout the night. Not only that, this young diploma holder and his wife went for a Delhi Darshan tour by private cab; all expenses paid. All this was adding insult to my injury. This young lad was recruited and sent to USA & Japan for training with collaborators. In return, he quit Gallium soon after and started a factory with a rich partner. They manufactured the same equipment as those of Gallium and became a competitor.

There were many such incidences which increased my frustration. I brought these to AKD's attention, but to no avail. It was a typical case of how some parents treat gifted and ordinary siblings differently. Things had gone beyond my tolerance limits. AKD on the other hand was assuming that I was the culprit of Migma's poor performance. As I stated earlier, AKD was a credulous person, and there were many people in Delhi who played Naradmuni. (A mythological character responsible for creating misunderstanding and petty quarrels among gods & goddesses.)

In the meantime, AKD suffered a mild heart attack. He was recuperating at Batra's house. That is where we discussed my separation. I resigned after my settlement was chalked out. Then I proceeded to our, sorry, their office, at Vasant Vihar.

It was around 2 pm. A postman delivered a letter from Maruti Udyog Ltd. which I opened and read. It said, "We are pleased to inform you that after 1000 hours of engine testing your camshaft has been found to perform satisfactorily and you are therefore requested to supply a pilot lot of 100 Nos. at the earliest."

I wish this goddamn letter had come a week earlier. Or I wish I were sick / bedridden for a week and my visit to Delhi had been delayed. But insha-alla it was not to happen. I had committed the second mistake of my life. I had resigned from Migma. I should have been a little more patient. I should have tolerated the situation for a week more.

If I was asked to evaluate my performance of Migma days, I would say I had created the base of a very good foundry. Though I was not a metallurgist and had no machine shop experience, I had still set up a green field project, developed difficult cast products at Pithampur which was only a desert land 35 kms. from Indore, practically without any funds.

EPILOGUE

I lost touch with Migma group soon after I left them, except for Pradeep Batra who visited my house once in a while. After I left, the Indore / Pithampur operations were handled by Anique Husain for some time. Then the reigns were handed over to Pradeep Batra, in spite of being a non-technical person, he brought the company to an externally good condition with Maruti camshafts to back him up.

Later Migma was bought by a German company at a premium. Migma & Gallium parted company with Pradeep taking up Migma. He is now the CEO of Mahle group in India and his net worth is in crores. He even has started another company in Haryana where he is the sole owner and is doing very well.

Gallium was sold to a Japanese company and is in deep financial trouble as I recently learnt from Arun Dutta whom I met during my last Calcutta visit. Anique Hussein was reportedly found to be making money on the side and hence was shown the door, AKD has retired from business. Arun Dutta is doing well as a builder in Calcutta.

--xxx---

THE THIRD MISTAKE OF MY LIFE

THIS CHAPTER IS DEDICATED TO

MY COLLEAGUES

WHO

HAVE SLOGGED WITH ME

AT STATIC TRANSFORMERS

The Third Mistake of My Life

BEFORE I TOOK OVER STATIC TRANSFORMER

Having left Migma I started working with Ashok and Kiran at Packtron. It was too small an outfit to earn enough for the three of us. But then I had no job in hand. Having worked as the MD of Migma for more than three years where I did the entire decision making, the idea of going for a job was a bit difficult to digest. Except for very major policy decisions, and once in a while following up on AKD's *fatwas* (orders), I had the last word; be it purchases, recruitment, or any other aspect of running the factory. This had made me plan to start something of my own. That is why I strongly feel that **"One Is What One Goes Through"**.

Packtron had by then diversified into vacuum moulding of plastic, to manufacture bathroom cabinets. Unfortunately, they had not made any attempts to improve on the sales figures. The first thing I did on joining them was to start a marketing drive.

Kiran was upset by my presence and within a couple of weeks asked for separation. Ashok joined him and I too wisely stepped out with my investment as I did not want to be stuck with a small-time business. Years later, on the verge of bankruptcy, Kiran and Ashok split up. While Kiran took to the bottle, Ashok stuck to vacuum moulding and struggled hard. Later, he struck a gold mine in the form of moulded parts for commercial vehicles. He is now rolling in crores.

I started an employment agency (refer "TALHUNT") and started taking up sundry consultancy assignments, though unsuccessfully. Later I also got into the construction business. This was during the period July 1989 to Dec 1991.

THE THIRD MISTAKE OF MY LIFE – PART I

At Talhunt, my income was drying up and my investment in the building was badly stuck. I was therefore looking for other avenues. Then I came across Ravi Abhyankar who had recently split from his longtime partner in a spring washer manufacturing factory. He therefore was in the same boat.

He and I learnt about Static Transformers Private Limited. This company was doing a business with annual turnover of around Rs 25 lacs. The company was formed in 1965 and had been manufacturing transformers/rectifiers for the Indian Navy, Centre for Advanced Technology (Indore), Instrumentation Ltd. (Jaipur), and a few other companies. The principal shareholder was one Mr. Nanal. He was quite old and wanted to retire.

Santosh Deshmukh, a CA by profession, was an advisor to the Company. Santosh was a self-made man and distantly related to Smita. I studied the company's balance sheet and it looked good. I asked Mr. Moghe, a retired JCO of Navy who was working as a director of the company, to provide me with market projections. My question was, "Can we cross a turnover of one crore in a couple of years?" and he promptly came up with the data to substantiate the marketing scope. After a considerable financial analysis and several meetings with Santosh, Moghe and Nanal, we decided to take over. All my savings were used up to pay for the shares of Static Transformers Pvt. Ltd.

THIS WAS THE THIRD MISTAKE OF MY LIFE WHICH I WAS TO REALISE ONLY OVER THE YEARS.

SETBACKS

Basically, the balance sheet of Static was all fraud. Rs. 6 lacs out of Rs 16 lacs receivables were Liquidated Damages deducted by the client for late deliveries. This I learnt when I sent Praveen, an intelligent young lad who looked after accounts, on an all-India collection drive. We were suppliers to shipyards covering the entire coastline i.e., Mumbai, Goa, Cochin, Vizag, Calcutta. This resulted in high travelling costs. Secondly, a nearby company which owed us Rs 2 lacs had gone bankrupt. I could have digested this, a loss of Rs8 lacs, as I never say die. But then an additional half of the receivables were towards material rejected by the clients.

In my opinion, the chartered accountants in India are not true to their profession. They only help their clients to camouflage the figures. This has been well established by Satyam's disaster a couple of years ago. Smita very rightly says that I believe everyone on face value. Well, there are two philosophies - you trust someone until he / she proves untrustworthy, or you do not trust someone until he/ she proves to be trustworthy. I unfortunately follow the first philosophy but then that is my nature. I had believed the audited balance sheet.

By the time I learnt all the facts, it was too late. Worse than all the above was the fact that all the bills purchased by United Western Bank were fake and that no payment was expected against those bills. The inventory did not match the working capital drawn from the bank.

I could even have overcome all this, but Static had no technology available for the products it claimed to be manufacturing. With such a background, I started working. In spite of all these odds, in the very first year, we jumped from Rs.25 lacs to 40 lacs turnover, and made profit, but it was not a smooth ride.

We had partially executed a thirty-five lacs order from ECIL for transformers meant for installation in a nuclear power plant. One lot of transformers, after thorough inspection by Papi Reddy of ECIL at Indore was sent to Hyderabad, but the same got rejected as some liquid was oozing out of it. Static, which boasted of manufacturing dry type transformers, had failed miserably. Fortunately, in spite of the cost of re-transportation of transformers to Indore, reworking and sending the material back, we did make some real profit.

93-94 & ONWARDS

In this financial year, again, our turnover went up from 40 to 55 lacs and we ended up with real profit. Next year we went up to Rs. 85 lacs, and further to Rs.98 lacs by 95-96. But then onwards things took a different turn.

DOWNFALL

Instrumentation Ltd. which was one of our major customers closed down. As a result, our turnover suddenly plummeted. We went into the red and entered a vicious circle of reduced volume of business, increased debt, additional interest cost and more & more losses. There was yet another reason which caused further strain and that was our attempt to enter into business with the Indian Air Force.

THE GPUS

Sometime in 1994 I visited group captain Jayanta Apte at his New Delhi residence. The idea was to explore a business opportunity with the Indian Air force as our order book was not very healthy and we had heard rumours of likely closure of Instrumentation Limited, Jaipur. I should not have used the word rumours as it really closed down soon after.)

Jayanta, my cousin, was a typical *fauji (army man)*. But unlike many, he was technically quite knowledgeable. He immediately responded by asking me if I could develop a 400 Hz light weight GPU for Jaguar & Mirage Aircrafts. Before I continue further, I will have to elaborate on 400 Hz and GPU.

400 HZ'S POWER:

The electric power we consume at home is 50 Hertz (Hz), 230 Volts AC. The power we consume for larger equipment (e.g., in factories) is generally three phase 50Hz, 415 Volts. The power consumed by aircraft equipment is 400 Hz 3 Phase, 200 Volts; the main reason being the motors which rotate, the transformers and other equipment which work at 400 Hzs. are many times smaller and hence lighter than the equipment which operate with 50 Hzs. I will not like to go into further details as this might be a bit too much for non-technical readers.

GROUND POWER UNIT (GPU)

Ground Power Unit is a source of power which supplies power to an Aircraft from outside through a cable. When a fighter aircraft starts, the pilot has to first switch on many avionic instruments and set these up. He has to check the functioning (performance) of a number of machines and instruments on board, such as a computer, radar, gyroscope etc. All these equipment take time to get set. The IAF calls this aircraft alignment. It takes around 10 minutes. Once the task is complete, the pilot starts the engine of the aircraft and aircraft's own power generation takes over, cutting off GPUs power.

IAF'S JAGUAR & MIRAGE FLEET

The fighter aircrafts normally operate from a base station. They are parked in blast pens when not in use. Blast pens for fighter aircrafts are what a garage is for a car. These Blast pens are spread along the airstrip and are far apart from each other. As a result, one GPU is required at every blast pen so that several aircraft can be started simultaneously as and when required. The requirement of GPUs is therefore sizable. Further, the aircrafts keep moving from one base to another for exercises. For example, a squadron shifts from Ambala to Gwalior. GPUs would then be required at Gwalior. The GPUS are therefore transported from Ambala to Gwalior using a transport aircraft like AN32.

The IAF was using imported GPUs which were quite old and had become quite unreliable. HAL Lucknow had also developed GPUs for these Jaguar & Mirage aircrafts. The problem faced by IAF in using these GPUs during that time was that they were quite huge and bulky. Each GPU weighed over 3000 Kgs. The weight and size of the GPU was such that one AN 32 could carry only one GPU in its belly at a time. And reportedly each trip of AN 32 cost as much as Rs.5 lacs. The second big problem faced by the user was frequency fluctuations on application of loads and removal of loads. The reason behind this was that these GPUs were rotating generators. They rotated at 2000 RPM (revolving 2000 times every minute). Say you are to drive a car at a fixed speed of 40 Km per hour. You are driving on a plain road and suddenly reach a slope of a flyover. Your speed is bound to reduce until you press the accelerator and do the correction. Similarly, when you come to the peak and start going down, you are bound to cross (exceed) your fixed speed.

To minimize this problem, they used a GPU with a capacity of 35 KVA (around 50 HP) while the actual power required by the aircraft was much less, around one third. One should visualize two passengers going in Nano, and other two in I20, both without breaks (there is no braking facility in diesel generators) at a fixed speed of 40 KMs per hour. When the cars pass under a tree, two huge apes jump onto the cars. The speed of the Nano car will drop more while I20's speed will be less affected. Similarly, if the apes suddenly jump out the cars speed of Nano will shoot up more than that of I20. So, more the power less the speed (and hence frequency) variation.

Jayanta Apte asked me if I could make a lightweight GPU with less frequency variation. My instant reaction was "Yes, why not?" He immediately took me to his boss, Air Cmdr. Arora (Refer chapter: Miraculous Memory) who happened to be my senior at NITIE. After discussion he ended up saying, "Mr. Joshi (we had not recognized each other then, else it would have been simply Shrikant) we cannot place an order with you just like that. However, if you make a GPU and demonstrate its capability to IAF, we will buy 108 GPUs." During that period the price of each GPU was around 15 lacs. Big market for a company with a turnover of less than a crore.

WHY YES

I am not an electrical or electronics engineer, but have reasonably good common sense. We used to supply transformers to Instrumentation Ltd. who were importing the control cards and other components from a Japanese company. They assembled and sold UPS. For the benefit of non-technical readers, I will have to throw some light on how a UPS works.

UPS or uninterrupted power supply provides power when the incoming power goes off. UPS uses Battery power to do this. The basic principle of working is that it first converts the incoming power from sinusoidal waveform to a flat waveform i.e., DC; and then it reconverts this back to AC power using a technology called PWM. This being done electronically; the parameters of power can be controlled very accurately. To give a vague analogy let us say you make a computer play 'Sa Re Ga

Ma Pa Dha Ni Sa - Sa Ni Dha Pa Ma Ga Re Sa' (the basic notes in Hindustani classical music) 50 times every second. The computer can keep this speed constant in spite of the listener changing the volume of the speaker.

I thought of making a GPU which synthesized power from ordinary power produced by an ordinary generator. The blueprint of my GPU was crystal clear in my mind.

KJELL ACKERMAN & VIBEKE

This Danish Couple owned two companies at Odense in Denmark. AXA Power & Axle Ackerman. Nilesh had once sent them a fax trying to source material required for manufacturing transformers. They had replied giving us addresses of suppliers and also giving details of products manufactured by them. They used to manufacture static frequency converters (SFCs) of 35 KVA or higher rating for the aviation industry. These SFCs used to be fitted in aircraft hangers and supplied synthesized power with a frequency of 400 Hzs to the aircraft in the hangar. In India however, only one attempt of using such SFCs in hangers was made by Indian Airlines till then. The attempt had reportedly failed. The equipment supplied by an Indian company had developed faults in a short period. Indian Airlines had given up trying to use these units.

MY VISIT TO DENMARK AND ITS SIDE BENEFIT.

For manufacturing the promised GPU, I had to have Ackerman's support. I therefore planned to visit Denmark. Earlier I had been to Denmark and had met Ackerman but only formally. This time however he was quite friendly. The couple accompanied me for all my meals including one dinner at their house. Vibeke also took great care to make my stay comfortable. She ensured that I got proper vegetarian food at the factory canteen.

One of the reasons why Ackerman was influenced / impressed with the Indian market was that though Air India and Indian Airlines were the only companies who operated aircrafts in India during those days, the Indian Air Force offered additional numbers. Another reason may have been that, during our factory visit, in spite of my being a mechanical engineer (and that too an Indian), I was able to give him a few suggestions which cut his manufacturing costs.

MY SUGGESTIONS

(Non-engineers may skip this section)

He showed me a product he called neutral compensator (NC in short). When installed it would equalise three phase voltages and even could produce a phase if the same was missing. NC also reduced wasteful neutral current and provided neutral in the event of a neutral break. Now, we at Static manufacture Neutral Compensators and market them in India.

He had fitted an overload relay on top to avoid the Neutral Compensator getting damaged due to overloading. I suggested them to use MCB instead. It was a cheaper option.

Secondly, he was making auto transformers (dimmer type) and selling them with KVA rating. As a result, he had to wind heavy gauge copper. It was a funny concept to sell autotransformers by KVA rating. I asked him why not sell at the current rating. He explained that that was the norm followed by the Danish market.

I suggested that he could get copper wire in variable diameter so that he could at least save half the copper. "At least break your winding in two or three parts so that at higher voltages, thinner wire could be used." I suggested. Though an electrical engineer himself, he called his design engineer Dhal, and in Danish talked to him. After their fifteen-minute discussion in Danish which was Greek / Latin to me, he turned around and smilingly told me that I was right.

By the end of my visit, he had agreed to develop a 4 KVA SFC which would work on 230 Hz 50 Hz power, a nonstandard item as their product range started at 35 KVA. He agreed to supply it free of cost. We had become project partners. We jointly planned to make a novel GPU based on SFC Technology for the first time in the history of the World's Aviation Industry.

THE GPU

Within a few months the SFC arrived at Indore. In size it was hardly bigger than a briefcase. We had bought a Honda 6 KVA petrol generator and had built a makeshift three-wheel trolley to carry the contraption as we were only to prove that it works. It was only meant for proving the concept, what is called 'Technology Demonstration'.

Jayanta Apte was by chance at Indore and we took him to our factory. As we switched on the unit, one component (IGBT) burst like a firecracker. Within the next few days, we procured a new IGBT. But the result was the same. Even Indian IGBT burst with the same sound effect. After the third unsuccessful trial we decided to send the unit back to Denmark.

Unplanned expenditure had already eaten into borrowed funds. We had no venture capital. Sending Neelesh was however necessary so that he would understand the unit better while it got repaired at AXA POWER. Nilesh carried the SFC to Denmark and returned with the repaired SFC within a week. Shortly we were ready for trials.

AMBALA TRIALS

After extensive in-house trials, we wrote to IAF that we were ready to demonstrate our technology. Normally no GPU is allowed to be tested on the aircraft without thorough trials at the factory by IAF's evaluation wing. Jayanta however pulled the right strings and we were asked to give trials at Air Force Station, Ambala.

I, along with my team, carried the GPU to Ambala. Our first couple of trials failed as the GPU used to trip instantly. After exchanging faxes with Akerman a few times via Indore, we tuned the SFC and informed IAF that we were again ready for trials.

The reluctant pilot climbed into the cockpit of a Jaguar aircraft to which we had connected our cable. We switched on our GPU power. One by one the pilot was checking the functioning of various equipment on board and after about ten minutes he pushed the start button. The sound of

Jaguar's engine was far more deafening than that of a Chetak helicopter which I had experienced earlier.

After a few minutes the pilot switched off the engine and all the loads one by one. This starting exercise was repeated two more times. The performance of our GPU was identical. Incidentally, the frequency of Honda generators varied from 45 to 55 but the frequency of our SFC remained dot 400 throughout. Even the voltage varied only marginally.

After the third trial the pilot opened the cockpit and removed his helmet. The pilot who had reluctance on his face while climbing into the cockpit was now beaming with a big smile. He raised his hand up and with a thumbs up pose said, "ROGER".

He climbed down and talked to us for twenty minutes. That the frequency had remained 400 Hz dot (it had to) and even voltage fluctuation was far less had amazed him. **For the first time in the world a non-electrical engineer had produced an Aladdin's lamp for the aviation industry, specially the IAF.**

Over the next few days, the trials were repeated on different aircraft. Only once did the trial fail. That was because the petrol tank was empty. We were too excited to watch the fuel level. We returned to Indore with a report of 40 successful trials.

Ripley's believe it or not: Incidentally I learnt a very interesting fact while I was at Ambala. In every sortie of a fighter aircraft, the pilot is physically so stressed that he loses as much as half a Kg weight. To compensate for this loss, they are given a special meal before the flight.

THE THIRD MISTAKE OF MY LIFE- PART II

Having yelled eureka, I thought I had done it. But it was this very project that was one major cause of our downfall. Having proven our concept with a 300 Kg makeshift GPU we were in a day-dreaming mode. And that was not without reason.

LORD GANESH

One day during that period I visited Uday's house. There I saw a poster of Lord Ganesh hanging on the wall. There was a list on the side giving hundred and eight names of the Lord. Though I am not a believer, I am a Hindu by culture and I knew that Lord Ganesh gets the privilege of getting worshipped before any other God, (including his father) in any religious function.

Our GPU too would have to be started before any Jaguar / Mirage – 2000 was to go for a mission. So, I suggested why not name our GPUs rather than using numbers for identification. Further we were hoping for getting an order for over 100 odd units. This suited us, as long as the numbers did not exceed 108. Accordingly, our first three GPUs were named GANESHA, VINAYAK & GANPATI. All other names have remained unused.

My daydreaming went a step further. We had already supplied Trishul Missile Launcher Starter Panel. We regularly supplied Helicopter Starting Rectifiers. We once had received an order for chokes for Bofors Guns and had supplied the same to Armament Factory at Jabalpur. We had supplied panels for AK 47 guns to be fitted on INS Betwa. We were also developing gas turbine starting rectifiers. And so, I thought: whenever we went for a public issue, our ad would be captioned 'WE START THE WAR'. Anyway, daydreams are not day-realities.

BACK TO REALITY

As I said earlier, having proven our concept, our getting into daydreaming mode was not without reason.

GPU based on our concept would have very low power consumption and hence would result in a considerable amount of saving of diesel. Cost of transportation from one base to another would reduce drastically as many GPUs could be accommodated in one AN32 transport Aircraft. Further the GPU, when used for powering aircraft parked in the hanger, could operate on ordinary power available there. That way they would not cause any noise and air pollution as the engine generator would be kept idle. And the most important factor was that there would be no failed starts, no damage to costly avionics equipment as the frequency would remain dot 400 Hz and voltage variation would be minimal (or nil).

In spite of all this, we were not to get any order for the next five years from the Indian Air Force. The efforts we put in for getting a developmental order of three GPUs were unprecedented. We had left no stone unturned but all our persuasion was futile. We must have spent more than ten lacs in travelling to meet various people. By the time we received the developmental order, our total investment in this project had crossed Rs. Twenty-five lacs without considering interest charges on the amount spent.

However, before I write further about our attempts to get the developmental order, I will try to answer an obvious question any reader, especially with an Indian business background might rightfully ask. Why did you not call off the project and stop spending more and more? Some would use jargon and say, "your good money was chasing bad money". Others would say, "you should have stopped spending money and considered whatever you had spent as sunk cost, cut back your losses and should have just called it quits." Some would criticise that I was emotionally attached to our product and behaved like an idiot.

There were many reasons as to why we did not drop the project; the most important one was my experience at Migma. The day I resigned and accepted the settlement, Maruti's letter confirming that our camshaft was approved was received. Migma had hit a goldmine. I had learnt a big lesson: **"Be patient, accept and make short term compromises for long term gains."**

Supplying a hundred or even twenty GPUs to IAF would again have been a goldmine. But then who knew that we would get the order only after around five years and that too for only three GPUs?

STATIC PROPOSES & IAF DISPOSES

On our return from Ambala, we sent our proposal for supply of GPUS to IAF based on our design. The same was promptly (i.e., in a couple of months) turned down. I therefore took an appointment with ACS Eng. B at AHQ (I still do not know what it stands for, however, it was he who had turned down the proposal) and met him. He told me I did not know what power the aircraft needed to start. This was in spite of having supposedly read the report.

Our offer had gone to Air HeadQuarters through Western Air Command where Jayanta was a group captain. During that time his boss was Air Commodore Janakiraman. From some other officer, I later heard that our proposal was turned down by the then ACS Eng. B as he was quite anti Janakiraman.

This rejection was a big shock to us. It had shattered our dreams. We had no clue as to what to do and whom to approach.

THE LONGEST WILD GOOSE CHASE

I will not be able to jot down various attempts we made to get an order for supply of GPUs chronologically as it would require a lot of research and it may not be worth the effort. I therefore plan to write about it as I remember it.

POLITICAL APPROACHES

I tried approaching IAF's top brass through politicians for quite some time. There is not much sense in narrating all of them, but in the process, I met Mrs. Sheela Gautam and Mrs. Sumitra Mahajan, both MPs, Baburao Paranjape, another BJP MP. George Fernandez and Mulayam Singh Yadav when they were the Defence Ministers, another Yadav, an MLA from Jhansi and late Shri Madhavrao Sindhia. However, none of my efforts yielded results.

Once I was to go to Delhi and had boarded the aircraft at Indore. It was an Indore- Bhopal- Gwalior- Delhi, hopping fight. We flew to Bhopal but the aircraft could not land as it was raining very heavily there. The aircraft returned to Indore. After half an hour we boarded again and flew over Bhopal.

This time a very senior congress MP was sitting next to me. He was to get down at Gwalior. As luck would have it, the aircraft could not even land at Gwalior and we went straight to Delhi. This MP was earlier a very senior minister in the congress Government but had resigned from the cabinet as his name was included in some scam. We talked for a while and I narrated my GPU case to him. He asked, "What is the value of your project?" In reply I said, "Thirteen crores, assuming we get an order for a hundred GPUs." While the plane was getting ready to land, he said, "The project is too small for me."

Sheela Gautam was curtly denied appointment by the IAF officers; Sumitra Mahajan knew George Fernandez well and hence directed me to him. He was the Defence Minister then. Babulal Paranjape and George Fernandez met at least once a week and were good friends. He also recommended my case to George Fernandez.

I must have met George Fernandez four times. The first time when I met him, he had just become the Minister. He used to pick up the phone himself. There were no gates at the entrance of his bungalow (He had got the same removed.) and he was accessible to all. I was also pleasantly surprised when he spoke to me in Marathi. This fire brand Defence Minister promised to get me justice and took the details of the case from me.

The last time I met him was when he came to Indore for canvassing for the election, four or five years after my first meeting with him. It was late in the evening. I was accompanied by Mrs. Sumitra Mahajan and her son, Milind. We went to his room in the Government Rest House. He said "Joshi, I tried, but they say that yours is a small company and cannot be relied upon." To which I said "Sir true, we are small, but we too are Indians and not Pakistanis and why should we not be given an opportunity?" At the end he replied, "I will try once again, but I cannot push them to the wall, else they will retaliate."

He did not become the minister in the next Lok Sabha. We had lost the last twig (There is a Hindi saying which means a floating twig is the last hope for the one who is drowning).

APPROACHES THROUGH IAF OFFICERS

I must have talked to and met n number of retired IAF officers who work as liaison agents, countless times but these yielded no results and there is nothing interesting to include their names or describe my visits. I even went to Dehradun to meet a retired Air Marshal who was known to be a close friend of the chief of air staff at that time.

Only two officers' stories I am including here. One relates to Air Marshal Tipnis who flew a MIG 21 (popularly known as Flying Coffin) even when he became Chief of Air Staff, and the other related to Air Marshal Janakiraman who was instrumental in getting us a developmental order for 3 GPUs.

AIR MARSHAL TIPNIS

A. M. Tipnis was the chief of Western Air Command during the time of our Ambala trials. One day I learnt from Jayanta that he was flying to Indore to meet his in-laws or some other relatives. Chief of WAC is a very senior post. If we could contact him, he could certainly help us get the order. We therefore planned to contact him one way or another.

Tipnis is a typical Maharashtrian surname. Normally, Tipnises are CKPs. (Chandrasenia Kayasha Prabhu). But this much information was too little to find a contact. We contacted all CKP friends and acquaintances but to no avail. There was no Google to help us then. AM Tipnis came to Indore & returned without any clue to us.

Then I checked with Sachhit Chitale whose wife was from a CKP family. He informed me that he knew Tipnis' brother-in-law at Nagpur, a Gujrathi gentleman. He even got me his telephone number. After talking to this chap on the phone I rushed to Nagpur to meet him. I do not remember his actual name, but everyone called him Pappu.

Pappu was an insurance agent and therefore a friendly person. He also knew half the population of Nagpur on a first name basis. He knew the top brass of United Western Bank's Zonal Office and offered me help to solve our banking issues which he did subsequently. Within an hour of meeting him, he called AM Tipnis at Delhi and fixed up an appointment for me the next day.

I flew to Delhi the same evening and went to Western Air Command the next day as per schedule. I was received at the gate, as if I was a king's relative. AM Tipnis gave me a patient hearing and agreed to help me. I am sure he must have tried but the end result was still a lemon.

Later, A.M. Tipnis went on to become the chief of Air staff, but it became very difficult to contact him. Once I was able to talk to him on the phone when he said something which meant that his officers had turned down the proposal. I recall that once, just to meet him, I attended Pappu's son's marriage at Nagpur. During that meeting too he expressed regret.

THE HONEST TAMILIAN

At the time we took trials at Ambala, Jayanta Apte was a group Captain at Western Air Command in Delhi. His boss was one Air Commodore Janakiraman. From Jayanta Apte, I had heard a lot about him. He was an honest Tamil Brahmin and a no-nonsense man. I had never met him till then.

By 1998, he had become Air Marshall and was stationed at Nagpur, one step away from becoming the AOM. We had become quite familiar with IAF's working and knew that he was to become AOM prior to his retirement. AOM stands for Air Officer Maintenance. Air Officer Maintenance at Air HeadQuarters is the second highest ranked post in the technical wing of the Air Force. For all major purchases of GPUs, amongst other equipment, his is the last word. He is practically the king.

As a future AOM, he was important to us and hence I called him from Indore. He did not know me and hence was surprised when I asked him for an appointment. I told him that I was not a supplier of IAF but for the Indian Navy. I did not give him any clue on phone regarding the purpose of my proposed meeting.

He agreed to meet me. I therefore went to Nagpur and by the end of our hour-long meeting he had understood my plight as well as our proposal. He was genuinely impressed by my perseverance and also had understood the advantages of our GPU. He said, "I can call Tipnis Sir now and tell him about your GPU, but then it is not right, I am not involved in the matter."

He then went on to become AOM and I met him once in his office in Delhi. He promised to help us. But then onwards our communication stopped as he refused to talk to me even on phone. It was a period when wives of technical officers of IAF were protesting against unequal compensation to technical officers as compared to pilots. They had come down on the streets to demonstrate. Later I learnt that he was afraid that even his phone could be tapped by Vigilance.

THE END RESULT

I have no clue as to what he did, nor what procedure was followed, but finally we got the tender for 3 SFC based GPUs of 12 KVA in the beginning of 2000 i.e., after four years of our Ambala trials.

We got excited but not thrilled. I immediately tried to contact Ackerman. He however did not respond to our mails. Without his support we could not have built the GPUs. We could not even quote. We called up AXA Power, only to learn that he was not available. Then one day we heard from the GM, Marketing of AXA Power stating that Ackerman had sold the Company to an American Company which basically was into manufacturing of nuts and bolts. Even in Snakes and Ladder no snake brings you back to square one. But this news did it to us.

Nevertheless, we quoted on the basis of an assumption of our would-be tie up with AXA Power and I planned a visit to AXA Power for working out collaboration details. We did come to a working agreement, but then we were to pay much more than what was agreed with Ackerman.

No other supplier had quoted for the tendered GPUs. Being the single party who quoted, we got the developmental order for around Rs.40 lacs. The power rating of the GPU was enhanced so that it could start two aircrafts at a time. The engine power was also enhanced so that the engine generator could work even at Leh (due to lack of oxygen, the power of the engine reduces at high altitude, and hence we had to go for an engine of higher capacity.) We received the order sometime in May 2000. We were relieved but not elated as we were already worn out. The costs had already gone up and profit margin reduced. Anyway, we thought 'all is well that ends well'.

THE THIRD MISTAKE OF MY LIFE- PART III

THE FIRST PROTOTYPE

We built a GPU which involved my visit to Denmark for negotiations, carrying out detailed engineering design. We encountered a mechanical failure during the first inspection, but then such events are part of the game. The GPU was finally inspected but not cleared for actual aircraft trials. Reason: we could not demonstrate that it switches off if the frequency drops below 380 or goes beyond 420 Hz. I was called to Delhi for a grand meeting to discuss this issue. I have narrated the discussions of the meeting in an earlier chapter; ultimately the GPU was cleared for field trials.

In the meanwhile, however, as our luck would have it, MBSB our bank (Maharashtra Brahman Sahakari Bank) got a court order and froze our assets which in turn froze all of us. The bank freezing our assets is yet another story and I shall write about it some other time. We had to convince the bank that frozen assets would not yield money, only liquid assets do. This took us a lot of time and after a gap of three months we got bank clearance and shipped the GPU to Gwalior.

THE GWALIOR TRIALS

The trials of 100 hours were completed without any problem. I was at Gwalior when the trials started. The only apprehension I had was whether our GPU would start two Mirage-2000 aircrafts simultaneously. But then on the very first day, our GPU worked as expected and surprised all the officers and others involved in the trials. The pilots were surprised to observe zero frequency variation.

Luckily a Jaguar detachment had landed at Gwalior for some exercise and so our GPU was tried out on Jaguars too. I returned to Indore a happy man.

THE AMBALA TRIALS T

The Gwalior trials ended in a month's time and the Jaguar detachment which was returning to Ambala carried our GPU with them. For the first time in my life GOI had paid for transportation which was in our scope of work.

HICCUPS AGAIN

It was time for us to plan for ETRP (Expected time for receipt of payment) for our supply of the first GPU. But we were not to receive the payment for the next two years.

Reports of our GPU were received from Ambala and Gwalior by AHQ & DGAQA (Quality wing for such items under MOD). Both the reports were excellent and had all the praise for our GPU, but for only two suggestions. Both the Stations wanted that the GPU should not comprise of two trolleys but should be built on a single trolley; and that the tires should be of solid rubber rather than air filled tires which we had used. This was totally contrary to the specifications. Had we built the GPU on a single trolley it would never have been approved for trials but would have been rejected on the basis of non-compliance to specification.

THE CUSTOMER HAS THE RIGHT TO BE WRONG

If I were a decision maker, I would establish a Supplier Court just like a Consumer Court. But then who am I? The DGAQA asked us to carry out these modifications, which meant bringing back the GPU to Indore, redesigning the mechanicals and re-building the GPU. In terms of time and money, it would have taken at least three months and more than two lacs to carry out the changes.

We faced a deadlock situation. The DGAQA was asking us for modification prior to clearing our payment and giving us a clearance to manufacture the next two units. We had no money left to do it and were theoretically right to claim the payment. In principle, they should have accepted the GPU as it was and asked us to build the second one with the required changes desired by IAF. It was however a no-go situation. In a meeting I therefore agreed to carry out the modifications in the first

GPU after the second and the third GPUs were supplied. (And after we received the payment). This was accepted and agreed by IAF as well as DGAQA.

In spite of giving this undertaking, we did not receive the payment for a long time. It was only after Air Marshal Desai, the AOM during July 2005, intervened and pressured the Secretary, Defence Production, that we got 95% payment for the first GPU. (Refer to the chapter "Miraculous Memory")

We then went on to build the second and the third GPU. These in my opinion were cute in design. We supplied and got a major payment. The remaining balance amount of one lac and few thousands was received only after three years, thanks to our babus!

Before we brought it from Ambala, this GPU had logged 1500 hours with an engine generator and operated for 5000 odd hours using ordinary power which theoretically had saved enough diesel to pay for its own cost. But then who is bothered about savings of ten lacs or so in a defence budget of over Rs 30,000 crores?

THE BULK ORDER

In spite of having supplied three GPUs which worked as expected and got highly appreciated, we never received any bulk order from IAF. As I said earlier, Lord Ganesha's one hundred and five names have remained unutilised. We have not received any maintenance call nor any order for spares which indicates good health of the GPUs.

Once we did get a tender for 17 GPUs which went up to the final stage of price negotiation, but was shot down by the then AOM for reasons known to himself. Only recently I learnt that somehow IAF has taken a decision not to buy GPUs below 40 KVA rating. It was probably briefcase technology which was at work.

EPILOGUE

Incidentally, based on this idea AXA Power started manufacturing and supplying large, i.e., 90/120/150KVA SFC based GPUs for passenger aircrafts like Airbus, Boeing 747, etc. They also incorporated another idea of varying the engine speed to match the power requirement. This we had already done in another GPU supplied to HAL, Nasik. To meet the increased power requirement, the engine speed was increased from standard 1500 RPM to 1800. During one of my visits to AXA Power, I had talked about our GPU and informed AXA's marketing manager about this improvisation. As of now AXA power has patented this technology and is probably the only supplier in the world for this kind of GPUs.

IAF has procured SFC based GPUs of 40 KVA rating from others during the last few years. We too received the enquiry, but the first unit was to be supplied on **NO COST NO COMMITMENT BASIS** by all suppliers and then after evaluation, price bid of all suppliers was to be opened. One of the suppliers was Wg. Cdr, Wig. We did not quote as we had no funds to invest, and we knew Wig's capabilities(?). Moreover, SFC technology was by then available in India, though the performance was no match to that of AXA units.

Though financially we lost heavily, I am extremely proud of the introduction of a new concept to the Aviation World. Was taking over Static and going for the mirage of IAF the third mistake of my professional life?

--xxx---

WHAT ALL CAN GO RIGHT AND HOW IT DOES NOT

THIS CHAPTER IS DEDICATED TO

MR. RAVINDRA S MAHAJAN EX. GM

MARINE DIVISION, EBG GROUP, L&T

WITH WHOM THE RELATIONSHIP WAS MORE THAN THAT OF VENDOR & BUYER (NOV-2021)

What All Can Go Right and How It Does Not (2021)

During the past few years, there was a boom in the shipbuilding industry in India. Thanks to Ajmal Kasab and the gang's terrorist attack, both the Indian Navy and the Indian Coast Guards placed orders to procure a large number of ships in various shipyards. A number of private shipyards have become operational in the country. Larsen and Toubro Limited, a company that needs no introduction, had also ventured into shipbuilding and had built a state-of-the-art shipyard near Chennai. All this had resulted in a sudden spurt in demand of marine electrical equipment.

L&T had also set up a new division to supply electrical systems and to carry out electrification of ships. This division (ESE Marine) was headed by Ravindra S. Mahajan, A brilliant electrical engineer with abundant PR Skills. I had made a couple of visits to his office at Powai for getting business from this division for our range of products. After a couple of meetings between us, RSM (Mahajan) planned to visit our factory at Indore.

Our meeting during his visit lasted more than five hours and our discussions drifted over to the vagaries of procurement and quality assurance agencies of the Indian NAVY and related shipyards. Our experiences were more or less identical, except in terms of scale. The difference was only in terms of quantum. For example, if our payment of say Rs. 10 Lacs was stuck with some shipbuilders for the same silly reasons, in case of ESE Marine the amount was Rs.10 Crore. By the end of the meeting the two of us become close friends.

After RSM's visit, we started getting a large number of supply orders from L & T. Our business started growing rapidly. We stopped quoting directly to the shipyards and Indian Navy's procurement agencies. Instead, L & T quoted and procured orders for us.

This was a Win -Win situation for both of us. Firstly, we got paid immediately on dispatch of material which otherwise would have taken months and perhaps would have entailed many visits to shipyards for follow up. Secondly, we would not be needed to submit 10% performance Bank Guarantee (which was now L&T's responsibility) and for which we had to make a FD (Fixed Deposit) of equivalent amount with the bank, hampering our liquidity which was a major problem for us. Thirdly, we got rid of "Commissioning of Equipment" which was now taken up by L & T's engineers. We were located in the centre of the country at Indore and all the shipyards were on the seashore - starting from Calcutta, Vizag, Port Blaire, Chennai, Cochin, Karwar, Goa, Mumbai and so on. With Indore's poor (Rail, Road, Air) connectivity and limited/ meagre manpower resources this was a big problem we had always faced. In some cases, L & T even extended large amounts to the tune of Rs.50 Lacs as advance payments without any bank guarantee, to enable us to execute the orders early.

On the other hand, L. & T got a reasonably good margin from the orders executed by us and they could provide a total electrical package to the shipbuilders. Net result: our honeymoon with L&T had begun.

Our business with L & T grew rapidly. We were proud that our products were sold with L &Ts logo. When I visited L &Ts works at Rabale Navi Mumbai, I was not required to have a gate pass. I could walk into the GM's cabin without any hurdles. I delivered lectures to groups of L &Ts electrical/electronic engineers and conducted training programs. In short, I enjoyed a special status. I, who had been rejected by L&T in 1975 for recruitment as Graduate Engineer Trainee. I, a mechanical / Industrial engineer, was being consulted for technical expertise by senior electrical/ electronic design engineers of L&T.

Our arrangement with L & T was working very well, though it had its own ramifications. The marine electrical business in India is a small world. Over the period every concerned officer of procurement wing of NAVY and shipyards, learnt about our joining hands with L&T. When we did not quote for the tenders where L & T was quoting, we were persuaded to participate in the tender and submit our offer. In order to tilt the order in L &T's favour, we quoted very high. In some cases where rules permitted L&T quoted for "Static Make' equipment. Objections were raised and this was viewed as if we were forming a cartel.

Simultaneously, between the two of us, issues started cropping up. For example, in one large order for supply of four systems (for four ships) which L & T had procured on the basis of our offer, L & T placed the PO for the equipment on us while proceeding to buy the cables directly from our vendor. This was not acceptable to us as the major profit margin was in supply of cables (these were zero halogen special cables). Our margin was drastically cut down as the big brother prevailed.

The second issue was related to induction of new equipment for fitment on board warships. As per standard norms, such equipment had to go through qualification tests covered under "Type Tests" and included EMI/EMC test. These tests involved considerable expenditure. Since L & T was officially supplying the equipment, the certification was obtained by them in their name.

As a result of all this, the flow of enquiries directly to us dwindled and there was a lurking fear that over a period of time the validity of our qualification test certificates might expire and our identity might get obliterated from the recommended suppliers list. My colleagues were all cautioning me that L & T might copy our design of equipment where we had a practical monopoly.

I was of the opinion that scope of supply of our products was too tiny for L & T and with their overheads they could not keep the costs down. With all this said and done, ultimately, L & T copied our design of one critical system and started manufacturing the equipment rather than placing the orders on us. Not that there was a great technology involved in that product but certainly during that period only Statics' product was performing as per desired performance requirements. I had incorporated a very innovative design which the contemporary electronics /electrical engineers had failed to do.

L&T copying our design was the breaking points in our relationship. A meeting was held at L&T's office at Rabale which was chaired by RSM and attended by senior echelon of the division. Most of the discussions took place in Marathi. When the topic of copying of our design came up,

I said "*This is nothing but, Raja Bhikari Mazi Topi Ghetli*" (A popular children's story in which the king snatches a mouse's cap, to which he jeers the king by dancing and singing "King is a beggar, he has taken my Cap")

We could still have continued to work together but their division had started facing funds problems and our payments started getting delayed to the extent of 90 days and beyond, defeating the basic purpose of our association.

To cut a long story short, we parted ways. Later this division of L & T was wound up. It was merged with another division. RSM retired (we are still good friends). Many staff members at L & T were given pink slips. Static continues to struggle for survival as ever.

--xxx---

All Is Well That Ends Well
(October, 2023)

Perhaps, this is going to be the shortest chapter of this book. Readers would realise that even the previous chapter was completed by me in a hurry. The reason may be a bit surprising, even shocking.

I was diagnosed with cancer of the liver in ….,2023 and hence could no longer procrastinate the completion of this book. Readers may wonder as to why I could mention such a serious matter so casually, seemingly contradicts the title of this chapter.

Well, here is the explanation: - When I started writing this book, I explicitly covered only professional matters and meticulously avoided mentioning personal, family and social issues. I also avoided writing directly about my financial woes. All such problems ended in acute lack of funds for various things in my life.

Anyway, until three years ago, our business unit had gobbled funds like a Black Hole. I had to sell my ancestral house worth more than a crore, as well as my factory (land and building) of more or less the same value and move to a rented shed. My son had further pumped in over 70 Lacs. Luckily, we were able to shift to my father-in-law's house as my wife was his only offspring. My father-in-law lived a healthy life until three years ago, when he passed away at the age of 103! Being an ex-army man, he drew a handsome pension which helped us manage our finances.

Anyway, at long last, we received and executed a highly profitable order which made me take the following steps: set aside sufficient funds for my wife as well as provide for financial needs for the rest of our lives; retire from business gracefully without any liabilities; and finally hand over the management to youngsters. I continue to work on a part time basis, and continue to design & develop new equipment. The above turn of events, in my mind, fully justify the title of the chapter.

I had planned to write about money sharks and the tricks of the trade adopted by them, and a few other interesting matters. But then…. as at the end of October, 2023, my health condition is ……. And I must stop now if I have to ever see a print copy of my book. Maybe, God willing, I will write more books……

--xxx---

www.ingramcontent.com/pod-product-compliance
Lightning Source LLC
LaVergne TN
LVHW061607070526
838199LV00078B/7200